AF394634

GODS MUST HAVE CURSED HINDUS

ONE THOUSAND YEARS OF DARKNESS

SUBHASH KAPUR
BHAWNA GOLA

OPUS

Published by OPUS Books
2/15 Ansari Road, Daryaganj
New Delhi 110002

ISBN 978-81-949640-4-9
© Subhash Kapur
First Edition 2021

MRP ₹595

Edited by Kanishk Shekhar
Typeset & Cover Design by Somesh Kumar Mishra
Printed by Vikas Computer and Printers, New Delhi

Peace Can Never Be Negotiated From The
Position Of Weakness. Only The Strong
That Have Power And Means Get A Fair
And Just Deal During Peace Negotiation.

SATYAKI

MAHABHARATA, Book 5: Udyoga Parva

In this world, fear has no place.
Only strength respects strength.

—A P J Abdul Kalam
Former, President of India

Strong Armed forces are necessary for an
atmosphere of peace, amity, harmony, and
brotherhood in the country, and that is the
foundation on which India would achieve new
heights of development.

—Narendra Modi
Prime Minister of India

China needs a strong military more than
ever, urging building the People's Liberation
Army (PLA) into a world-class armed force with
confidence and capacity to defeat all invading
enemies and safeguard world peace.

—Xi Jinping
People's Republic of China

Russia needs Strong Army to defend peace.

—Ruslan Tsalikov
Deputy Minister of Defence, Russia

Prologue

Vasudhaiva Kutumbakam—the world is one single family, *Atithi Devo Bhava*—the guest is equivalent to God, and *Ahimsa Parmodharma*—non-violence is the greatest religion; Hindus are firm believers of these three ideologies but somewhere along the way they have lost the true context behind them. As a result, they have continuously been persecuted for more than 1000 years. The biggest irony is that we Hindus are still sleeping leaving everything to destiny, while our ignorance is erecting a fence of thorns around us yet again; even the Gods who helped us in the previous *Yugas* seem to have forsaken us; or worse, 'They have cursed us for our ignorance, passiveness, and fatalism.'

How did we forget those vicious invaders who pushed our ancestors into a thousand years of darkness, a darkness that is still blurring our vision? Should we not ponder over this fact to prevent history from repeating itself?

The persecution of Hindus has been the biggest holocaust in human history. However, it is so underrated that we find it necessary to draw to it the attention of not just the world, but the Hindus themselves, as even they are unaware of the horrific aspects of their history. The persecution lasted not for a decade or a century but for more than a millennium. Numerous invaders came to this land as guests, looted it leaving our ancestors struggling to stand once again and restore the lost wealth, only to be persecuted by the next persecutor.

The chapter that began in the 7th century with Muhammad Bin Qasim, the first Muslim invader from Middle East as documented, has not ended even now in 2020 when during a global crisis like COVID-19, a specific group was caught entering the country illegally, violating the lockdown rules (the only rescue measure to fight the pandemic), and misbehaving with the female medical staff who were trying to treat them.

For centuries Mother India has welcomed the world with open arms especially those seeking help or refuge irrespective of their origin or religion. But, ironically few wild beasts also landed here and captured this land that was once called a Golden Sparrow for its abundance and self-sufficiency. They wrote a tale of persecution with the blood of those who embraced them, the Hindus. The believers of *vasudhaiva kutumbakam, atithi devo bhava* and *ahimsa parmodharma* had to undergo extreme atrocities—enslavement, forced conversions, amputation of limbs, rape, murder, self-immolations and so much more that is way beyond human imagination. This land of the holy Ganges was drowned in the blood and tears of the Hindus.

Though no exact count is available, it is estimated that nearly one fourth of Hindus were slaughtered by the invading swords, one fourth were forcibly converted to Islam and a section of them converted to Christianity. Those whose ancestors managed to protect their identity by enduring the atrocities are the ones practicing Hinduism today but they too are captivated by the imprints of the invaders' ideologies; which is a big danger buzz.

Persecutors have constantly invaded and looted this venerable land in different ways, with different intentions, and from different parts of the world. Sometimes they were Persians, sometimes Arabs, Khiljis, Turkish, Mongols, Lodis, Mughals, Portuguese, or British but the victim remained the same, the Hindu. The question is why? There must be some reason why so many invaders trampled all over our country for more than a thousand years. There must be some fault in us that we have always suffered and are still suffering.

Whether we accept it or not, the Hindu is still paying the dividend for his past ignorance. His identity has been suppressed under his quest for peace. He is unaware that sometimes peace has to be defended with power. Even today the population of Hindus in the world is constantly declining, surprisingly also in a country like India. Forced conversions are a reality even today. On one hand, Hindus have been killed for refusing to convert to Islam as it was during the Muslim Rule, on the other hand, Christians are bagging the Hindu population by their manipulative means as it was during British Rule. But can we blame them?

No. Because the Hindu is sleeping on a mattress of fancy terms that have been his means of escape from responsibility towards his religion. We still feel that nothing can challenge the Hindu religion in spite of innumerable past experiences. Those who endorse this view must know that the Hindu religion exists today because of the warriors who dared to give a tough fight to the invaders. We have no idea what we have lost and what we are still losing. So many countries that were once Hindu countries have been transformed into Muslim or Christian countries now. Are we aware that along with Pakistan and Bangladesh, Maldives, Malaysia, Indonesia, Brunei, Tajikistan, and even Afghanistan were Hindu countries in the past?

It is often argued that the British Era was an era of darkness but is it the whole truth? The last 1000 years have been a period of darkness with the Muslim rule being the scariest and bloodiest. But why did it happen? Are we Hindus facing a curse? We pray to the Almighty in so many different forms but none came to our rescue. Did the Gods curse us? If they did, then why?

Maybe because we always blame others but seldom look inward, introspect, and identify our own weaknesses. Along with *vasudhaiva kutumbakam* and *atithi devo bhava* we were also taught *Karmanye Vadhikaraste, Ma Phaleshoukada Chana, Ma Karma Phala Hetur Bhurmatey Sangostva Akarmani.*

Lord Shri Krishna said that every Karma(action) has its consequence. But we have conveniently defined Karma as destiny instead of action. We started taking everything for granted and attributing everything to God's wish? It won't be wrong to say that the biggest persecutors of Hindus are Hindus themselves—not Muslims not Christians but Hindus. Caste differences, lack of integrity, superstitious belief systems, gender biases and most importantly, fatalism has paralysed the Hindu community since forever.

We have clearly forgotten that Hinduism was never about fatalism. In our scriptures, it is clearly stated that it is important to fight and slay evil in order to enforce truth and justice. This is also emphasised in our mythological stories. Are we then hiding behind terms like non-violence while forgetting that nonviolence can't be synonymous to indolence, inaction, and cowardice? Killing of Mahishasura by Goddess Durga, killing of Ravana by Shri Rama and the assassination of the entire Kuru family by Pandavas in the divine presence of Sri Krishna exemplifies that our ancestors were never short of courage and never endorsed fatalism. They believed in standing firm against *Adharma* (what is not right), no matter what? This is why only in Hindu temples worldwide we see deities wielding weapons in their hand. Goddess Kali wears a garland of skulls, and carries a bowl of blood and sword in her hands.

It is widely believed that India attained freedom because of Mahatma Gandhi's philosophy of non-violence. But is that really true? If yes, then what about Rani Lakshmibai, Subhas Chandra Bose, Chandra Shekhar Azad, Bhagat Singh and the other freedom fighters who sacrificed their lives for the freedom of this soil? Did they all not welcome the British bullets on chests broadened by courage? What about the sacrifices of the Azad Hind Fauj? Which slogan brought India freedom *Ahimsa Parmodharma* or *tum mujhe khoon do, main tumhe azaadi dunga* (You give me blood; I will give you freedom)?

We hesitate to speak against those who pushed our daughters into the fire of Jauhar, who plundered our temples, set our literature ablaze, assassinated our monks, soaked our sacred threads in blood, and erected towers of skulls just because they were Hindus. It has been more than ten centuries of darkness—betrayals, beatings, cries, failure, cowardice, ignorance, and pain but we are still unable to free our captivated minds. How ironic is that?

We feel superior while talking in English, following

British culture, and adapting their racist mentality. Hasn't caste discrimination paralysed our country enough? Rapid conversions of Hindus to Christianity with monetary incentives and sneaky invasions like love jihad to convert Hindu girls and prevent the growth of Hindu population is on the rise. But we are too busy with our IIT admissions, MBA degrees, H1B Visas, jobs in United States, foreign brands, and exponentially growing consumerism. Yes, they are important but they may become irrelevant if this issue is not addressed with an action-oriented approach.

We long for the creator to manifest and intervene but he may be waiting for us to act. We are not concerned with what is going on in the country. Patriotism is only contracted to the army and politicians and we fulfil our duty by simply criticising the government while sitting in our living rooms with a cup of coffee. We don't exercise our right to speech and right to vote carefully. We don't want to pay taxes. We don't mind bribing government officials and continue to fuel the monster of corruption that manifests into the biggest of the scams and endangers national security. We continue to glorify the persecutors of our religion as taught to us by the fraudulent education system drafted by the British and their sycophants.

We should learn from the Europeans who have erased and are still erasing the imprints of a narcissist like Hitler. No book or movie has projected him as a positive ruler. Instead they did the exact opposite. But in India we sing glory to the persecutors. We write books idealising Akbar, Shahjahan, and Jahangir whose lives were tainted with our ancestral blood. Our provinces are still home to the graves of those who sucked the blood of our ancestor till their very last breath. We also sing glory to those who cheated Indians in the name of freedom—those very people who sliced the country into three pieces where one piece has been hurting the other till date standing for what was taught to them by the deceiving invaders. As a result, our border areas are terrorized by the assassinations of innocent people and we still blindly stand for non-violence on Twitter, Facebook, and other social media. Doesn't this seem like a curse of the Gods?

Though, we can't prove all that actually happened with what is available as history of India, it is a known fact that history was tampered with and manipulated in favour of those who ruled. However, neither the Arabic nor the English pen has been able to completely disguise the pain of Mother India.

This book, *The cursed Hindu: One thousand years of darkness*, is the struggle between what has been documented and what the actual truth is. We have made an effort to dig out the truth hidden under a pile of fallacious stories by Muslim historians and biased British educationists like Macaulay. Because if they were not fallacious, our heroes would have been Subhas Chandra Bose, Bhagat Singh, MartandaVarma, Chandragupta Maurya, the Chalukyas, and Cholas and not Akbar, Shahjahan, Jahangir and some other prominent names of Indian politics whose actions compelled us to doubt the integrity of our leaders.

In a nutshell, the foundation of this age-old, diversified, liberal, all-inclusive, and all-embracive religion is crumbling due to repeated attacks, looting, and persecution by both, those who came from outside and those who reside within.

According to us, anyone whose ancestors lived near the river Sindh, that has become our identity today, is a Hindu. This includes not only the Hindu who goes to a temple but also the Hindu who was converted to Islam, the Hindu who was converted to Christianity, and anyone who resides from Sindh to the Bay of Bengal.

The Cursed Hindu aims to inspire introspection in both Hindus and ex-Hindus to pause and think about what is going on right under their noses. How we are repeatedly making the same mistakes for the last 1000 years and wandering in darkness. We all need to ponder over past mistakes and make sincere efforts to correct them before history repeats.

We hope that after 1000 years when we bid farewell to this world, no author is writing a book on 2000 years of darkness but is sharing a narrative of a Golden era based on learning and integrity.

Jai Shri Ram!

Contents

Prologue   *vii*

Introduction   1

The Most Persecuted Hindu   6

The Eternal Dharma: Why?   15

Hindu's Portrait 5000 Years Ago   23

The Vedic Evolution   29

The Golden Sparrow   36

The Dacoit from the Middle East   43

The Biggest Pathological Robbery:
Shivalingam into Pieces   57

Hindu Will Spare, but they will not   68

What Goes Around Comes Around   74

And, It was too late: Very late   77

Muslim Genes and Hindu Wombs   86

A Religious Bulldozer on Hindus and Humanity   91

Monster growled in the valley of Kashmir   93

No Space for Secularism: Only Death for Seculars   95

The Not So Great Mughals   98

Monster extends to South   126

Persecution by the Portuguese:
Leave, Convert, or Die   129

The Greedy Dutch   141

The Brutish British   143

Power Hunger of Politicians: India into Pieces   168

Indian Independence: Truth or Myth?   177

India's obsession with self destruction:
Mistakes after Independence   186

The Surviving Persecutors: Terror and Horror   208

Defense Appratus: We haven't learnt,
we haven't learnt, and we haven't learnt!   213

The Indian Persecutors: Threat to future   217

Religious Exodus of Hindus: The Biggest Challenge   223

The tired Hindu Shoulder: Superficial Secularism   225

The Ex-Hindu: Who are you fighting with?   238

The Captivated Indian Mind: Modern
& most dangerous Weapon of Persecutors   242

Call to Action: Wake up Hindu   262

Citations   275

Introduction

—Lord Krishna
Shrimad Bhagwat Geeta

—Translated By
Swami Vivekananda

ABOVE IS A Shloka from the pious Shrimad Bhagavad Gita that reminds us of Lord Krishna's promise to Arjuna and the whole humanity, thousand years ago, in Kurukshetra.

But…Hasn't virtue subsided as yet? Or is the prevailing wickedness not enough for the Lord to manifest himself. This land has seen much more in this Yuga than in any other Yuga ever; compulsion, theft, deceit, murder, slaughter, abuse, and rape of innocent women. It also manifests in the form of cruelty shown towards her, the vulgar dances on this land. Then why he, the Almighty never came to this world? Why did he break his promise? Why did he back off from his words? Is it because he cursed us for we disregarded the wisdom he had shared with us through the scriptures like the Puranas, the Vedas, the Upanishads, the Geeta, and in person during his various incarnations? Did he curse us because we forgot both Rama and Krishna who were the living examples of an ideal code of conduct for mankind?

India, a country of culture, heritage, spiritual bliss, and incarnations has a longer history than has been documented. Not only the references from the Hindu scriptures but the recent archaeological discoveries have found the records of Hindu civilization to be much older than what is believed.

The dates of the Hindu Mythological texts or the stories passed down amongst the Hindu families from generation to generation are often measured and debated with the official documents. None of the historians could ever confirm the exact dates. They could see Hinduism only since the last five thousand years. Though, the Hindu scholars claim it to be a civilization that is almost a million year old. This is not a difference of few years but of millions of years which increased our curiosity to delve deeper into our history. It is an ocean of unlimited depth with diversified tales.

The mythological scriptures of the Hindus are substantiated by the historical evidences in various forms that compel us to think how multifaceted, old, refined, liberal, and grand was the story of the Hindu legends.

But we Hindus could neither value what we were blessed

with nor could preserve it. We could not use it as much as we misused it and allowed others to misuse it too. And after everything we blame others to have robbed our civilization instead of blaming ourselves. It is the truth that the ones who robbed us were sinful and nasty but there have been a lot of flaws from our end too. Our religion teaches us to look inward for the truth and not outward as that is somebody else's karma but as with all the other fundamental teachings we forgot this one too.

Whatever the case may be, the foundation of this age old, diversified, liberal, and all inclusive religion is suffering because of several attacks, loot after loot, and persecution after persecution by those who came from outside and those who resided inside.

We are fully aware that history is written by those who are in power, so would it be right to rely on it? Adding to this the history of India is especially filtered through multiple perspectives, interests, and biases that is not only incorrect but unjust to teach the same to the future generations and contaminate our civilization further.

If we closely analyze the facts written in the history text books, many times the content does not prove itself to be the ultimate truth. Reality has a lot of grey shades. The amplification of the stories of the powerful invaders while suppressing the narratives of the brave Hindu kings is often seen as what we call 'history of India'. The exaggeration of their nobility and deceiving reality of their cruel deeds is the real face of the Indian history that comes on the surface, screaming of the lies and fraud that historians have committed to contaminate the thought process of the future generation of India. They wrote what was convenient to write instead of facts. There are very few historians who could dare to reveal little bit of a reality while saving their interest at the same time leaving a hint for the future generations to dig out the facts that are left behind.

Above all, the anesthetics that are injected into the Hindu blood from multiple directions have made the problem even worse. But that doesn't stop us from making our efforts to dig out the truth hidden under a pile of fallacious stories. Here, the term 'Hindu' includes everyone whose ancestors have lived near the river Indus that became our identity today. This includes the Hindu who goes to a temple, a Hindu who was converted to Islam, a Hindu who was converted to Christianity, and everyone who resides from Sindh to the Bay of Bengal.

The foremost weakness of a Hindu has been his lack of Integrity which is still a major cause of suffering. We had a vast heritage of knowledge, geographical advantage, and the divine bliss. This country was known as the land of incarnations since time immemorial. In a small area; we saw multiple worshipping places with multiple deities worshipped in diversified manners. Every temple had its own decorum but followed the common practices from north to south India. We had the same deities, we chanted the same mantras, and we conducted the same rituals that were an integrating force amongst us. In short, the scenario was not much different from the current circumstances with a little difference.

Like today, we never bothered to identify ourselves with that single common thread amongst us which was our religion; may be because we never had a concept of religion. As per Hindu religion the term Dharma which is used as a literary translation of 'religion today' means a *universal code of conduct* or one's *universal duty* for every being under this earth. We never differentiated each other on these grounds. Though, we did not divide on the basis of religion, it could not prevent us from splintering the motherland on other criteria.

We identified ourselves as Brahmin, the priest class, Kshatriya, the warrior class, Vaishya, the trading class, Shudra, the service class, and Dalit, the outcaste since ages. If we compare with the current scenario, the only difference was that today we are consolidated at least on paper with a centralized governance which was missing in the past.

We identified ourselves with the kingdom we belonged to, the language we spoke, the attire we wore, the customs we followed but never did we weave ourselves into a garland of a religious entity. This statement is both negative as well as positive. We call it our religious liberty but it also came with a responsibility that we forgot to fulfil. While staying limited to our own boundaries, we forgot to unite on the basis of our faith, culture, and civilization. We never claimed a name for it so the others cut us in bits and pieces. It was only when the foreigners came to India, they named us as Sindhu and Hindu relating us to the river Sindhu.

The other name for Hinduism was 'Sanatan Dharma' which means the 'Eternal Dharma'. This Eternal Dharma too could not consolidate the Indian people under one nation. We knew that our dharma is eternal but we never collectively identified with it.

This became the reason for the persecution of Hindus for centuries to come. And may be this was a curse of Gods for all the Hindus.

The Most Persecuted Hindu

PERSECUTION MEANS HARASSMENT. 'Religious Persecution' means harassing an individual or a group of individuals on the basis of religious background; the methods of his worshipping, the deity he worships and his sacred places. This includes a 360 degree persecution in all aspects whether it is economical, social, political, or human. This includes the mental, emotional, and physical torture to enforce one's belief system (religion) on others.

According to David T Smith, *"Persecution refers to violence or discrimination against members of a religious minority because of their religious affiliation. Persecution involves the most damaging expressions of prejudice against an out-group, going beyond verbal abuse and social avoidance. It refers to actions that are intended to deprive individuals of their political rights and to force minorities to assimilate, leave, or live as second-class citizens. When these actions happen persistently over a period of time, and include large numbers of both perpetrators and victims, we may refer to a "campaign" of persecution that usually has the goal of excluding the targeted minority from the polity."*

The irony is that Hindus were not even classified as

minority that could be persecuted. Then why did it happen? Was it because of a curse?

Nazila Ghanea-Hercock in 'The Challenge of Religious Discrimination at the Dawn of the New Millennium' defines persecution as follows:

"In the aspect of state policy, it may be defined as violations on freedom of thought, conscience, and belief spread by systematic and active state policy and actions of harassment, intimidation, and punishment that infringes or threatens the right to life, integrity or liberty. The distinction with religious intolerance is that the latter in most cases is in the sentiment of the population, which may be tolerated or encouraged by the state."

Seen in light of the above definitions, the Hindu community is possibly the most persecuted community in the entire world. It's even more than the Jews and the irony is that the persecution is still continuing. The world does not even know about this persecution. Even in independent India with a majority of Hindu population and more than 80% of the tax collected by the Hindus, the Hindu community is getting persecuted knowingly or unknowingly. As repeated in this book again and again, all this happened because of us. We cannot blame others for it. We allowed them to persecute us and we are still doing the same. Earlier it was more on knifepoint and now it is done socially and politically along with terrorism, which remains the biggest threat to India.

We have been crouching within our society, community, and caste. We forgot that when any Hindu would be persecuted then even the Brahmin, the Kshatriya, the Vaishya would be persecuted, and the already persecuted Dalit for ages would be persecuted to another level.

As a result, the entire Hindu community was persecuted irrespective of caste, gender, region, class, language, or community. Men and women were persecuted equally. States especially in the North West regions faced religious persecution. The South could protect itself due to the geographical advantage of being located at a distance from the vulnerable North-Western borders. Though later, the invaders reached there too and the royals had a hard time protecting the Southern provinces from their wicked hands. This persecution still continues in South India and Indo-Sri Lankan borders.

It's high time that the Hindu opens his eyes. It is not only required but urgent also because we are under a severe threat today and the irony is that we are not even aware of what is going on under our nose.

On one hand the population of Hindus is constantly declining in the world, on the other hand susprisingly the graph of the Hindu population in India, a country that is supposed to have a majority of Hindus is also bending downwards. The Hindu vote bank has been shrinking which was a cause of concern for everyone but we were hardly aware of what was going on and what happened in the past?

Though, we saw a major shift in the psychology of Indians during the 2019 elections when people voted for the government that took bold steps like demonetization and establishing the center's rule in Kashmir by withdrawing article 370 and 35A, we would consider it as just a beginning. This was just one candle that we lit to win over this darkness. We need millions more to brighten this land once again like the way it was done by the people of Ayodhya when Lord Rama returned from exile after killing Ravana.

Few historians discuss that in spite of so much of persecution and holocaust, Hinduism stood firm for ages and still continues to exist which is a very big assurance that this religion is based on such a strong foundation that could never be challenged. It is true but can we ignore the data and facts? We cannot shut our eyes to the fact that there is no Hindu country in the world because they turned into Muslim or Christian countries.

Half of the Hindu population was converted to Islam during the Muslim Rule and the British became the basis of creating Pakistan and Bangladesh from India. A major section was converted to Christianity. Now in India too population of Hindus has declined from 84.1 per cent in 1951 to 79.80 per cent in 2011. Nearly 50 per cent of Hindus were converted in last 1000 years and many more were killed.

Please refer to the table below as extracted from Census 2011 data published on the Hindu.com:

Year	Percent	Increase
1951	84.1%	-
1961	83.45%	-0.65%
1971	82.73%	-0.72%
1981	82.30%	-0.43%
1991	81.53%	-0.77%
2001	80.46%	-1.07%
2011	79.80%	-0.66%

Now let us see the state-wise population of Hindus which is also rapidly declining leaving few states as Muslim majority states like Kerala and Kashmir and few states have majority of Christians.

Region	Hindus	Total	% Hindus
Andaman and Nicobar Islands	264,296	380,581	69.45%
Andhra Pradesh	74,824,149	84,580,777	88.46%
Arunachal Pradesh	445,876	1,383,727	30.04%
Assam	19,180,759	31,205,576	61.47%
Bihar	86,078,686	104,099,452	82.69%
Chandigarh	852,574	1,055,450	80.78%
Chhattisgarh	23,819,789	25,545,198	93.25%
Dadra and Nagar Haveli	322,857	343,709	93.93%
Daman and Diu	220,150	243,247	90.50%
Delhi	13,712,100	16,787,941	81.68%
Goa	963,877	1,458,545	66.08%
Gujarat	53,533,988	60,439,692	88.57%
Haryana	22,171,128	25,351,462	87.46%
Himachal Pradesh	6,532,765	6,864,602	95.17%
India	980,378,868	1,210,910,328	79.9%
Jammu and Kashmir	3,566,674	12,541,302	28.43%
Jharkhand	22,376,051	32,988,134	67.83%
Karnataka	51,317,472	61,095,297	84.00%
Kerala	18,282,492	33,406,061	54.73%
Lakshadweep	1,788	64,473	2.77%
Madhya Pradesh	66,007,121	72,626,809	90.89%
Maharashtra	89,703,056	112,374,333	79.83%
Manipur	1,181,876	2,855,794	41.39%

Region	Hindus	Total	% Hindus
Meghalaya	342,078	2,966,889	11.53%
Mizoram	30,136	1,097,206	2.75%
Nagaland	173,054	1,978,502	8.75%
Odisha	39,300,341	41,974,218	93.63%
Pondicherry	1,089,409	1,247,953	87.30%
Punjab	10,678,138	27,743,338	38.49%
Rajasthan	60,657,103	68,548,437	88.49%
Sikkim	352,662	610,577	57.76%
Tamil Nadu	63,188,168	72,147,030	87.58%
Tripura	3,063,903	3,673,917	83.40%
Uttar Pradesh	159,312,654	199,812,341	79.73%
Uttarakhand	8,368,636	10,086,292	82.97%
West Bengal	64,385,546	91,276,115	70.54%

Along with Pakistan and Bangladesh, we should know that Maldives, Malaysia, Indonesia, Brunei, Tajikistan, and even Afghanistan was a Hindu country. We can see few names mentioned in the age old Hindu epics. For instance, Kandhar which has been famous for terrorist activities of late actually was Gandhara. The princess of Gandhara, named as Gandhari was married to Dhrutrashtra who was the King of Hastinapura as mentioned in the profound Hindu epic, Mahabharata.

Sindh has been the foundation of the Hindu culture as it is named after the river that flowed besides this desert known as Sindhu. The Indus Valley Civilization prevailed there which is considered as the foundation of Indian civilization by historians. There are so many places in that area that have religious relevance in the Hindu history but today we need a visa to visit them.

Philippines first fell to Islam, then to Christianity. The Tarim Basin was once independent and a Hindu region but presently is a part of China. India which was supposed to be different from Pakistan on religious grounds could not claim the status of a Hindu country, whereas Pakistan claims the status of a Muslim country. India is still bound by the Sharia law that sometimes goes contradictory to Indian constitution and is marked by anti-Hindu outlook to governance and law. This is only because of its secular status. This has also been a reason for the chaos that has plagued the country on a national and social front since ages.

So much has happened and the target was the Hindu. Why? Doesn't it sound like realization of a curse on the Hindu? If history is reviewed, it seems that all troubles were invited by our own people. We opened the door for the monster of darkness so he came in. Why do we blame others?

The day may not be far when we will have more and more Muslim majority states. The same is in Kashmir and many other states. More than anything, even today we know that forced conversion is a reality in India. Hindus have been killed for refusing to convert to Islam. Videos of such incidents go viral on the internet but nothing changes. On the other hand, Christians are bagging the Hindu population by other means. For instance, granting them various aids for converting into Christianity. The poor Hindus are trapped for a few facilities offered to them whether it is for cash or in kind and agree to give up their age old identity. And this is not in few numbers but in thousands and millions which is a red alert for Hindus.

Not only this, the rest of the Hindu population is constantly suffering from terrorist activities and dying in bomb blasts, adding to the declining graph of their population.

Millions of Kashmiris and Goans were thrown out of their own land tainted with the blood of their own family members even after partition. They were made to live like refugees in their own country waiting for government to do the needful so they acquire their previous status.

If the Hindu does not wake up to this data and facts then shall we not consider that Hindu identity is merely restricted to our genes now and the Hindu soul is dead? We don't even bother about what has happened, what is going on, and what will happen? May be we have accepted that being persecuted is the natural state of Hindus and we have to live with it leaving the way for more intense and fierce persecution to take place in future. Are we waiting for the time when the Hindu religion becomes history and Hindu heritage is confined to a museum?

Millions of people have been tortured, killed, raped, and converted on knifepoint for centuries. The only choice given to them was to convert, leave, or die, whether it was given to Hindus in India before independence, or in Pakistan, Bangladesh, Kashmir or Goa. Persecutors changed but persecution was constant and it was majorly on the basis of religion. Why? Is it because the Hindu is cursed?

There must be a curse that after so many attacks the Hindus continue sleeping.

Only a few could manage to survive and those were our ancestors and we are the proud children of those people who have protected and maintained the religious inheritance by sacrificing their blood. We owe so much to them. This freedom and identity that we enjoy today has been given to us on a golden platter but this gold was not a metal but a narrative of a dark past that is demanding light from us. We need to introspect and question the mistakes that brought them to this phase and what we should learn from them.

Are we waiting for the time when no mantras will be chanted here, water of Ganga will not be poured on our sacred rituals , no bells will ring in the temples, more scriptures would be burnt or would be stolen, more Hindu wombs would be forced to deliver Aurangzeb and Jahangir…And much more!

The idols of our deities, the scriptures, the bells of temples, and the other cultural tools are only found in a museum, is that what we are waiting for?

The numbers may not seem important but heritage, civilization, and culture are important. Isn't it? The irony is that it is not just the problem of the Hindus, but that of humanity, which will lose the vast inheritance left by our forefathers and is considered a bliss for the whole world and not just the Hindus. It would also lose the only religion that is accommodative of all other religions, rituals, deities, and values. This trait of Hindusim avoids conflict as it never claims holier than thou status. It is the only religion that could be an answer to these childish games of idiotic fanatics in which they are simply using Gods as their toys and trying to dominate the others in his name. The idea of Divine is all inclusive not exclusive.

The Eternal Dharma: Why?

WAY OF LIFE, eternal religion, universal belief system, however you may address Hinduism, it is a religion that sets a human free to have his own belief system and respect the others, maintaining harmony on this planet and integrating them only as humans. It does not impose his God, Mantra, Practice, Ritual, or Culture on others.

It is a religion that allows a human to rise above what is taught to him as religion and grants him freedom to question everything including the Gods. It does not differentiate him from others but connects him with the other beings and with the Almighty.

This may be the reason that in Hinduism, we do not have a word called religion. The term dharma that we use to refer to religion in modern language was not used to refer to a community. For us, Dharma means the lawful code of conduct which is mandatory for maintaining harmony amongst all beings. We have no word which could literally translate the term religion because in our civilization we did not have a concept of having different religions. Yes, one could pray to the Almighty in whichever form he wants to, in whichever way, at whichever time and place. And still he belongs to us. We never discard anyone for praying to a different deity, in a different way, and at a different place nor for marrying in a different religion.

Hinduism is also called the Sanatan Dharma that differentiates us from other religions in practice. But this too means the 'Eternal Dharma' that connects us to 'One God in various forms'. It is the only dharma that shows that we are God in human form and that God is not just outside but within us. To change the world we have to change ourselves. We are not just a human body but a part of Brahma, the divine. Once we know this truth, we break free of this imaginary matrix of life that suffocate us like a bird in the cage trying to open a door that is locked from inside. The key to unlock this lock was knowledge which was provided to us in form of scriptures like the Puranas, Vedas, Upanishads, Smritis, and others. Worldwide, the Hindu scriptures are known to be an ocean of knowledge and wisdom that have proven their relevance on scientific, spiritual, and ethical benchmarks time to time. That we Hindus don't bring this knowledge into actions is a different story.

Vedas: the supreme source of knowledge

We are a knowledge based religion, which is why the four pillars of the Hindus are the four scriptures, the Vedas on which the entire concept of Hinduism prevails. The term Veda comes from the Hindi word *'Vid'* that means *'to know'*. These Vedas that are based on science are divided into four parts to include, *Samveda, RigVeda, Yajurveda,* and *Atharvaveda.* And if we want to refer to these Vedas in precise format, we could refer to *'Shrimad Bhagavad Gita'* which is the nectar of these Vedas and many other Hindu scriptures. This powerful scripture which is as short as seven hundred verses holds the solutions to all our problems; individual, social, national, or global. It is said that there is nothing about human life that is beyond Shrimad Bhagavad Gita.

So many leaders, kings, scholars referred to Bhagavad Gita for taking strategic decisions in the past, whether it was Mahatma Gandhi, Albert Einstein, Annie Besant, Jawaharlal Nehru, Narendra Modi, and many more. Even some Muslim kings have been reported to have sought solutions from this great scripture.

Vedas that are regarded as the revealed knowledge and not what was written by any human shows acceptance of monotheism, polytheism, and even atheism. It allows a human to use his or her intellect to draw his own theory with respect to his faith. According to Vedas, a human is only bound by his actions that yield him sweet or bitter fruits. There is no compulsion to believe in the Lord or not to believe in him.

These books are a jumble of hymns, prayers, rituals for sacrifice that brightens the human intellect to prosper in this life and also rise above what is called life. Though, there is no idol worship in them or the temples for the Gods but they do leave a room for a human to formulate his own philosophy of religion.

From astrology to astronomy, economics to Ayurveda, all disciplines are told in depth in the Hindu scriptures. Apart from the Vedas we have many other valuable books to include the *Arthashastra* from Chanakya, the *Charak*, the *Upanishadas*, the *Puranas*, the *Manusmritis* and texts like *Kama Sutra* that exemplify the far-sighted and liberal thinking of our scholars.

Millions of our books were destroyed by the invaders, many of the universities were burnt, and a number of Gurukuls were plundered but India's intellectual heritage till date ranks higher than any other country.

The one common preaching that was given to us in every form was the superiority of *'Karma'* – *'the action'*. A human is assigned a responsibility of accomplishing his karma as a duty from the Almighty not only in his individual interest but also in social, national, and global interest. Still, we Hindus say everything is destined and use it as an excuse to be self-centered and indolent, which is referred as a sin in our religion. We do not realize that we have turned fatalist which is nowhere mentioned in Hinduism. *This is the reason and the result of the curse of Gods on the Hindus.*

Millions and billions of scriptures, mantras, mythological history, spiritual knowledge, geographical bliss, still we are a poor country not merely by money but by knowledge also because owning scriptures and actually knowing them are two different things.

These scriptures are not just books but a way of governance. They are a way of life, life cycle itself, life itself. There is nothing beyond Vedas in this world, nothing behind, and nothing ahead. They were relevant yesterday, they are relevant today, and they will be relevant in future. They are the absolute knowledge that is a key to unlock all locks in this world. They are researched in the difficult circumstances in the wild surroundings of the woods by the sages who devoted their lives to the Almighty to gather such knowledge. The acute and obtuse knowledge and the multidimensional perspectives constitute the Hindu scriptures. Each and every word is absolute in itself. The poems are written in perfect meters. It depicts the immense knowledge of the composers who adapted high quality diction and meters while writing them. It takes a highly developed language and culture to be able to write such content. As per scholars, the Vedas that we have today are mere one third of what we had originally. Passing from generation to generation for thousands of years, even now they remain the ocean of knowledge in today's world. They are called the ultimate truth.

Each and every word of the Vedas reveals such deep secrets of life that they are still worth contemplation for modern science. For instance, the Gayatri Mantra:

'om bhūr bhuva suva
tatsa vitu rvare ya
bhargo de vasya dhī mahi
dhiyo yo na prachodayāt'

Many great scholars have tried to translate it from their own wisdom.

We meditate on the glory of that Being who has produced this universe; may He enlighten our minds.

Translated by Swami Vivekananda

We choose the Supreme Light of the divine Sun; we aspire that it may impel our minds.

Translated by Sri Aurobindo

Sri Aurobindo further elaborates: The Sun is the symbol of divine Light that is coming down and Gayatri gives expression to the aspiration asking that divine Light to come down and give impulsion to all the activities of the mind.

Let us adore the supremacy of that divine sun, the god-head who illuminates all, who recreates all, from whom all proceed, to whom all must return, whom we invoke to direct our understandings right in our progress towards his holy seat,

Sir William Jones

Oh God! Thou art the Giver of Life, Remover of pain and sorrow, The Bestower of happiness. Oh! Creator of the Universe, May we receive thy supreme sin-destroying light, May Thou guide our intellect in the right direction.

Maharshi Dayananda Saraswati
(founder of *Arya Samaj*)

Just one mantra and few words translated by many people from different perspectives. But they all churn out the divine reality of the universe without offending any religion. It is personal yet universal, all embracive and all inclusive. It unites, integrates and consolidates not only humans but all the living and non living beings on this planet.

This has been the vastness of the Hindu Religion. It is universal, eternal, and liberal. The irony of this divine land is to witness the darkness overshadowing the light of the Vedas. It is difficult to imagine how unfortunate we have been. This is why we are compelled to think that Gods must have cursed the Hindus.

What should be done?

Past is past but what to do in present and in future to protect our heritage? Shall we still address Hinduism as a way of life with open ended boundaries? Haven't the all inclusive approach of Hinduism also made it vulnerable over a period of time that did not differentiate between friend and foe.

Though sensitivity of religion and its doctrines should be strength for humanity but somewhere it backfired because the others took it as our weakness; or shall we say that we made it our weakness. Flexibility and adaptability made it fragile and influenced everyone easily.

In other words, this vulnerability has been the reason for Hinduism to reach nearly a collapse, time to time, offering the Hindu heads to the sword of the religious fanatics. All these values led us to transform our identity into somebody else's completely. Why? Because somewhere we could not draw the line between tolerance and cowardice.

Major sections of the Hindu population were swept away to a strange dominion especially in the name of religion for many centuries. We changed so quickly that any new practices which were neither based on science nor on divinity overpowered us and hollowed our foundation like a parasite.

So the question is that shall we not erect firm boundaries around our religion to deal with the wrong influences just like the other religions because while accepting everyone, the Hindu religion has been losing its own identity and getting threatened on several grounds. Should we not stop calling it a way of life, but name it as a well-defined religion that has a firm code of conduct, which is not open to misinterpretation and manipulation? Should we not finally draw the line?

In other words, the point is that shall we stop addressing Hinduism by various fancy terms and identify it as one single religion which is distinctly defined so that we identify with our ancestral heritage and stand for it to eliminate the vulnerability of this eternal dharma from foreign influences?

Let's travel back to the beginning though we are unsure when exactly the beginning was but as per the documented facts let us take off from the Indus Valley Civilization till today.

Hindu's Portrait 5000 Years Ago

THOUGH OUR KNOWLEDGE and intellect both agree to the reality of Hindu civilization to be much older than what historians validate, still while walking on and around the path that historians have constructed for us, we see the first civilized inhabitation on the Indian subcontinent in the Indus Valley Civilization, which is again an example of a vast and rich cultural heritage of this divine land.

As documented, modern humans arrived on the Indian subcontinent between 73,000 and 55,000 years ago. By 4,500 BCE history counts evidences of a settled habitation that eventually evolved into the Indus Valley Civilization, an early civilization of the Old World, contemporaneous with ancient Egypt and Mesopotamia.

This age is also noted as the Bronze Age in the Indian history and the cities here were noted for their urban planning, baked brick houses, elaborate drainage facilities, water supply systems, clusters of large non-residential buildings, and new techniques in handicrafts, carnelian products, seal carvings and metallurgy including copper, bronze, tin and lead as we see in any modern planned city in India.

The concept of apartments and condominiums was considered and adapted by them in that time. The large cities of Mohenjo-Daro and Harappa very likely grew to accommodating between 30,000 and 60,000 individuals and the civilization itself may have contained between one and five million individuals.

As per Wright 2010, *along with Ancient Egypt and Mesopotamia, the Indus valley region was one of three early cradles of civilization of the Old World.*

Of the three, the Indus Valley Civilization was the most expansive, and at its peak, may have had a population of over five million, says McIntosh, Jane in *The Ancient Indus Valley: New Perspectives.*

The civilization was primarily located in the northern provinces of India which was spread into what is now called Gujarat, Haryana, Punjab, Rajasthan, Uttar Pradesh, Jammu and Kashmir in India and Sindh, Punjab, and Balochistan in Pakistan. Some sites in Afghanistan are also believed to be the trading colonies during the Indus Valley Civilization. A total of 1,022 cities and settlements had been found by 2008, mainly in the general region of the Indus and Ghaggar-Hakra Rivers, and their tributaries; of which 616 sites are in India and 406 sites are in Pakistan; of these 96 have been excavated.

The uniformity in infrastructure and many other produces shows that people were governed by state at that time. The excavations also found seals of those times which indicate that there existed, inter-state trade. The terracotta toys hint that the lifestyle was prosperous enough to find time for recreation activities and designing toys for their children. These toys included carts that confirm that wheels and carts existed at that time so people had the facility of using vehicles for travelling and transporting goods and services. The toys of dancers hint that the culture had elements of dancing in those days.

The trimmed beard and fancy attires of these statues imply that people lived a luxurious lifestyle in which they gave utmost importance to fashion and luxuries like wearing ornaments and beads of different density and size that again shows that there was standardization in a variety of matters in terms of their weight, size, and shape. There was embroidery, stone blades, and stitching that is observed through the statues found.

The seals usually were carved out of stone with animal imprints showing the animal loving nature of people. The pottery carried the black designs and cotton was found during the excavation of Mehrgarh. They had refined garments, art and culture at a time when most of the world was walking nude, struggling for its survival.

It is the oldest documented planned city of India which was approximately five thousand years ago. Not only this, but the city was constructed into the grid structure following a common architectural plan. The cities were divided into two parts, big and small, which was meant for different strata of the society as per their dominance. Concept of a great bath with bricked lining, plastered finish, water tight with tar, steps from two sides, and rooms on all sides in circular set up were also found during the excavations. The houses were single as well as double storey with separate space for bath. House wells in a few houses were also seen. The covered as well as interconnected drainage system with proper scope for investigation proves the finesse that went into the refined sanitation system in the cities.

This was the platform from where the civilization of

Hindus that was driven by the word Sindhu was oriented. Such profound planning, execution, and architecture still surprises the globe with the standard from which the Indian civilization took off.

'The Indus Valley Civilization', writes Professor Childe, 'represents a very perfect adjustment of human life to a specific environment that can only have resulted from years of patient effort. As it has endured; it is already specifically Indian and forms the basis of modern Indian culture.'

The archaeological survey reports over 1,000 Mature Harappan cities and settlements, of which just under a hundred have been excavated. However, there are only five major urban sites to include Harappa, Mohenjo-Daro, Dholavira, Ganeriwala, and Rakhigarhi. The early Harappa cultures were preceded by local Neolithic agricultural villages, from which the river plains were populated.

The idol of the Pashupati Nath implies that people must have been spiritual and would have followed Lord Shiva at that time, though it's not a documented fact but just an assumption drawn from the artifacts. Also these idols depict praying to both male and female deities showing gender equality. They also prayed to the natural elements like sun, moon, water, and air giving utmost importance to nature.

Inkpots, lipsticks, and other tools clearly indicate that their standard of living was no less than our modern lifestyle. Mesopotamian cylindrical seals were found during the excavations that indicate bilateral trade existed between Mesopotamia and India. Fire altars were found showing the system for producing baked bricks. Bones of the horses in Surkotada shows that not only horses were found at that time, but they were also imported from the other states hinting of export and import. The large letters of Harappan scripts on white stones at Dholavira proves the presence of script.

There were common ceremonial halls showing the existence of community living there. People must have celebrated festivals together and believed in social life.

At the sites of Lothal, dockyards were discovered that confirms the existence of ships and trade through water at that time. People were connecting with the other subcontinents not only by road but also through the ocean. This dockyard carried allocated spaces to preserve and save the ships from tides of the ocean at the time when the ship was not sailing.

The collapse of the Indus Valley Civilization is still a mystery but it compels us to question what went wrong that the same land saw darkness for years to come, which is also the motive to write this book.

River Saraswati had dried and the collapse of this rich civilization followed. But why did the river dry? Was it the beginning of a curse that followed Hindus for centuries to come?

There is no record of any survivors of the Indus Valley Civilization, but few historians claim that the South Indians identify few of their traits with them. Maybe, the residents would have shifted downward seeking survival during calamities.

Post the Indus Valley Civilization, there were many Hindu dynasties that ruled the Indian subcontinent and the tales of their governance surprise us with the perfection and grandeur about our ancestral heritage which was spread beyond the boundaries of Afghanistan till Tamil Nadu. The Hindu kings had ruled for not just few decades but for centuries. This will be discussed later in the book after the Indo-Aryan period that was recorded 2000 years after the Indus Valley Civilization.

However, none of them could undo this curse which acted like a monster that only grew in size with time.

The Vedic Evolution

HISTORY FINDS THE Rigvedic Era and the Aryan dominance in the Indian subcontinent from 1500 BC to 1000 BC. One of the four dominant Vedas of the Hindus called Rig-Veda was conceived during this era. It is still a question if the script existed at that time or not because the content was transferred generation to generation by the word of mouth and they were explored by the sages in form of verses and hymns. It is also said that these hymns and verses were deliberately not recorded on paper as they found it auspicious to share this knowledge by word of mouth. As per historians, the remaining three Vedas were written in the later Vedic era from 1000 BC to 500 BC. They were Samaveda, Yajurveda, and Atharvaveda.

Cattle rearing and cow worship began during this period. Few historians claim that the gap of two thousand years between the Indus Valley Civilization and the Rigvedic Era was so huge it surprises everyone that from such refined and prosperous lifestyle people went back to cattle rearing and agriculture? What went wrong that pushed it behind by centuries? In this context, the Hindu scholar's point of view seems appropriate that our history is much older than what is documented. How can people who were rearing cattle speak, talk and conceive books like Vedas that too in a difficult language Sanskrit, which is recognized as one of the most profound languages in the world. Even NASA has recommended the use of Sanskrit.

It is difficult to believe that in the era where people spoke Sanskrit, conceived Gayatri Mantra and wrote the very first Veda, the Rig Veda, people were dependent on rearing cattle; quite surprising!

This substantiates the contradictions in our knowledge of history. As mentioned before, it gives more weight to the claim that the Hindu civilization is way older than mere five thousand years though we don't have a document to substantiate the same so we have to rely on the other perspective that is documented.

The later Vedic era saw some evolution which was the conception of the other three Vedas which is useful even today and for centuries to come and also much more. Earlier people were worshipping natural elements like air, water, and fire. People now began to worship the idols and that still continues. These idols were majorly of the trinity, Brahma, the creator, Vishnu, the preserver, and Mahesh, the destroyer. People now understood that life is a cycle, what is created is preserved and then it is destroyed and created further. They also knew that this is all done by a supreme power that governs all beings.

The concept of temples began from here. These Gods did not only include the male Gods but also the female Goddesses indicating the equality between the genders in Vedic era too. It is evident that people perceived men and women as equally powerful so gave equal weight to both when it came to worshipping. Cow was considered a wealth and an object of worship for spiritual reasons or may be because they knew the divine benefits of cow products. It is claimed that the cow urine heals a number of ailments that sometimes the modern allopathic medicines can't cure. Cow milk is a natural source of multiple nutrients and it also possesses antibiotic properties. This proves the claim that Vedic knowledge and Hindu rituals are based on scientific reasoning.

Adding to this, almost all of the Hindu practices are based on scientific reasons. For instance, mantra chanting produced the desired vibrations that affect the universe outside and the system within while manifesting various objectives. The jewels worn in different parts of bodies are based on the principles of acupressure that enhance blood circulation. The sacred fires were lit for purifying the physical and emotional surroundings and for many other things. Each and every scripture and mythological epics account for endless principles based on science.

As per Hindu mythology, Ramayana was written during the transition period from the Rig Vedic era to the later Vedic era. From here, the Hindu civilization was fully flourishing in social, economical, political, and cultural arena. The Hindu incarnations exemplified the ideal code of conduct of a man that still motivates Hindus. An ideal man, an ideal woman, an ideal king, an ideal brother, an ideal mother, and an ideal friend, all are seen in this great epic. It is still a foundation of the Hindu religion. Since, the historian's point of view and the Hindu scholar's point of view is extremely contradictory, every Hindu can formulate his or her opinion about his history drawing his reference from the content provided from different sources.

Though Ramayana and Mahabharata are considered as mythology by the historians but excavation has found records of the states that were mentioned in Ramayana like Ayodhya, Lanka, Kishkindha, Dwarka, Mathura, Vrindavan and many others. Mahabharata too was recorded during this phase when one of the supreme scripture, Shrimad Bhagwad Gita evolved as a major guiding principle of life for Hindus and others till date and times to come. During the time of Ramayana and Mahabharata we could see the level of evolution, technological, social, and economical advancement. The knowledge of various disciplines was present to an extent but couldn't be traced fully by the modern scientists and scholars.

The concept of astronomy and astrology evolved in this phase surprises the scientists today. Modern discoveries were mentioned in the scriptures of those days. Millions and billions of scriptures were recorded with variety of scientific, social, economical, moral, astrological and religious principles which are still a wonder for the modern world.

The armaments were advanced and high tech. Concept of airplanes has been mentioned in our epics. We see the ships and the dockyards from the Indus Valley Civilization. We see numerous evolved beings that we Hindus consider as Gods like Rama, Krishna, Arjuna and thousands others who blessed us with wisdom on how to lead a successful life. Though the time had its own flaws, no one could deny the talent and the prosperity that our ancestors possessed.

The communities were divided into classes based upon their occupations. This was to distinguish the classes for producing the skilled manpower and supporting system through families. This was later manipulated for individual motives. The division transformed into discrimination that became a parasite for the Hindu civilization, the horrible caste system in the long run that is uncured till date.

Gradually, the Society was divided into the four *Varnas* and this division was named as 'the caste system' that followed the hierarchical order. This was the root cause of all troubles. This new definition placed *Brahmana* on the top who were the priests and scholars, the second was the *Kshatriya*, the warriors, third was the *Vaishya*, farmers and merchants, and the fourth was the *Shudra,* laborers who were considered the lowest rank. Later the untouchables who handled meat and waste were tagged as outcastes and were rejected and humiliated by the four others.

Originally, this caste system was merely a reflection of one's occupation but people interpreted it to be determined by one's birth and one was not allowed to change castes till death. At one time, it became so strong that one was not even allowed to marry in the other caste. It became a generation by generation phenomenon that Indian society is still dealing with. In short, originally it was Karma based but was manipulated into Birth based discrimination. This understanding was a reflection of the belief in an eternal order of human life dictated by a supreme deity which was completely fallacious.

We Indians always manipulated our texts and preaching as per our own convenience. Caste discrimination is one of them, which was amplified to its greatest extent in modern world substantiated by the reservation system. It could be titled as the leprosy of the Indian civilization that ate our resources in the long run and is still continuing.

While the religious beliefs that characterized the Vedic

Period are considered much older, it was during this time that they became systematized as the religion of Sanatan Dharma which means the 'Eternal Order' evolved. This also reminds us of the idol worship and chanting mantras giving religious identification to a culture which is now called as Hinduism.

It is known as Hinduism in modern times, but as we know the term Hindu is derived from the Indus River where worshippers were known to gather. The outsiders named them as Sindhus and then gradually 'Hindus' that had nothing to do with their religion but was their geographical identity. Sanatan Dharma is based on a belief that there is an order and a purpose to the universe and human life and, by accepting this order and living in accordance with it, one will experience life as it is meant to be properly lived with the divine bliss. Also a believer of Sanatan Dharma believes that there is a power that governs this entire cosmos and we must worship him to constantly attain the guidance towards happiness and truth. It is still debatable whether it is a polytheistic religion consisting of many Gods, or it is a monotheistic religion, believing in one God, Brahma. It is Brahma who decrees the eternal order and maintains the universe through it. This belief reflects the stability of the society in which it grew and flourished.

During the Vedic Period, governments became centralized and social customs integrated fully into daily life across the region. Besides the Vedas, the great religious and literary works of the Upanishads, the Puranas, the Mahabharata, and the Ramayana all came into existence as mentioned above too. All the Gods and Goddesses that we pray in the temples find relative records in the Vedic age except Lord Shiva whose hints are also found in the Indus Valley Civilization.

What an irony! Such rich culture, value system, refined knowledge went in vain when the Hindu could not justify his eligibility for the same in the long run; curse of Gods.

The Golden Sparrow

AFTER THE VEDIC period, most of records mention that India was fragmented into multiple kingdoms. It was never united to endorse one common belief system or religion, which is why it has always been a target for greedy invaders. Alexander the Great in 327 BCE also succeeded in conquering a part of northwest India. Foreign influences gave rise to Indo-Greek and Greco-Buddhist culture which impacted all areas of culture in northern India from art to religion.

In 3rd century AD, we see a number of kingdoms but the most dominating and widespread was Magadha. After a long and fierce struggle amongst the kingdoms, it was Magadha that succeeded in dominating most of the others especially in the North-West Frontier region.

After turning few pages of the ancient history, we see the first and the most powerful empire of the Hindu origin that consolidated and dominated the entire Indian subcontinent under one single flag was the Great Mauryan Empire from 322-185 BCE.

On the other side, Chera dynasty, Chola dynasty, and the Pandyan dynasty ruled parts of southern India and they too were quite dominant Hindu rulers in India. They were followed by the Satavahanas who overpowered most of the Hindu rulers in the Indian history. Not only south but rulers in the north and the foreign land bowed their head to the Satavahanas, especially during the reign of Gautamiputra Satakarni, a renowned ruler of the South.

Under the reign of Chandragupta Maurya from 322-298 BCE, Mauryans conquered the entire north, stretched arms to east, west, and a part of the Deccan region. They also maintained cordial relations with the southern rulers so found no need to conquer them.

Not only south but the Mauryan Empire maintained diplomatic relations with the Greek world and other neighboring continents. These relations rested on the solid foundation of mutual commercial interest.

Chandragupta Maurya founded an empire that lasted from about 322 to 185 BCE under the guidance of the great scholar of that time named as Chanakya who is also known as Kautilya or Vishnugupta.

There was hardly anything Chanakya would have refrained from doing to achieve his goal which was national prosperity and public welfare. He was a patriot with great diplomatic skills. He changed the definition of a Hindu sage by enforcing the principle of national prosperity by all means; politics also. *Sama* (negotiation), *Dama* (reward), *Danda* (punishment), and *Bheda* (divide), whatever it takes, country and dharma should be supreme as per this foresighted scholar who is an inspiration for even today's policymakers and will continue to be; may be forever. He played the role of a guide, philosopher, economist, policymaker, jurist, and royal advisor during the Mauryan

Rule. He is also known for authoring the famous Chanakyaniti and Arthashastra.

"He (Chanakya) is considered the pioneer of the field of political science and economics in India, and his work is thought of as an important precursor to classical economics"

As L K Jha writes in International Journal of Social Economics in 1998.

Chanakya also enforced an idea of war for what is right and not sit defending non violence waiting for fate to decide a country's future. This is a very important learning that modern India should reflect upon.

According to Chanakya, *"War is only a continuance of state policy by other means. It is basically a means to ensure that law and order is not challenged and people should abide by them in all circumstances"*, as mentioned by Pt. Jawaharlal Nehru in Discovery of India.

Here we see the two non Kshatriyas winning over most of India together with a combination of 'masculine intellect and bravery'. This shows that the biggest of the social and national reformers were not tied with the sick Caste system of India.

Chandragupta did not belong to a Kshatriya caste by birth but he did not only conquer most of the kingdoms defeating the Kshatriyas but also the foreign rulers who made attempts to strengthen their ties with Chandragupta. Many of them offered their daughters to maintain the harmonious relations with Chandragupta which exemplifies India's escalated reputation internationally in ancient times.

After Chandragupta, his son Bindusara reigned between 298-272 BCE and extended the empire throughout the whole of India. After Bindusara's death, his son 'Ashoka the

Great' ruled the Mauryan Empire for approximately 37 years. During his reign the empire flourished and was at its zenith. He contributed to the Indian heritage by building some of the greatest monuments and architecture. Like Chandragupta, Ashoka ruled like a lion in the Indian subcontinent. He conquered the undefeated eastern city-state of Kalinga which lead to a scary bloodshed and more than a hundred thousand deaths.

Though he won Kalinga, the destruction had a huge impact on him and awakened a human in a ruthless king who only knew victory till then. Ashoka embraced the teachings of the Buddha and decided to endorse Buddhism to make his contribution for humanity and peace. He established many monasteries and gave lavishly to Buddhist communities. His ardent support of Buddhist values eventually caused a strain on the government both financially and politically. Even his grandson, Sampadi, heir to the throne, opposed his policies. By the end of Ashoka's reign the government treasury was severely depleted through his regular religious donations and, after his death, the empire declined rapidly. In other words, his passive approach to governance, Brahminical opposition and unrest amongst the Vedic Believers lead to the dilapidation of the Mauryan Empire.

This deteriorated to such an extent that a Brahmin minister of the Mauryan Empire named as Pushyamitra Shunga overthrew the last heir of the Mauryans to establish the Shunga dynasty.

Shungas ruled for ten generations and after them the country once again splintered into many small kingdoms and the borders became vulnerable to be attacked or invaded by many foreign rulers. This era saw the increase of trade with Rome following Augustus Caesar's conquest of Egypt in 30 BCE. Egypt had always been India's constant partner in trade in the past. This was a time of individual and cultural development in the various kingdoms which finally flourished in what is considered the Golden Age of India under the reign of the Gupta Empire that ruled from 320-550 CE.

The Gupta Empire was founded by Sri Gupta who probably ruled between 240-280 CE, though this is an evaluated fact by the historians. But the ruler that evolved as a dominant one from the Gupta clan was Samudragupta who took the Gupta Empire to a new height completely. Gupta's rise to power was not swallowed by the caste system in India hence was opposed by the other classes especially the Brahmins because he came from the Vaish (Trader) family, who are entitled to pursue only trade and not to rule. However, the dynamic rulers of the Gupta clan laid the foundation for governance that would stabilize the society in many ways. As a result, every aspect of culture reached its height under the reign of the Guptas.

Till here we saw that India has been majorly ruled by the non Kshatriyas in the ancient times discarding the caste system that paralyzed India after the golden age when other castes were barely involved in the country's security and were dependent only on Kshatriyas and few rebellions to save their land.

Gupta period witnessed a lot of prosperity. Philosophy, literature, science, mathematics, architecture, astronomy, technology, art, engineering, religion, and astronomy; nearly all flourished during this period, resulting in some of the greatest of human achievements. The *Puranas of Vyasa* were compiled during this period and the famous caves of Ajanta and Ellora, with their elaborate carvings and vaulted rooms were also established. The artists set many milestones in many streams. For instance, Kalidasa, the poet wrote his masterpiece *Shakuntala* during this period. *Kama Sutra* was also written or compiled from earlier works, by Vatsyayana. Varahamihira explored astronomy further. Aryabhatta, the mathematician made his own discoveries in the respective field and also recognized the importance of the concept of zero which he is credited of inventing and which became a breakthrough in nearly all the modern inventions.

After Samudragupta, Chandragupta II contributed to the fame of the Gupta Empire that empowered the title of Golden Sparrow to the Indian Land because of the level of prosperity and abundance here. But many of the social evils continued to pluck the feathers of this sparrow. Brahminical unrest, caste system, gender discriminations, and lack of integrity amongst Hindus began to serve the purpose of the foreign elements.

The empire collapsed around 550 CE after the succession of weak rulers in the last one third of their tenure. Though after the Gupta Empire, King Harshavardhana held the command of this land for forty two years, after that again the boundaries of this subcontinent became vulnerable.

Harshvardhana was a literary man of considerable accomplishments. He authored three plays in addition to other works. He was also a patron of the arts and a devout Buddhist who forbade the killing of animals in his kingdom but he too recognized the necessity to sometimes kill humans in warfare to enforce peace and order.

This quality shows the essence of Hinduism. He was a highly skilled military tactician who was only defeated in the field once in his life that too by a Hindu emperor of the south whose name was Pulakeshin. Under his reign, the north of India flourished but his kingdom collapsed following his death. The invasion of the Huns, who were from what is today China, had been repeatedly repelled by Harshavardhana similar to Guptas in the past. Everytime they attempted to get inside the Indian borders, these Hindu kings would push them far away. But with the fall of his kingdom, India fell into chaos and fragmented into small kingdoms once again but this time not to be united by an Indian King but to be persecuted by the Muslim rulers; destiny was tired of giving a helping hand to the Hindu.

The Dacoit from the Middle East

TILL NOW THE birds flying in the Indian sky saw abundance and prosperity under them because the states were dominant, strong, and attentive, but now they had to soak their feathers into the blood of the offsprings of these warriors, who matched their DNA but their vigor and valor was lost to materialism and fatalism.

Thus, the phase of darkness began. As stated before, the platform for the monster of darkness was set up much before this by the caste hierarchies, gender discrimination, other shades of racism, and religious differences but the consolidation of states, strong governance, and armed strength of the kings pushed it back everytime it tried to spread its shadows on the Indian subcontinent.

But from the 7th century somewhere the boundaries of the nation and religion began to dilapidate creating a scope for foreign forces to latch on to the never ending wealth of India.

Until the end of 600 AD, Afghanistan, Pakistan, Nepal, Tibet, Bhutan, Bangladesh, Burma, Indonesia, Cambodia, Vietnam, Malaysia, Java, Sumatra, Maldives, and many other states were part of the Indian Subcontinent or were intensely influenced by the kings like Chandragupta Maurya, Ashoka, Guptas and Harshvardhana, as told by historians. Though it was not a consolidated nation, it did fall within the common boundaries while sharing the similar value system in terms of religion, society, and economic system. The people majorly followed the Hindu religion while leaving reasonable scope for other religions to grow for its liberal and embracing philosophies. As a result, Buddhism and Jainism grew to huge heights and were accepted by the Hindus.

All these regions were ruled by different emperors and there were occasional raids from groups of foreign origin especially Middle East. There were internal battles for expansion and other reasons within different states but on the whole the common people enjoyed a prosperous and peaceful life. But looking at the larger picture, the continent was fragmented into multiple small kingdoms and Indians could never realize that the small routine differences in the name of caste, region, language, religion, and most importantly lack of integrity will feed them into the mouth of the monster of darkness for a term that would be more than 1000 years.

As discussed above, between 606-647 AD India continued to enjoy harmony and prosperity during the rule of King Harshavardhana who ruled the country for approximately 41 years. During this period, in the Arab world, Islam as a religion came into existence which was a major turning point for the history of India; in fact the world. After this the pages of history needed no ink to be written because there was ample blood of Hindus to write the history of this dawn.

After the reign of Harshavardhana, there were occasional attacks by the Persians and Arabs but these attacks were secret and usually in the remote corners of India. The rulers of those times did not consider them as threats until Mohammad bin Qasim marched towards Sindh, though merely for loot, but this was the transition when India began facing major trouble from foreign attackers.

In the beginning of the medieval period, the Indian and the Arab subcontinent maintained quite cordial relations. There was harmony between the country and healthy trade relations. Arabs would come to India to exchange goods from the rest of the world and earned their living mostly by the profit margins.

But over a period of time the borders of this country began witnessing raids and trials of invasion along with business. Though these attempts were there before the 6th century too, our strong emperors threw the invaders away from time to time. As per historians, this time they did not aspire to rule here but to loot the wealth and resources and take them back home.

There were two eminent reasons of these loots.

First, their soil was not fit for agriculture so scarcity of edible resources compelled them to locate other resources of survival. They majorly depended on their role as mediators into trade between west and east before the sixth century. They would buy sandal, textiles, spices, cloves, camphor, black pepper, diamond, ivory, bamboo, and lead from India and sell that in the West. In return they would bring silk, weapons, horses, dates, alcohol, etc to Indians. They prominently dealt with Africa, Europe, and Egypt. Japan and Korea were also in the list.

Second, they depended on animal husbandry but rearing animals was also a rare possibility in the absence of adequate agricultural produce. As a result, they always had an eye on Indian soil that was an embodiment of fertility in every way. It was abundant in resources and precious stuff. Just as how the disadvantaged look at the advantaged; what he doesn't have, he wants to snatch from the one who possess it in abundance.

They did not foresee much scope of increasing their wealth in future. The only means to survive and increase their wealth was to snatch it from others especially India that was an enviably self reliant country possessing every means of survival, exactly opposite to the land of their origins.

A lot of trials took place between 636 to 637 AD in the caliphate of Hazrat Umar, but Indian kings would defeat them badly and push them away from their fences; majorly all trials of invasions failed. At that time, they would only come to the villages and loot the civilians and by the time soldiers would hear of them, they had already run away. But they continued with minor attacks in routine on civilians of small regions like Debal, Khari, and Baluchistan to steal their belongings.

The two generals, Al Haris in 662 AD and Al Muhallav in 664 AD, formally attacked under the guidance of the caliphs but they were defeated by the royals of those times.

Till now the motive behind all the attacks had been for either resources or power but with the birth of Islam, a completely different reason evolved. The concept of religion in these countries was now politicized, manipulated, and contaminated to a great extent. They would substantiate their political aspirations with twisted religious beliefs. It was difficult to differentiate between religion and politics. Religion had begun to be used as a powerful weapon to fulfill the political aspirations at the cost of the unaware people. The religious entities were seeking power hence they directed the warriors to increase the muscle power, wealth, and density of

Islamic population (basically their followers) while advocating divine reality that had no substantial meaning behind it. They bribed them with a dream of not only overpowering the other continents but also attaining heaven, the fairies, and other material comforts after death. In every case, they wanted Islam to grow so Islamic community dominates the world and they gain monopoly over the other religious beliefs.

A lot of international threats today are apparently the amplification of the same strategy.

Guided by such entities, it said that the royals of the Arab subcontinent began to focus on spreading Islam through the Islamic followers. Initially, it was to ensure that more and more people accept Islam as a religion but later it turned into a power struggle in which the believers of the monotheistic religion did not hesitate in forcing their belief on others worldwide, even if it takes holocausts of millions and billions mercilessly in the name of the Almighty; height of insanity. Who was behind this is not known but certainly those anti-human brains who did not mind using religion for their individual gains. The price was paid by the entire humanity for years to come; till date.

Gradually this became a visible reality of these countries. The kings of these countries consulted the caliphs for political decisions and the caliphs wanted dominance of Islam worldwide. The real essence of religion got lost in the power struggle and this power was not desired by exemplifying virtues but by sword; a bitter truth to swallow.

Hence, their political aspirations, practical approach, and religious fundamentalism pushed their cavalries towards a subcontinent whose habitants were ignorant of the approaching demon of darkness. They believed in virtues like *'Atithi Devo*

Bhava', Guest is God and '*Vasudhaiva Kutumbakam*', world is family. Nobody could imagine that due to these virtues, this Golden sparrow, as India was named in those days, was going to be shattered where wild beasts were waiting to pluck her feathers mercilessly for centuries to come unless Gods returned their blessings on her and her children and healed them with the patriotic ointments.

Removal of Article 370 & 35A and 2019 elections have been few drops of this ointment but a lot more is required.

Nobody knew that this bird would witness her people being enslaved, children being exploited, forced conversions, religion struggling for existence, land coloured not by mustard seeds but human blood, women being raped or committing self-immolations, skulls erected into pyramids, knowledge burnt to ashes, and temples plundered; a nude dance of the bare sword of brutality was performed in front of her eyes by the merciless invaders who knew no ethics or humanity. She did witness this, but still is trying to get up again and fly with her golden wings to restore her history.

The other corners of India have been secured mostly leaving only the north western borders to be the armor of the rest of the regions. Most of the invaders tried to enter this country from these borders that included Sindh, Punjab, and few more regions that is modern day Pakistan. What an irony, it was people of these regions who fought for the Hindu virtues and now they are persecuted to an extent that they either don't stand for their religion or some of their offsprings don't even want to accept that they are of Hindu origin. It is this deep that the claws of the monster have injured Hinduism.

In 600 AD, King Dahir, the ruling emperor of Sindh ignored

the initial trials, while underestimating the danger to his fences. This opened the door for the dacoits to loot the border areas. They did not know that the Middle East was preparing soldiers to plunder the Hindu civilization in the long run.

The first of this series of invaders was Mohammad Bin Qasim. Qasim first attacked Debal, an area located on the western frontiers of Sindh in 711 AD, but the king did not bother to protect it and continued saving the eastern borders, leaving the western fences to the amateur army men and civilians.

Few historians claim a story behind the formal attacks by Arabs. They say that Al Hajjaj requested King Dahir to recover their ships from the pirates of the sea who robbed them in the area of Sindh ports. These ships were loaded with precious gems and resources and were sailing from Sri Lanka as gifts for the Arab royals.

These ships were looted on the way and Al Hajjaj wanted King Dahir to catch the pirates and surrender the ships to him but the later refused to intervene into the matter. Though the Arabs were already planning to realize their greed of encroaching upon Indian borders, they now had a formal reason to attack King Dahir for their grudge against him.

As told above, after many successive attempts, the very first invader who successfully invaded the boundaries of Sindh was a seventeen-year-old Umayyad general Muhammad bin Qasim. He conquered the Sindh and Multan regions along the Indus River, which is now Pakistan, for the Umayyad Caliphate.

Qasim was born and raised in the city of Ta'if , which is modern-day Saudi Arabia. It is said that he was a full grown man for his age, a refined strategist of war tactics, brave and a profound soldier.

He had lost his father in early childhood and his mother raised him in the supervision of his paternal Uncle Al Hajjaj, who was also his father-in-law. He trained him in the armaments and military practices which became a reason for this young blood to defeat an old and experienced king like Raja Dahir.

His strategies followed no rules in war just like other invaders. They believed in victory by hook or by crook unlike Indian warriors. The story goes that he injured the Hindu king's elephant and when he fell down, a huge cavalry attacked him with arrows when he was carrying no weapons in hand. Multiple arrows pierced Dahir on his own land and the eclipse on Indian sky overshadowed the full moon for an unlimited tenure.

The irony was that Qasim's conquest of Sindh and southernmost parts of Multan opened the doors of Indian subcontinent for further Muslim conquests by boosting their confidence. These invasions were not to rule the country but to loot the resources and valuables and to spread Islam as it was instructed to them. Mohammad bin Qasim was one of those Muslim invaders who came from the jihadists' system of beliefs. They were fanatic and extremist because their trigger was in the hands of people who claimed them to be the messengers of the Divine.

They wanted to live or die for spreading Islam worldwide because this is what they were raised learning.

"My ruling is given: Kill anyone belonging to the combatants; arrest their sons and daughters for hostages and imprison them. Whoever submits…grant them protection and settle their tribute as dhimmah."

Instructions given to Muhammad bin Qasim by Hajjaj-Derryl N. MacLean, *Religion and Society in Arab Sind.*

The above quote leaves no scope of doubt that these invasions were erupting out of minds of religious fanatics who endorsed killings and slaughter of innocent people if they do not admit to their belief system. This was a conch horn of the devil.

Dr B.R. Ambedkar writes in his book *Pakistan or The Partition of India* that "Muhammad bin Qasim's first act of religious zeal was forcibly to circumcise the Brahmins of the captured city of Debal; but on discovering that they objected to this sort of conversion, he proceeded to put all above the age of 17 to death, and to order all others, with women and children, to be led into slavery. The temples of the Hindus were looted, and the rich booty was divided equally among the soldiers, after one-fifth, the legal portion for the government, had been set aside.

Another quote that approves of his jihadist ideology is the statement of the Hajjaj as under:

> I am appalled by your bad judgment and astounded by your policies. Why are you so intent on giving aman, even to an enemy whom you have tested and found hostile and intransigent? It is not necessary to give aman to everyone without discrimination.... In any case, if [the Sindis] sincerely request aman and desist from treachery, they will surely stop fighting. Then income will meet expenditures and this long situation will be concluded.... It is acknowledged that all your procedures have been in accordance with religious law [bar jadah-yi shar] except for the one practice of giving aman. For you are giving aman to everyone without distinguishing between friend and foe."
>
> —From a letter by Hajjaj to Muhammad bin Qasim.
> MacLean, *Religion and Society in Arab Sind.*

After Debal he attacked Rawar, Sehwan, Dhalila, Brahmanabad and Multan. The Hindu soldiers and men with arms were slain and so were the common men who refused to accept Islam. Few of them fled, and, if flight was not possible, accepted Islam. Many women of the higher class performed Jauhar, a Hindu custom of self-immolation, to save themselves from sexual horror and others became a prize of the unjustified victory. It is also said that Qasim had taken Raja Dahir's daughters, Parimal Devi and Suraj Devi, who were the beautiful princess, to be gifted to Al Hajjaj. Later these princesses were killed for conspiring to create a misunderstanding between Qasim and Al Hajjaj.

The queen also committed Jauhar to save her sanctity. In reality, this was the time when the tradition of Jauhar actually started in India as per the documented records. Sati tradition was not an eternal reality of our country but came into practice when women had to save themselves from the wild invaders especially Muslims.

Women and children were enslaved and converted. Some of them, were dispatched in batches to the Caliph in regular installments who sold them into the Arab market for wealth. After being sold these people were forced to live a life that was worse than animals and which is beyond our imagination. Even in this 21st century, we have social media reports on how they still continue to ill-treat their slaves. Though, this is not a general statement but true for at least a group of people.

Kufi, the author of the *Chach Nama* says that the total loot was distributed into five sections. Four sections were distributed amongst the soldiers and one section was sent to Hajjaj, the Governor of Iraq for onward transportation to the Khalifa.

The *Chach Nama* gives the details.

After the capture of the fort of Rawar, Muhammad bin Qasim "halted there for three days when he massacred nearly 6,000 men and their dependents like women and children were taken prisoners."

According to historians, the total number of prisoners taken were between thirty and sixty thousand amongst whom thirty were the daughters of the chiefs.

The head of Dahir and a fifth part of the prisoners were sent in charge of the Black Slave Kaab, son of Mubarak Rasti. In Sindh itself, female slaves captured after every campaign of the marching army, were forcibly married to Arab soldiers who settled down in colonies established in places like Mansura, Kuzdar, Mahfuza, and Multan.

The standing instructions of Hajjaj to Muhammad bin Qasim were to "give no quarter to infidels (hindus), but to cut their throats", and take the women and children as captives. In the final stages of the conquest of Sind, "when the plunder and the prisoners of war were brought before Qasim… one-fifth of all the prisoners were chosen and set aside; they were counted as amounting to twenty thousand in number… (they belonged to high families) and veils were put on their faces, and the rest were given to the soldiers". Few lakhs of women were enslaved and distributed amongst the elite and the soldiers.

Lal, K. S. (1992). *The legacy of Muslim rule in India.*

Such was the erosion of demography and prosperity that after the capture of Brahmanabad, "all people, the merchants, artisans, and agriculturists were divided separately into their respective classes, and ten thousand men, high and low, were counted. Muhammad bin Qasim then ordered twelve dirham weight of silver to be assigned to each man (for rehabilitation), because all their property had been plundered.

It is recorded that the Brahmins, the attendants of the temples were likewise in distress. For fear of the Muslim army, they were deprived of the basic utilities hence they were reduced to poverty. The temples had been plundered so the priests and their dependents had no employment and no income. It is documented that it was ordained by Qasim that the Brahmins should wander like beggars with a copper basin in their hands and go to the doors of the houses to take whatever grain or other things that would be offered to them to survive.

Qasim died an early death before even completing 20 years of his life. Regarding the death of Qasim, the story goes as follows. As it is not confirmed, a lot of facts floating around as history have question marks against them. This gives us the freedom to share what we learnt while researching this topic. This is because it helps us explain that the reasons behind this cruelty were never for religious or social reform but for filthy personal greed.

It is said that the two princesses longing for revenge narrated a false story to the Suleman that they were already molested by Mohammad bin Qasim before they reached him. For that, Suleman ordered Mohammad bin Qasim to reach him wrapped in a leather bag fully enclosed. Qasim captivated in his obedience and loyalty to his master, followed the instructions word by word because of which he died on the way out of suffocation. The princess on knowing this unveiled their lie to Suleman who later ordered their killing.

According to Tarek Fateh, a scholar and columnist of Pakistani origin, Raja Dahir is the hero of Sindh who gave refuge to Prophet Mohammad's family and saved him from the murderer from Arabia. In spite of this, in ignorance of reality, there came rapid conversions of Hindus into Islam. To save their life and their daughters from rape, the Hindus accepted Islam and became Muslims. To remind these are those persecuted Hindus who are currently known as Pakistanis.

The ones who resisted were slaughtered. There was no sin that was not committed in the name of religion. They looted the civilians, killed them, and raped their women.

The ray of positivity was always blinking in this dark sky though it could not completely eliminate the darkness. There were kings during this entire period who gave a tough fight to these outsiders but their number was not enough. Most of them surrendered to their fate, fear, or to their greed.

It is recorded that when Bappa Rawal, the influential and undefeated King of Mewar, came to know about this, he defeated Mohammad bin Qasim and threw him out of Sindh like a dog as told by historians. This defeat was so miserable that for many years invaders did not even think of invading Indian borders. However, later Qasim had died his own death to put a temporary break on the series of invasions. Also the Rajputs, the Jats, and the Gurjars all gave these thieves a tough fight there. Even though their mouth was watering for Indian resources they were pushed far behind the Indian soil.

Today, our history does not serve much information of Raja Dahir who had an important role in setting an example of secularism in India during those days and his story unveils many realities hidden in past that should be a learning lesson for Hindus and Muslims both. We don't even remember the Jauhar of his wife or the killing of his daughters along with thousands of Hindu princesses in the 7th century; thanks to our biased historical records.

All the above leads us to believe that Gods must have cursed the Hindus.

The Biggest Pathological Robbery: Shivalingam into Pieces

AFTER MOHAMMAD BIN Qasim, it took more than two hundred years, when the Islamic invaders gathered the courage to attack Indian borders once again. And this was during the reign of Mahmud of Ghazni who was the first independent ruler of the Ghaznavid dynasty.

He was the grandson of Alptegin who in 10th century founded an independent Turkish state in Ghazni, near Afghanistan.

He was succeeded by his son-in-law named Sabuktigin who made his first attempt to attack India. He attacked King Jayapala who was the ruler of what is currently known as Afghanistan which was a Hindu territory. The battle concluded into a peace treaty where both the rulers decided not to attack each other's kingdoms to maintain harmony.

Jayapala's capital was Vaihind which was also known as Udbhandpur and Peshawar, the cities that are based in modern day Pakistan. In short, the attack by Sabuktigin could be called as an unsuccessful attempt to invade India by the Turkish rulers.

Finally, the son of Sabuktigin, a man of Ghazanavi from Yamini dynasty attacked India 17 times as per records. He is described as a brave ruler who was difficult to be defeated. His attacks were not targeted to rule the country, but to loot the precious belongings and resources. However, he did dominate the Hindu territory by his barbaric war strategies.

He was the first emperor who entitled himself with a title of Sultan that means the supreme authority to exemplify the extent of his power while also preserving an ideological link to the suzerainty of the Abbasid Caliphate. During his rule, he invaded and plundered parts of the Indian subcontinent mostly the east of the Indus River.

In his first attempt, he attacked King Jayapala, with whom, his father Sabuktigin too fought in the past. But this time, the history was different.

Ghazni defeated King Jayapala which was a big shock for the latter. It was unacceptable for him to be defeated by the son of Sabuktigin who could not defeat him in the past. In 1000 AD, he attacked Afghanistan and Punjab that was the most fertile land fit for abundant agricultural resources. Historians give mixed opinion about Ghaznavi's motive behind these attacks. It was to take revenge for his father's defeat but also to encroach upon Punjab and Afghanistan's territory to loot and capture their resources and establish the dominance of Islam in the world.

Shocked by his defeat by a young king, Jayapala committed suicide. Historians of Mahmud of Ghaznavi condemn Jayapala as the "Enemy of Almighty". This shows the Jihadist bent of mind of this Muslim emperor like all others. Their fanaticism and will to impose their beliefs of monotheistic religion made them forget all rules of humanity.

During 1005 AD, Ghaznavi attacked Multan, Punjab, and

Afghanistan and plundered whatever came their way, living and non living.

Anandapala, the son of Jayapala succeeded him and continued the struggle to avenge his father's suicide. He assembled a powerful confederacy by joining hands with Gwalior, Kannauj, Ajmer, and Ujjain to defeat Ghaznavi in 1008 AD, but he suffered a defeat. It is said that his elephant turned back from the battleground at a crucial moment turning the circumstances into Mahmud's favor once more at Lahore in 1008 AD. This brought Mahmud into control of the Shahi dominions of Udbandpura which is modern day Peshawar. This again hints of a curse on Hindus when destiny turned her back on them for an unknown reason.

Following the defeat of the Indian Confederacy and after deciding to retaliate for the combined resistance of the Hindu warriors, Mahmud then set out on regular expeditions against them. Later, while leaving the conquered kingdoms into the hands of his Hindu vassals he annexed only the Punjab region. He also continued to raid and loot the wealthy region of northwestern India every year to add to his wealth. He also plundered a number of temples of this state during his raids.

In 1013 AD, during Mahmud's eighth expedition into eastern Afghanistan and Pakistan, the Shahi kingdom which was then under the King Trilochanapala, son of King Anandapala, was overthrown.

In 1014 AD Mahmud attacked Thanesar. In 1015 AD, he attacked Kashmir. Mahmud's army sacked Lahore but his expedition in Kashmir failed due to inclement weather. In 1017 AD, he attacked the kingdoms along the side of Yamuna River. This included Kannauj, Meerut, Muhavun, Mathura, and various other regions along the route.

In 1018-1020 AD he sacked the town of Mathura and defeated a coalition of rulers there while also killing a ruler called Chandrapala. During this attack, he plundered innumerable temples of Krishna and slaughtered the Brahmins and warriors who came his way.

During this period, Mahmud of Ghaznavi made another attempt to encroach upon the Indian territories by attacking Kannauj with his army. But the King of Kannauj, Rajyapala who was terrified by Ghaznavi, ran away without facing the battle. Aggravated by the cowardice of Rajyapala, Vidhyadhara, the King of Chander, a kingdom which was near Bundelkhand, formed a union of the Hindu empires. The union decided to locate Rajyapala and get him killed for his flight from a warrior's responsibility.

Vidhyadhara was a popular king who was famous for his bravery and vigor in the Hindu Kshatriya (Warriors) arena. Mahmud of Ghaznavi got furious with this episode because a king who ran away due to his fear was killed by an unknown king in punishment. Hence, in 1020 AD, Ghaznavi directed his forces towards Vidhyadhara but was unable to defeat him. The battle went on many days and at last Ghaznavi proposed for a peace treaty with Vidhyadhara. It is recorded that he also rewarded Vidhyadhara with fifteen forts. Every time the kings got united to fight against the invaders, they surrendered, but they were few in number. Unfortunately not many Vidhyadhars fought against Gaznavis else history would have been different.

He also attacked the Jat people of Jud. The Indian kingdoms of Nagarkot, Thanesar, Kannauj, and Gwalior were all conquered and left in the hands of Hindu, Jain, and

Buddhist kings as vassal states. He was pragmatic enough not to neglect making alliances and enlisting local people into his armies at all ranks. Since Mahmud never kept a permanent presence in the northwestern subcontinent, he engaged in a policy of destroying the Hindu temples and monuments to take away their wealth from time to time.

These facts of history were enough for a Hindu to be awakened but the curse continued and there was so much to happen ahead.

One of the last and the most important attack that no Hindu can ever forget and should not forget was the attack on Somnath temple in Gujrat. In this critical scenario, the king of this territory was Raja Bhimdev Solanki who fled leaving the city to its fate, which unfortunately favored Mahmud that time; perhaps to awaken the sleeping Hindu. The story of this attack is so painful that not only the Hindus but any human will burst out in tears.

Somnath temple was one of the twelve Jyotirlingas of Lord Shiva. Located in Prabhas Patan near Veraval in the Saurashtra region in the West coast of Gujarat, the temple was the Mecca of Hindus. The temple was located in such a way that there is no landmass in a straight line between Somnath seashore until Antarctica, as mentioned by a Sanskrit inscription found encrypted on an Arrow-Pillar called Baan-Stambh that is erected on the sea-protection wall. It mentions that the pillar stands at a point on the Indian landmass that is the first point on land in the north of the South Pole at that particular longitude.

According to the ancient scriptures, the Somnath temple was first built by Raja Somraj in gold in the Satyayuga, then by Ravana in silver in Tretayuga, in wood by Krishna in

Dwaparyuga, and finally in stone by Bhimdev Solanki in what is called Kaliyuga.

Somnath temple is a rich cultural heritage that held extreme importance for Hindu sentiments. Records show that the pilgrim faced a number of attacks in a row. Every time the invaders would come, plunder a part of this huge temple, and loot the precious gems. The kingdoms would every time restore its decor and wealth.

Gazni's attack on this culturally, religiously, spiritually, and historically rich pilgrimage site was probably the most drastic and painful attack on the soul of Hindus. Though, he wanted to rob the unlimited wealth of the temple, he also plundered it multiple times as mentioned in the narratives.

Ghazni's last attempt became history that could never be restored. All the limits were crossed this time. It is recorded that Ghaznavi broke the pious Shivalingam with a hammer multiple times and took the pieces of this divine idol with himself as an emblem of his victory. People encircled the lingam and laid on floor to stop him from doing so but in no time they were brutally killed. Later, he embedded the pieces of the lingam into the staircase of a mosque known as Jama Masjid situated in Ghazni. This pathological robber also took along with him the huge sandalwood doors of Somnath sanctorum that were later used to adorn his tomb when he died 4 years later in 1030 AD at the age of fifty nine.

Ghazni's expedition was triggered by illicit will and continued for few years while he was emptying India's wealth and civilization to the core. The Islamic entities honored him with the title of 'Ghazi' for this victory. Ghazi means the one who kills the infidels. For them, anyone who believes in any other religion except Islam was an infidel and the Hindu was on top of their list. The other title he was honored with was of 'butshikan', the one who plundered idols, which he substantiated by plundering the great Shiva Lingam of Somnath temple by his own hands.

Al Biruni described the Temple's destruction as follows:

In January 1026, Somnath Lingam was smashed, after killing 50,000 devotees, and the loot amounted to 20,000,000 dinars, each containing 64.8 grains of gold. The smashed Shiva Lingam was carried to Ghazni where some of the fragments were turned into steps of the Jama Masjid in the city, while the rest were sent to Mecca, Medina, and Baghdad to be desecrated in the same manner.

The savagery was described by Minhaj-i-Siraj in *Tabakat-I-Nasiri* (Tabaquat-i-Nasiri) as, "When Sultan Mahmud ascended the throne of sovereignty, his illustrious deeds became manifest unto all mankind within the pale of Islam, when he converted so many thousands of idol-temples into masjids, and captured so many of the cities of Hindustan, and overthrew and subdued its Raes, Jaipal, who was the greatest of the Raes of Hind, he made captive, and kept him [a prisoner] at ManYazid, in Khurasan, and commanded that he might be ransomed for the sum of eighty dirams. He led an army to Nahrwalah of Gujarat, and brought away Manat, the idol, from Somnath, and had it broken into four parts, one of which was cast before the entrance of the great masjid at Ghazni, the second before the gateway of the Sultan's palace, and the third and fourth were sent to Makkah and Madinah respectively."

According to Persian Geographer Qazvini, "When Sultan Mahmud, the son of Sabuktigin, went to wage religious war against India, he made great efforts to capture and destroy Somnath in the hope that the Hindus would then become Mohammedans. He arrived there in the middle of Zu-l-ka'da, 416 AD. The Indians made a desperate resistance. They kept going into the temple weeping and crying for help; and then they issued forth to battle and kept fighting till all were killed. The number of the slain exceeded fifty thousand. The king looked upon the idol with wonder, and gave orders for the seizing of the spoils and the appropriation of the treasures. There were many idols of gold and silver, and countless vessels set with jewels, all of which had been sent there by the greatest personages in India. The value of the things found in the temples and the idols exceeded twenty thousand dinars."

Somnath as mentioned earlier was a glittering jewel in the eyes of robbers. After that also, it was destroyed three more times from 1297 AD to 1395 AD by the Sultanate of Delhi. The last time it was plundered and looted by the Mughal ruler, Aurangzeb in 1706 AD who made his identity in history by persecuting Hindus and their pathological belief system.

This has been the extent of persecution of Hindus in the past and there are millions of other examples that would bring tears into humanity's eyes but we as a community are still struggling to identify how the past is repeating in modern times. We neither realized then nor do we realize today. We used our knowledge and wisdom to manipulate what was taught to us and accept what is going on as natural course of action because we do not want to stand for our religious and cultural wealth. This could be nothing but a curse; curse of Gods.

The Hindu temples were always targeted by these illiterate pathological robbers. This was obviously due to the effulgence of Indian wealth that blinded their greedy eyes since forever. Such wealth was beyond their dreams in societies where they came from. They had no intelligence and sensitivity to understand the sanctity and subtlety of Hindu culture which was the reason for this age old civilization to sustain and recover even after being persecuted from across the world relentlessly. Archaeological findings suggest that Somnath Temple was rebuilt at least three times before Mahmud Ghaznavi's raid.

In independent India, the restoration of Somnath temple was not easy. It was opposed by the Muslims as well as the Hindu policymakers like Jawaharlal Nehru who feared annoying the Muslim segments. This was because Muslims have been the vote banks of Congress for long and so they always refrained from standing for the Hindu religion. However, it's a different thing that when politically it was required, they were noticed in the temples wearing the sacred threads in renowned holy places to create a buzz for their Hindu identity. This was nothing but a strategy to bag the Hindu voters.

It is still surprising why Muslims of independent India would oppose restoration of the symbol of the Hindu's religious sentiments? But we could see the same opposition in the Babri Masjid issue where construction of the Ram Mandir was not supported by them for decades. Is secularism only a Hindu's obligation? How can restoring what is rightfully yours especially when it has a sentimental value attached be annoying for any being in this world. But it happened; a truth that can't be digested.

The irony is that after 1000 years of holocaust also, Indians still found a scope for debate on reconstructing the Somnath Temple after Independence for which the sons of this motherland sacrificed their lives. It is interesting to note that Mahatma Gandhi was in favor of rebuilding the temple though he did not want this to be constructed with the State funds. His excuse was not to attempt anything that could threaten Muslims. The irony is that Muslims have been getting the subsidies for Haj for decades and the Hindus never got threatened. But if a Hindu temple is constructed with the same taxes that Hindus pay, the Muslims would be threatened; this could only be a curse of Gods.

The appointed archaeology expert expressed his worry about the safety of the fast decaying structure of historical relevance so he suggested constructing a new temple at a different location. This was because they were concerned that the concourse of devotees coming from all parts of India and rushing through the dilapidating building will lead to its speedy decay. Thus, the Junagadh State Administrator, who was a British, suggested preserving it as an archaeological site and not as a temple. The Education Ministry gave its consent to this view for it was headed by Maulana Azad. However, Home Minister Sardar Patel wanted to restore and preserve the temple along with necessary safety provisions.

Well, after few debates, it was finally decided to rebuild the Temple—where it always stood. On January 23 1949, with consent of Mahatma Gandhi, who was initially in dilemma as he did not want to annoy Muslims, Sardar Patel and other leaders managed to erect this dilapidated religious emblem once again. In 1970, a statue of Sardar Patel was inaugurated in the temple because he was the main person who made it happen convincing and arguing with the Hindu and non-Hindu leaders.

Politician, writer and educationist from Gujarat state Shri

Kanaiyalal Maneklal Munshi, in his book Jay Somnath, writes as follows:

The Shrine Eternal: In the beginning, some persons, more fond of dead stones than live values, pressed the point of view that the ruins of the old temple should be maintained as an ancient monument. We were, however, firm in our view, that the temple of Somnath was not an ancient monument; it lived in the sentiment of the Whole nation and its reconstruction was a national pledge. Its preservation should not be a mere matter of historical curiosity. Some of my scholar friends had hard things to say about me, for my 'vandalism'. They forgot that I am fond of history, but fonder still of creative values. When the question was pressed by the Archaeological Department, Sardar expressed his views as follows:

He also quotes a statement of Mr. Sardar Patel

"The Hindu sentiment in regard to this temple is both strong and widespread. In the present conditions, it is unlikely that, the sentiment will be satisfied by mere restoration of the temple or by prolonging its life. The restoration of the idol would be a point of honour and sentiment with the Hindu public."

The museum would have restored the dead body of the Hindu Heritage and the soul would have been missing. Thankfully we had leaders like Sardar Vallabhbhai Patel who stood for Dharma and infused life into it from time to time which is why this religion exists today, else, the other Hindus were enough to persecute them as they did for ages.

Hindu Will Spare,
but they will not

AS MENTIONED EARLIER, till the 10th century these attacks were merely restricted to loot, killings, and conversions to an extent. The thieves intended to come and steal the wealth of India but they did not dare to establish themselves here. Their aspirations amplified by the time 11th century came to its third quarter.

In 1175 AD Mu'izz ad-Din Muhammad Ghori, born as Shihab ad-Din attacked the region of Multan which is currently at the border of Pakistan. Later in 1178 AD he directed his army towards the Chaulukya capital of Anhilwara which is modern day Patan in Gujarat where he was badly defeated by Mularaja II who is also known as Bhim Singh II in the battle of Kayadara. Bhim Singh II imprisoned Ghori for few years but later granted him freedom assuming that he would not dare to look at India again.

Asoke Kumar Majumdar in his book, *Chaulukyas of Gujarat* states while referring to the 13th century Persian chronicler *Minhaj-i-Siraj*, that Muhammad of Ghor marched towards Nahrwala, the Chaulukya capital Anhilwara via Uchchha and Multan. The "Rae of Nahrwala", the

Chaulukya King was young, but commanded a huge army with elephants. In the ensuing battle, "the army of Islam (Ghor) was defeated and put to rout", and the invading ruler had to return without any accomplishment.

He also refers to an account by Nizam-ud-din that states that Muhammad of Ghor marched to Gujarat via the desert.

The 16th century writer Badauni also mentions the invader's defeat, and states that he retreated to Ghazni with great difficulty. Firishta also states that the ruler of Gujarat defeated the Muslim army 'with great slaughter', and the remnant of the defeated army faced many hardships during his return journey to Ghazni.

This was probably the biggest mistake of the victorious king who had the power to prevent the country from these barbaric attackers who knew no humanity or ethics. Was this not an effect of the curse of Gods? Our ancestors could easily have prevented the monster of darkness from growing further but they did not, despite the ample opportunities to do so. They commited the same mistake again and again; overlooking the danger. Had Bhim Singh II killed Mohammad Ghori, India would have been saved by these brutal chapters of Muslim invasions because it was this particular invader who implanted the seeds of Muslim rule in India. This was the first defeat of Ghori in India that could have benefitted the nation big time.

The most repetitive mistakes of our ancestors were their forgiveness. They forgave so many invaders so many times constructing a bridge for the demon of darkness to reach the bright culture of India. In the past, Bappa Rawal released Qasim after defeating him. Apart from this too we can see many occasions when Hindu kings spared the lives of invaders similar to the leaders of the independent India who missed many opportunities of teaching a lesson to Pakistan.

In 1186 AD, Ghori along with Ghiyath, ended the Ghaznavid dynasty after having captured Lahore and focused on planning a series of invasions against India. Later in 1191 AD, Ghori, through the Khyber Pass in modern-day Pakistan, managed to reach Punjab and captured a fortress in Tabar-e-Hind which is currently known as Bhatinda.

Bhatinda was the northwestern frontier of Prithviraj Chauhan's kingdom. Prithviraj, then, was a teen prince who acquired the throne of Ajmer. He defeated the Chandels in the battle of Mahoba in which two brothers named as Alha and Udal were killed. These two brothers also find a lot of fame in the history of Hindu warriors.

The king got the information of Prithviraj's army approaching Bhatinda to besiege the fortress. The army led by his vassal prince Govind Tai was known to be a huge composition of soldiers, cavalries and elephants. Hence, he directed his army to prevent him from reaching Bhatinda. The two armies eventually met on the way, near the town of Tarain, which is modern day Ambala, and was 14 miles from Thanesar in present-day Haryana. The battle was marked by the initial attack of mounted Mamluk archers to which Prithviraj responded by counter-attacking from three sides and thus dominating the battle. Ghori was seriously wounded so his army retreated and Prithviraj won this battle that is famous as the first battle of Tarain. Hammir-Mahakavya states that Prithviraj imprisoned Ghori but he spared him instead of killing him for he was already mortally injured; another mistake of the Indian Rulers who allowed a cancer to develop in the future of India.

After this, Ghori returned to Ghazni. However, he did not sit back but continued with his preparations for another attack on Prithviraj Chauhan who was one of the biggest challenges on his mission to establish their rule in India. This is a learning why a soldier should not spare his enemy because he would bounce back with much more strength and a spirit to take revenge.

The same is repeated by the governments when they leave the terrorists or stretch the criminal cases against them for a long time inviting trouble for the entire nation.

As expected, Mohammad Ghori planned to attack now with much more strength and with much more precision this time. The motto of this invader was to win by hook or by crook. Although, Prithviraj's army was one of its kind in those days and as historians say, defeating it was considered next to impossible.

According to Firishta, the Rajput army consisted of 3,000 elephants, 300,000 cavalry and infantry where as Minhaj-i-Siraj, stated that Ghori brought 120,000 fully armored men to the battle in 1192.

Prithviraj invited the entire Rajputana to assist him in defeating this invader and sending him far behind the boundaries of the Indian subcontinent. Where few stood with the young king, few like Jaichand refused to assist him keeping personal grudges over the welfare of his countrymen. This was because the rulers of India never perceived this land as one integrated country connected by the single religion which was Hinduism, common scriptures called Vedas, common mythological history, and common interest.

As observed in our famous epics like Ramayana and

Mahabharata, the Indian soldiers followed strict rules and regulation in war also as we are a country of ethics and civilization. Since the Dasraj Yudha, to Mahabharata, our warriors religiously followed these constitutional directives. As mentioned there, the Indian soldiers never attack any army post sunset and these rules were not broken even in the greatest epic called Mahabharata which is a tale of a fierce battle as per Hindu records. But Muslim invaders like Ghori had no dos and don'ts in their dictionary which is an identical reality of all the Muslim invaders.

This was the historical fact of this war. In fact, a game changing move of Ghori. Knowing of this rule of the Indian Army, Ghori attacked the Rajput army before dawn when everyone was in deep sleep. Although, they were able to quickly form formations, they suffered losses due to the surprise attack before sunrise. Few historians also say that Ghori's Army did not attack from the front but from behind which was another objectionable war strategy for Hindu soldiers. Given these circumstances, the Rajput army was eventually defeated and Prithviraj was arrested at the bank of river Sarasvati. Later he was taken to Ghazni.

The mistake here was that they expected the Muslim invaders to abide by the rules and regulations forgetting about the massacres and plunder by Qasim and Ghori who had already shown the wild face of their value system.

The story after this incident shows a lot of contradictory facts. Historians have diversified views regarding the same.

As Professor Hasan Nizami says, he (Prithviraj Chauhan) accepted the overlordship of Muhammad but, when found guilty of a conspiracy against Muhammad, was punished with death. The second battle of Tarain proved to be one of the decisive battles of Indian history. It settled the future course of India.

After the fall of Prithviraj Chauhan, Ghori captured the Hindu kingdoms like Saraswati, Samana, Kohram and Hansi with not much difficulty and finally, he directed his forces towards Delhi.

As Dr D C Ganguly writes: "The defeat of Prithviraja in the second battle of Tarain not only destroyed the imperial power of the Chahamanas (Chauhans), but also brought disaster on the whole of Hindustan."

The battle led the way to the conquest of India by the Turks. Ajmer and Delhi both were occupied by Muhammad which paved the way for his further conquests in India. Besides this, the battle definitely weakened the morale of other Rajput rulers to stand against Turk invaders.

Soon after that, within a year's time, Ghori took control of northern Rajasthan and the northern part of the Ganges-Yamuna Doab. Though, he returned to Ghazni to deal with the threat to his western frontiers from the unrest in Iran, he appointed Qutb-ud-din Aybak as his regional governor northern India. This is how the slave Dynasty was established.

What Goes Around Comes Around

QUTB-UD-DIN AYBAK consolidated the Indian conquests of Muhammad, and suppressed the revolts of the Chauhans at Ajmer. He made Delhi the capital of the kingdom in India in 1193 AD after conquering Ranthambhor, Meerut, Bulandshahar, Aligarh, etc. in the absence of Muhammad.

Muhammad came back to India in 1194 AD. This time his target was the kingdom of Kannauj ruled by Jayachandra, who had enmity with Prithviraja III due to which he did not help him in the second battle of Tarain against Ghori.

As a result, now it was his turn to face Muhammad Ghori alone. It is rumored that Jaichand for his personal grudges helped Ghori in defeating Prithviraj Chauhan; by doing a secret treaty with Ghori. However, there is no evidence of this treaty and this narrative is considered as superficial by history.

Mohammad Ghori ditched Jaichand also while punishing the king for trusting this cheat outsider instead of supporting the Rajput king Prithviraj Chauhan who was also his son-in-law. 'What goes around comes around'. This was probably a reminder by the universe to wake up and get integrated before an outsider takes advantage of domestic differences but unfortunately as always the message was missed.

The battle between Muhammad and Jayachandra took place near Chandawar on the river Yamuna between Etawah and Kannauj. Jayachandra was killed in the battle affecting the morale of Rajputs. Taking advantage of the same, Muhammad proceeded to Banaras and occupied all the important places of the kingdom of Kannauj.

Leaving Qutb-ud-din Aybak again, Muhammad went back. Aybak consolidated his conquests as usual and suppressed the ongoing revolts taking place at Ajmer, Aligarh, and other corners of India. In 1195 AD, he conquered Bayana and attacked Gwalior.

After this, Muhammad could not come back to India for some years and the responsibility of consolidating his conquests in India rested on Qutb-ud-din Aybak. A serious revolt in Rajasthan was suppressed by Qutb-ud-din Aybak after much difficulty. Thereafter, Aybak attacked Gujarat and plundered its capital Anhilwara in 1197 AD Aybak also conquered Badaun, Banaras, Chandawar, and consolidated the conquest of Kannauj.

The Chandela ruler, Paramaladeva of Bundelkhand was now the only independent Rajput ruler in central India. The fort of Kalinjar was regarded as an impregnable fort but Aybak attacked that too in 1202-03 AD

Paramaladeva died during the course of this warfare but the Chandelas continued with their revolt under the leadership of his minister Ajayadeva. Ultimately, the Chandelas had to leave the fort. Later, Qutb-ud-din Aybak also occupied Mahoba and Khajuraho.

Thus, Muslims dominated central India and Hindus continued to sulk in the corners captivated by the monster of darkness that was now openly hovering over the country.

And, It was too late: Very late

FAR AWAY FROM north, Bengal and Bihar were targeted by Muhammad Bakhtiyar Khilji who began his career as an ordinary soldier and received some villages as Jagir from his master Hisam-ud-din Aghul Bak, the governor of Oudh.

There he gathered a small army of his followers and raided the nearby territories of Bihar. The astonishing fact is that nobody tried to oppose him anywhere which boosted his morale. In 1202-03 AD, he attacked Odantapuri and plundered the Buddhist monastery. Next, he conquered Nalanda and Vikramasila as well where he plundered the world class universities giving a big setback to Hindu intellectual wealth. Plundering of Nalanda and Vikramashila universities are the deepest wounds on the Indian Civilization. These universities were the epitome of knowledge and produced thousands of intellectuals who kept the foundation of Indian heritage in various disciplines from Ayurveda to Astrology and mathematics to science. Not only from India, but the international community also sent their students to be trained in these universities.

Lakshmana Sena, the ruler of Bengal, took no steps to

stop him so far. As a result, Bakhtiyar-ud-din attacked Nadia, the capital of Bengal in 1204-05 AD During the same period in north-west, the Khokhars tried to capture Lahore when Muhammad had come to India. He fought a battle against the Khokhars between the rivers Chenab and Jhelum. Though Khokhars fought fiercely, they were defeated and punished mercilessly.

On the way, while he was engaged in his evening prayers, an unknown entity stabbed him on 15 March, 1206 AD at Damyaka on the banks of the river Indus. The body of Muhammad was carried to Ghazni and buried there. Whether the assassins were Khokhars or fanatical Shias of the heretical Ismaili sect still remains a mystery.

Aybak initiated the construction of Delhi's earliest Muslim monuments known as the Quwwat-ul-Islam mosque and the Qutub Minar. Though this fact is also debated by the scholars of the right wing with an argument that Qutub Minar was founded by Hindu monarchs and not Muslims for the encrypted walls and the pillars aside resembles the architecture of Ashoka's reign. However, there are rare proofs to substantiate their argument.

Aybak's reign as the Sultan of Delhi was not for a very long time as he died in 1210 AD and his son Aram Shah rose to the throne as the second Sultan who ruled from 1210 to 1211 AD But he too was assassinated for an elite group of forty nobles known as the *Chihalgani* conspired against him. Chihalganis could be referred as the pressure group that influenced the Delhi Sultanate with an intense power on the policymakers. They invited Shams-ud-din Iltutmish, then Governor of Badaun, to replace the existing Sultan. Iltutmish defeated Aram in the plain of Jud near Delhi in 1211AD.

Thus, Shams-ud-din Iltutmish became the third sultan of Delhi who reigned from 1211 to 1236 AD. He shifted the capital from Lahore to Delhi and troubled the exchequer. Rukn-ud-din Feroze followed Iltutmish and reigned from April 1236 to November 1236 AD. He ruled for only seven months under the guidance of his mother, Shah Turkan. Both mother and son were assassinated by the Chihalganis.

The fifth Sultana was the first female Muslim ruler in India known as Razia al-Din who had the titular name of *Jalâlat-ud-dîn Raziyâ Sultana*. She reigned from 1236 to 1240 when she managed to impress the nobles and administratively handled the Sultanate well but was resisted by Muslim nobles who were against the female monarch; the gender biased belief system.

The powerful nobleman Malik Altunia defeated her whom she later agreed to marry but her half-brother Muiz-ud-din Bahram, however, managed to snatch the throne from her with the help of the Chihalgani and defeated the combined forces of the Sultana and her husband. It is said that the couple went to Kaithal, where they both were assassinated by Jats on 14 October, 1240.

After this the Sultanate was ruled by many not so strong rulers for short intervals such as Muiz-ud-din Bahram, Ala-ud-din Masud, Nasir-ud-din Mahmud and Ghiyas ud din Balban.

The last Sultan of the Delhi sultanate was Muiz-ud-din Muhammad Qaiqabad who reigned from 1287 to 1290. But he was later murdered in 1290 by a Khilji who brought Slave dynasty to an end opening the door of Delhi to the Khiljis who wrote another chapter of brutality in India.

The slave or Mamluk dynasty ruled from 1290 to 1320

AD where on the other side a group from Hindu arena was trying to recover from their losses. The Hindu princes and chiefs were discontented at their loss of independence and had recovered Kannauj, Banaras, Gwalior, and Kalinjar that were lost during Qutb-ud-din Aybak's reign. Ranthambore had been re-conquered by the Chauhans during Aram Shah's rule.

It is not that the entire Hindu community was sitting quiet but the ones who rebelled were very few in number. They too only rebelled when it came to their own empire and not for the other Hindu rulers leaving the Hindu belt struggling alone with the Muslims. They did not cross their borders giving hand to the other rulers and crush the Muslim invaders at the seed level. Hence, the poisonous seeds grew into the gigantic trees with its roots hollowing the soil of India till date.

As we said earlier, had all the Hindu kings raised their swords with Raja Dahir and Prithviraj Chauhan, the golden sparrow of India would have been flying with the added feathers in the world and the holocausts of Hindus would have remained only a dream for the Invaders.

Khilji dynasty was known for its ferocity and conquests into the south. They are also credited for successfully fending off the repeated Mongol invasions of India.

Sultan of Delhi, Ghiyas ud din Balban made way for Khiljis in India when Bakhtiyar Khilji established the Muslim rule in east India as mentioned above.

Later, Jalal ud din Firuz Khilji, the seventy years old sultan who is also known as the founder of the Khilji dynasty assumed the throne of Sultan of Delhi after assassinating the seventeen-year-old Mamluk successor, Muiz ud din Qaiqabad. Muiz ud din Qaiqabad was the last ruler of the Mamluk dynasty.

Historians describe Khilji as a humble and kind monarch to the general public. He managed to sow the seeds of the Khilji's rule in the Delhi Sultanate that his nephew, Alauddin Khilji who was also his son-in-law, inherited from him. From here the Khiljis began spreading their influence on the entire Indian subcontinent including a part of the south. He raided the Deccan peninsula and Deogiri, the capital of the Hindu state of Maharashtra. After that he returned to Delhi in 1296 AD. Later, he murdered Jalal-ud-din also and assumed power as Sultan of the Delhi Sultanate only to advance the chapter of barbaric Muslim rule in India.

He continued expanding Delhi Sultanate into South India with the help of generals such as Malik Kafur and Khusrau Khan who attacked and raided multiple Hindu kingdoms of that period. This was to gather wealth in order to strengthen the army of Khilji. They collected the war spoils from the Hindu kingdoms and paid a section of it to the Sultan's treasury.

The throne of Delhi bore the burden of this Muslim invader for twenty years to witness him attacking and seizing the Hindu states of Ranthambhor in 1301 AD, Chittorgarh in 1303 AD, and Mandu in 1305 AD. He badly plundered the wealthy state of Devagiri along with other accounted and unaccounted wealth of Hindus.

Each and every attack of Khilji is a tale of nasty bloodshed and terror, especially for women who had to turn into ashes or drown into the river to save their sanctity.

He also managed to guard the boundaries of India from the Mongols at that time. The invader was famous for the slaughters he committed in the attacked kingdoms after wars. Historians describe him as a tyrant to anyone who was suspected of being a threat to his power. He would brutally assassinate suspects and the women and children of that family.

Vincent A Smith in *The Oxford History of India: From the Earliest Times to the End of 1911* mentions that in 1298, between 15,000 and 30,000 people near Delhi who had recently converted to Islam were slaughtered in a single day due to fears of an uprising.

William Wilson Hunter in *The Indian Empire: Its Peoples, History, and Products* also account for his brutality. The author writes that Alauddin also killed his own family members and nephews in 1299-1300 AD after he suspected them of rebellion by first gouging out their eyes and then beheading them.

In 1308 AD, Alauddin's commander, Malik Kafur, a Hindu converted to Islam captured Warangal. He overthrew the Hoysala Empire located at the south of the Krishna River and raided Madurai in Tamil Nadu. He plundered and looted the treasury in capitals and from the temples of south India.

Alauddin Khilji was one of the very few invaders who could reach south India unlike other Muslim rulers till thirteenth century. Kohinoor, the largest known diamond in human history was also looted by Malik Kafur who returned to Delhi in 1311 AD laden with loot and war booty from Deccan peninsula, which he submitted to Khilji. This made him the favorite of Alauddin Khilji.

To maintain his growing army, Khilji crushed the commoners with the burden of multiple taxes that were threefold and at times tenfold than what was reasonable; though, expecting something reasonable in the Muslim rule was insane.

Alauddin Khilji enforced four taxes on non-Muslims in the

Sultanate. This included jizya: the poll tax, kharaj: the land tax, Kari: the house tax and Chari: the pasture tax.

He also instructed his Delhi-based revenue officers to assist by local Muslim Jagirdars, Khuts, Mukkadims, Chaudharis and Zamindars to collect half of the total produce by the farmers. Those who resisted had to bleed and bury themselves under the soil. Historians say that the Tax system introduced during the Khilji dynasty had a long term influence on Indian taxation system and state administration. We see its impact in the 19th century and the 20th century too.

The Cambridge Economic History of India: c.1200-c.1750 states that "Alauddin Khilji's taxation system was probably the one institution from his reign that lasted the longest, surviving indeed into the nineteenth or even the twentieth century. From now onwards, the land tax, kharaj or mal, as it was called, became the principal form in which the peasant's surplus was expropriated by the ruling class."

Not only the taxation liability was unjustified but the collection policies were also far away from humane. Failure in the tax submission lead to slavery and torture. Along with the people who were seized during raids and attacks, people who were tax defaulters were also enslaved with family.

Institution of slavery and bondage labor was a common feature of the Muslim rule and Khilji rule was no exception, but an extension of the illicit tradition. Male slaves were referred to as banda, qaid, ghulam, or burdah who were treated worse than the animals and female slaves were called bandi, kaniz or laundi who were not just tortured but were molested and sexually abused to the depth of their soul. The daughters that we pray on *'Kanyapoojan'* and touch their feet were turned into the concubines of these wild beasts.

We can't imagine how many cries are buried under the foundation of these monuments built by Muslim invaders who painted our history with blood of humanity and will always occupy a space reminding us of the cries of our own people.

Though, the authenticity of the narrative of Padmavat is questioned by few historians but as the trend of self immolation was a sure shot reality of the Muslim rule in India, there is more possibility of the story being true.

Many princess and queens had to burn themselves into ashes to save their dignity from the cruel nasty invaders like Khilji who would have scratched their pure bodies like vultures.

The Khilji dynasty ruled the Delhi Sultanate before 1320 AD.

After the death of Khilji in 1315 AD, Malik Kafur rose to the throne of Delhi but he was assassinated in a very short span of time. Thereafter, for the next three years, three more sultans assumed power but were killed in coups. Following Malik Kafur's death, the Amirs installed a six-year-old named Shihab-ud-din Omar as sultan and his teenage brother, Qutb-ud-din Mubarak Shah, as regent. Qutb killed his younger brother to appoint himself as sultan. To win over the loyalty of the Amirs and the Malik clan, Mubarak Shah offered Ghazi Malik the position of army commander in Punjab. After ruling for four years, Mubarak Shah was murdered in 1320 AD by one of his generals, Khusrau Khan. Amirs persuaded Ghazi Malik who was still army commander in Punjab to lead a coup. Ghazi Malik's forces attacked Delhi to capture Khusrau Khan and beheaded him. Upon becoming sultan, Ghazi Malik renamed himself Ghiyath al-Din Tughluq who became the first ruler of the Tughluq dynasty.

The irony is that the last ruler of this dynasty, Khusrau Khan was a Hindu who had been forcibly converted to Islam. He served the Delhi Sultanate as the general of its army for some time. Khusrau Khan, along with Malik Kafur who also was a convert, had led numerous military campaigns on behalf of Alauddin Khilji to expand the Sultanate and plunder non-Muslim kingdoms in India. Both of them had the Hindu DNA but they both lived and died to finish the Hindu religion from India. Gods must have cursed the Hindus.

Muslim Genes
and Hindu Wombs

GHAZI MALIK ACQUIRED the throne under the title of Ghiyath al-Din Tughluq establishing the Tughluq dynasty in Delhi.

The dynasty expanded its territorial reach through a military campaign led by Muhammad bin Tughluq who was known for his torture, cruelty, and exceptionally brutal behavior towards Hindus. He was of Turko-Indian origins. His father was a Turkic slave and his mother was a Hindu but he exemplified an extreme intolerance towards the Hindu community. This is another example that a Hindu-Muslim marriage did not convert a Muslim heart into a Hindu but only a Hindu womb into Muslim womb.

It was in the reign of Ghiyas-ud-din Tughluq when Tughlakabad, a city near Delhi was constructed. The city was planned with a fort in order to protect Delhi Sultanate from Mongol attacks.

The ruler reduced the tax rate on Muslims and raised the taxes on Hindus as written by his court historian Ziauddin Barani to make sure that they might not be blinded by wealth or afford to become rebellious. Withdrawing their financial powers was a far-sighted policy to weaken the Hindu community in future. This was to be able to persecute them further.

In 1321 AD, his eldest son Ulugh Khan went to Deogir to plunder the Hindu kingdoms of Arangal and Tilang which is modern day Telangana. After few attempts, Ghiyas-ud-din Tughluq succeeded in plundering Arangal and Tilang. Arangal was renamed to Sultanpur and the wealth was transported to Delhi Sultanate.

There are many controversies on how Ghiyas-ud-din Tughluq was killed but his son Juna Khan ascended to power as Muhammad bin Tughlaq and ruled for twenty-six years.

Delhi Sultanate temporarily expanded to most of the Indian subcontinent during Muhammad bin Tughluq's rule. He attacked and plundered Malwa, Gujarat, Mahratta, Tilang, Kampila, Dhur-samundar, Mabar, Lakhnauti, Chittagong, Sunarganw and Tirhut. His distant campaigns and attacks on non-Muslim kingdoms brought more and more wealth from captured people. He raised taxes to levels where people found it impossible to manage especially in the fertile lands.

In the area between Ganges and Yamuna rivers, the land tax rate on non-Muslims ascended by tenfold in some districts and twentyfold in others. Along with land taxes, non Muslims were required to pay crop taxes by giving up half or more of their harvested crop. These extremely high crop and land tax led entire villages of Hindu farmers to quit farming and escape into jungles. They refused to grow anything or work at all because it was no longer beneficial to them. As a result, famines followed and on the other side the Sultan expanded the arrests, torture, and mass punishments. He slaughtered people as chickens and goats. The Hindu blood was flowing like a river. Few historians say that Muhammad bin Tughluq was cruel and severe not only with non-Muslims but also with certain sects of Muslims like *Shias, Sufis, Qalandars*, and others. His court historian Ziauddin Barni noted in *Tarikh-I Firoz Shahi*:

"Not a day or week passed without spilling of much Musalman blood."

The above statement shows that these invaders were not rulers, in fact not even humans. *They had no divine mission, neither in the name of Hindu religion nor in the name of Islam.* All they wanted was destruction and prevalence of anti-human activities to resume power. This is similar to the terrorist groups who till today justify their actions using a religious philosophy behind plundering the common property and murder of others.

Not only this, but his reign touched the zenith of cruelty when he founded a new city called Jahanpanah that means Protection of the World which connected older Delhi with Siri. He ordered that the capital of his Sultanate be moved from Delhi to Deogiri in present-day Indian state of Maharashtra by renaming it to Daulatabad. He ordered a forced mass migration of Delhi's population and the ones who refused were killed.

It is said that one blind man who failed to migrate to Deogiri was dragged for the entire journey of forty days till the time he died and his body fell apart. It was only one of his tied legs that reached Daulatabad, where the rest of his body split into pieces to narrate the story of Tughlaq's torture.

However, the capital move failed for the lack of foresightedness of the Tughlaqs. Daulatabad did not have enough drinking water to support the new capital which was not anticipated or confirmed by those who run thirsty for blood. Hence, the capital was brought back again to Delhi. But the influx of the then Delhi residents into Deccan region during his reign led to the growth of Muslim population in central and southern India which was limited to Northern region till now.

After this, the Vijayanagara Empire originated as a direct response to the attacks from the Delhi Sultanate liberating the southern India from Muslims. In 1336 AD, Kapaya Nayak, son of Musunuri Nayak defeated the Tughlaq army and reconquered Warangal. By 1339 AD, the warriors of the eastern regions under local Muslim governors and southern parts led by Hindu kings also stood for themselves and revolted against Delhi Sultanate declaring them to be independent states. But people in India experienced a huge loss in economical and social sphere. Historian Walford also mentions that Delhi and most of India faced severe famines during Muhammad bin Tughlaq's rule making the survival of Hindus impossible.

As per *Tarikh-i Firoz Shahi* and *Shams-i Siraj Afif,* after Muhammad bin Tughluq died, his relative, Mahmud Ibn Muhammad, ruled for less than a month when he was replaced by Muhammad bin Tughluq's 45 year old nephew, Firoz Shah Tughlaq, who ruled for thirty-seven years.

As documented in the above mentioned book, Firoz Shah was of Turko-Indian origins. His Turkish father Sipah Rajab was infatuated with a Hindu princess named Naila who initially refused to marry him and her father too refused the marriage proposal. But Sultan Muhammad bin Tughlaq and Sipah Rajab sent their army with a demand for one year taxes in advance and a threat of seizing all their property and people for this rejection. During that phase the kingdom was already suffering from famines. Hence, the princess offered herself to save her people from these cruel and shameless invaders who did not mind marrying against a woman's will.

Sipah Rajab and Naila were married and Firoz Shah was born as their first son. The Hindu blood in his veins did not stop him from carrying the legacy of his ancestors of spreading Islam and holocaust of Hindus.

As his court historian, Shams-i Siraj 'Afif, states that Firoz Shah Tughlaq burnt Hindus alive for secretly following their religion and for refusing to accept Islam. Firoz Shah Tughlaq also, in his memoir, listed his accomplishments in which converting Hindus to Sunni Islam was one of the main achievements. This was by announcing an exemption from taxes and jizya for those who converted and raising the same for all Hindu Brahmins.

History of India has clearly seen that a Hindu womb could not change much in the Muslim DNA. In fact, many of the Hindu wombs could not infuse a tint of Hindu values in the children of Muslim invaders who proved that they had no mercy for the maternal community or religion. The Hindu women were simply used as an invaded territory to implant a Muslim seed into another persecutor of the Hindus.

These marriages resemble what is today called Love Jihad which means producing Muslim children by Hindu women in the name of love and marriage.

A Religious Bulldozer on Hindus and Humanity

EXTENDING ANOTHER LEVEL of cruelty, came the Turko-Mongol ruler Timur Lung to further amplify the slaughter and atrocities in the Indian subcontinent especially on Hindus on a massive scale. Though, he did not intend to rule here but he raided and looted Delhi while sparing only the Muslim neighborhoods of the city. The graph of enslaved and massacred Hindus ascended rapidly.

Burgan Michael writes in his book, *Empire of the Mongols* that "one hundred thousand Hindu prisoners were killed by his army before he attacked Delhi for fear of rebellion and many more were killed afterwards".

He attacked and sacked the important cities like Sirsa, Fatehabad, Sunam, Kaithal, and Panipat, while plundering the regions coming his way. The residents of these regions who were mostly non-Muslims tried to flee but were chased by his army only to be assassinated. From there he travelled to Fatehabad and did the same with the inhabitants there. The Ahirs and Jats resisted him at Ahruni and regions around, but were defeated leaving their land to turn into ruins. Then, he marched towards Delhi through Kaithal while chopping the commoners coming his way like vegetables and fruits.

As quoted by Elliot & Dowson, it is mentioned in *Zafarnama* written by Sharafuddin Yazdi that

"Timur's soldiers grew more eager for plunder and destruction. On that Friday night, there were about 15,000 men in the city who were engaged from early evening till morning in plundering and burning the houses. In many places the impure infidel gabrs (of Delhi) made resistance. Every soldier obtained more than twenty persons as slaves and some brought as many as fifty or a hundred men, women and children as slaves of the city. The other plunder and spoils were immense, gems and jewels of all sorts, rubies, diamonds, stuffs, fabrics, vases, and vessels of gold and silver. Amir Shah Malik and Ali Sultan Tawachi, with 500 trusted men, proceeded against them, and falling upon them with the sword dispatched them to hell."

A thief turned into a soldier only amplified the level of his thefts to the bigger raids, loots, and slaughter. This man and his army ran on Delhi as a bulldozer demolishing a building to the ground while not differentiating between the stones and humans. The alleged descendent of Genghis Khan justified his barbarism as a holy war similar to Khilji who declared himself to be a prophet of Mohammad as per the historians.

Monster growled in the valley of Kashmir

AFTER THE EXIT of Timur, different Muslim Sultans were involved in a tug of war for the throne of Delhi Sultanate, where in Kashmir another sultan named Sikandar was fighting his own dirty but so-called holy war. He was known for his religious intolerance while converting the Kashmir habitants from Hindus to Islam by force. This earned him a sobriquet of Butshikan, the idol breaker. He imposed Islam on Hindus and if they resisted he killed them. He plundered the temples, pilgrims, hermitages, and all other community places meant for Hindu and Buddhist religious practices. He banned all Hindu religious activities such as prayers, dance, and music while also burning the religious texts of Hindus to prevent them from reaching the future generation.

The *Tarikh-i-Firishta* records that Sikandar persecuted the Hindus and issued orders proscribing the residency of anyone other than Muslims in Kashmir. He also ordered the breaking of all "golden and silver images". The *Tarikh-i-Firishta* further states: "Many of the Brahmins, rather than abandon their religion or their country, poisoned themselves; some emigrated from their native homes, while a few escaped the evil of banishment by becoming Mahomedans. After the emigration of the Brahmins, Sikandar ordered all the temples in Kashmir to be thrown down. Having broken all the images in Kashmir, (Sikandar) acquired the title of 'Destroyer of Idols'".

He strived to destroy the idols of the infidels. He demolished the famous temple of Mahadeva at Bahrāre. The temple was dug out from its foundations and the hole (that remained) reached the water level. Another temple at Jagdar was also demolished, as mentioned by Khwājah Nizāmu'd-Dîn Ahmad.

Sikandar burnt all books the same way as fire burns hay. All the scintillating works faced destruction in the same manner that lotus flowers face with the onset of frosty winter, as mentioned by Srivara, *Zaina Rajtarangini*.

Lawrence, Walter Roper (1895) states in the *The Valley of Kashmir* "Encouraged by Islamic theologian, Muhammad Hamadani, Sikandar Butshikan also destroyed ancient Hindu and Buddhist books and banned followers of dharmic religions from prayers, dance, music, consumption of wine and observation of their religious festivals."

Several ancient temples in Kashmir that were considered architectural masterpiece of those times were demolished during this period to make sure that the Hindu heritage is completely eliminated from the valley of Kashmir.

Today's Kashmiri Muslims majorly constitutes those Kashmiri Hindus who were converted out of fear of invaders like Sikandar Butshikan. The irony is that these converted Hindus are still in the captivity of those Sikandar and Khiljis. They are carrying forward the same Jihad that was the reason for their ancestors to bend in front of the monsters and accept their undue demands; Gods must have cursed the Hindus.

No Space for Secularism: Only Death for Seculars

ON THE OTHER side, the people and lands within Delhi Sultanate were left in severe political disturbance. As observed from the historical records, the Sayyid dynasty was comparatively less intolerant, but they too continued with the plundering and persecution of the Hindu community as is described in *Tarikh-i Mubarak-Shahi*.

Over 1414 AD through 1423 AD, according to the Muslim historian Yahya bin Ahmad, the Islamic commanders "chastised and plundered the infidels" of Ahar, Khur, Kampila, Gwalior, Seori, Chandawar, Etawa, Sirhind, Bail, Katehr and Rahtors.

The Hindus retaliated strongly at that time. They were trying to get united to push the Muslim rulers away from their regions. They formed their own armed groups and attacked forts seized by Muslims. For example, Jalandhar was retaken by Hindus in 1431 AD and all Muslims inside the fort were placed in prison.

It may sound repetitive, but the same religious violence continued to persecute the Hindus during the reign of the Lodhis. Bahlul Khan Lodhi and Sikandar Lodhi too executed the massive killings of Hindus in the name of religion in Bengal, Bihar, and Uttar Pradesh.

The religious priests and Islamic scholars played a dominant role in religious violence by the Muslim rulers. They continued instigating the rulers to persecute Hindus in the name of holy war. The surprising fact is that they were not only against the Hindus but also the emerging groups of the secular people.

As mentioned in many records and the *Zubdatu-t Tawarikh* in 1499 AD, a Brahmin of Bengal was arrested because he had attracted a large following among both Muslims and Hindus with the following teaching: "the Mohammedan and Hindu religions were both true but different paths by which God might be approached." Sikandar, with his governor of Bihar Azam Humayun asked Islamic scholars and Sharia experts of their time whether such pluralism and peaceful messages were permissible within the Islamic Sultanate. The scholars advised that it is not, and that the Brahmin should be given the option to either embrace and convert to Islam or be killed.

Sikandar accepted the counsel and gave the Brahmin an ultimatum but the Hindu though a secular person refused to change his view and was killed.

As written in *Tárikh-i Dáúdi,* "He [Lodi] was so zealous that he utterly destroyed diverse places of [infidel] worship... he entirely ruined the shrines of Mathura, [and] the minefield of heathenism. Their stone images were given to the butchers to use...as meat weights and all the Hindus in Mathura were strictly prohibited from shaving their heads and beards, and from performing ablutions. He stopped the idolatrous rites of the infidels there. Every city thus conformed as he desired to the customs of Islam."

The idols that Hindus anointed by the panchamrita, sacred water of the holy Ganges, turmeric, sandalwood paste, and which was adorned by flowers and rare fragrances were given to the butchers, the prohibited areas for the Hindu worshippers. There was no limit to the smashing and crashing of the religious sentiments of the Hindus that history would never forget. It is quite surprising how the Hindus forgot it. This must be because of the curse of Gods.

The Not So Great Mughals

AFTER A SERIES of Muslim invasions, persecution of Hindus, and slaughter of humanity, history was ready to be penned down by another empire of the Islam followers who invaded the Indian subcontinent never to return, but to stay here forever and dig a foundation of what India is today and what it will be for the Almighty knows how long. These people were the grand Mughals who are the said descendents of the Mongols.

Barbarism of Babur

Babur, yes the founder of the Mughal Empire in India is also a founder of Babri Mosque that he built after plundering the Rama temple of Ayodhya in Rama's birth place. He began a new chapter of the persecution of Hindus by killing them, converting them, and plundering their wealth which they called a holy war like all other Muslim invaders.

The raid, loots, rapes, murders clearly explain that the reasons behind these invasions were thoroughly materialistic. However, they continued to snatch somebody else's wealth and land, coating them with religious names; bad luck for the liberal Muslims who pay the price of this contamination of their religion by having a reputation that is suspected by every other country of the world.

According to *Tuzak-i Babari*, Babur's campaign not only targeted the Hindus and Sikhs but the non-Sunni sects of Islam. Whether it was building the "towers of skulls of the infidels" on hillocks or plundering their beloved pilgrims.

The eldest son of Umar Sheikh Mirza, the governor of Fergana and great-great grandson of Timur, defeated Ibrahim Lodi at the First Battle of Panipat in 1526 AD and founded the Mughal Empire. However, he had to face the Rajput rulers before he could ascend to the throne of Delhi. Rana Sanga of Mewar gave him a tough fight, but the invader was a meticulous general with advanced military resources, who managed to defeat the Rajput ruler in the Battle of Khanwa on 17th March, 1527 AD.

As K.V. Krishna Rao writes in *Prepare Or Perish: A Study of National Security* that Babur won the battle because of his "superior generalship" and modern approach: the battle was one of the first in India that featured cannons. Rao also notes that Rana Sanga faced "treachery" when the Hindu chief Silhadi joined Babur's army with a garrison of 6,000 soldiers. Our Hindu soldiers constantly became the arms of the Muslim Invaders which has been the biggest reason that they dared to establish themselves in India. We can see this in all the battles since 7th century.

Babur was also the first invader to use gunpowder in India. Where India was neither integrated nor advanced in the military arena, it was easy for him to push the great warriors like Rana Sanga away from his way to the throne of Delhi.

The incident should be a learning not only for India but for all the countries that in absence of military resources and national integrity, a nation is bound to perish, no matter how strong the economy is.

Many activists claim that Indian economy is growing at a fast rate and one should be happy with it by not bothering much about the defense arena. They must analyze Indian history, India was always a rich economy. From the Harappas to Mauryas to Guptas, all the empires had enviable resources but the land had to face a dark era only for two reasons, lack of integrity and weak military resources.

The dangerous buzz for modern India is that we are still overlooking these two pillars of a sustainable freedom of the country. United States of America is planning to create robotic warriors. China is also busy in bringing advanced defense equipments and a country like Pakistan is constantly threatening of a nuclear attack on India. In this scenario, overlooking the defense arena could be nothing but mass suicide. Along with Rana Sanga, Medina Rao of Chanderi also stood against Babur by refusing his proposal for a peace treaty by exchanging Chanderi for Shamsabad. As a result, Babur attacked Chanderi fort where the women and children were prepared with fire of Jauhar to immolate in order to save them from Babur's slavery and abuse.

After a series of destructive attacks, persecution of Hindus and bloodshed, eventually, Babur occupied Delhi and Agra. He escalated himself to the throne of Lodi and laid the foundation for the rise of Mughal rule in India.

Babur also left a burning issue for India which took ages to resolve. There have been bloodshed and riots in the 20th century too because the Hindus were waiting for their plundered Rama temple to be restored in Ayodhya. This became possible recently after a long trial in the Supreme Court. However, the leftist community of India with few Muslims are still challenging the integrity of Supreme Court's judgment that has kept the matter at bay for decades. This was just because it favored the Hindu. Actually, it is not about Hindus or Muslims, but about right and wrong. But who cares? Gods must have cursed the Hindus.

Mughals did not rule in continuity. In 1537 AD, when Babur's son Humayun was elsewhere on an expedition, Sher Shah Suri overran the state of Bengal and established the Suri dynasty in India. Sher Shah, born as Farid Sur was known for his brilliant administrative skills and military expertise. During his seven-year rule from 1538 to 1545, he set up a new economic and military administration. He issued the first *Rupiya from Taka*. He is also known for re-organizing the postal system of the Indian Subcontinent and for few reforms on strategic level that set the foundation of the Mughals in future as per historians.

Later, Mughal emperor Akbar too adapted a lot of Sher Shah's strategies to establish a long lasting rule in India. But the story of Hindus was the same. Sher Shah extended this tale of persecution of Hindus in his own way. There were massacres, conversions, and plundering of Hindu wealth during his reign also. There are historical evidences of the cruelty that Sher Shah Suri dealt Hindus with.

According to `Abd al-Qadir Bada'uni and other Muslim historians, Sher Shah Suri is known for destroying old cities while founding new ones on their ruins after his own name. Shergarh, which was a deserted town with a fort in ruins, is a prime example of this. In old times, this place was a thriving spot where Hinduism, Buddhism, and Jainism co-existed peacefully but Muslim rulers were not only against Hindus but were against secularism also. We see so many evidences in the past that Muslims never ever supported secularism because they did not believe in any belief system beyond their own. The counselors of these invaders too supported the desecration of the Hindu pilgrims.

Elliot and Dowson state in *The History of India, as Told by Its Own Historians - The Muhammadan Period* "As with theologians and court officials of Delhi Sultanate, his advisors counseled in favor of religious violence. Shaikh Nizam, for example, counseled, "There is nothing equal to a religious war against the infidels. If you be slain you become a martyr, if you live you become a ghazi."

When those who should throw light and prevent the destruction of humanity only turn against it, then who would come to its rescue?

Sher Shah Suri is also known for his attack on the Hindu fort of Kalinjar ruled by Kirat Singh in 1545 AD. As per *Tarikh-i-Sher Shahi*, the ruler died in an explosion. Although, he handed over the fort to his nobles before his death, his forces recaptured the fort by afternoon and killed everyone who came their way. After few years Humayun's son Jalal-ud-din came into power and was raised to the throne of Delhi.

The Pioneer of False Secularism

Here comes the most important chapter of the Persecution of Hindus. It was most crucial phase that turned around the foundation of Hindu history and the Hindu till date is unaware of it.

Abu'l-Fath Jalal-ud-din, the grandson of Babur acquired the throne at a very young age. He initially ruled behind the shadow of Bairam Khan after killing a Hindu king known as Raja Hemchandra Vikramaditya, also known as Hemu, who acquired the throne of Delhi Sultanate. King Hemu was a Hindu king who reached the throne of Delhi Sultanate after pushing the invaders behind but the irony is that very few pages of Indian history glorify this fact.

After the merciless killing of Raja Hemu, Akbar became a successful general and a well known Mughal Emperor, who occupies maximum space of the Mughal history. The emperor must be credited for his political wisdom and foresightedness that created a base for the Mughal Empire in India that none of the Muslim invaders could attain.

He is portrayed as a hero in our history for his religious tolerance and liberal governance which is not a complete truth. It is said that he established Din-I-Ilahi, the religion of one God. His liberal upbringing had sown the seeds of religious tolerance and open minded political approach for he was born and raised in a Rajput family in their provinces when Humayun was absconding after his battle with Sher Shah Suri. Few historians also claim that there was no term called Din-I-Ilahi in Akbar's reign which is another topic of debate.

At that time it was called *Tawhid-i-Ilāhī*, the divine monotheism, as it is written by Abu Al Fazal, a court historian during the reign of Akbar. So it can be assumed that it was not a religion but a political strategy to promote religious pluralism in the subcontinent. In other words, it can be said that it was a political system to bring unity in plurality rather than a religion to strengthen the roots of Mughal Empire on a Hindu land. It won't be wrong to state that for a strategist like Akbar, political aspirations weighed higher than the religious limitations. For this he did whatever it took him to establish very strong political grounds for the Mughals.

He formed matrimonial alliances with the Hindu Rajput princesses and nurtured the cordial relationship with the Rajput rulers who were ready to cooperate with him. He allowed the princess to follow Hindu religion after marriage. However, it was nothing but a political strategy, but all's well if it ends well. Rajput royals found it as an opportunity to strengthen their relations with the Mughals and also protect their territories from the Mughal armies. They themselves proposed the matrimonial alliances of their daughters for their political interests or Akbar would have compelled them to do so directly or indirectly.

Though before Akbar too, there were marriages between Hindus and Muslims but there was no prominent connection of these personal alliances with political strategy. But during Akbar's reign it seems very evident as the kings who married their daughters to the Mughals were given due importance, nearly equal to the Muslim nobles and they were also given the politically dominant position in the Mughal empire. Similarly, he made many strategic and sharp moves to win over the Hindus in the long term and it literally paid off too. For generations, not only Hindus but the entire world sung glory to this so-called secular politician and cannot see the motive behind till date.

Schimmel, Annemarie writes in her book called *The Empire of the Great Mughals:*

"Akbar promoted tolerance of other faiths. In fact, not only did he tolerate them, he encouraged debate on philosophical and religious issues. This led to the creation of the *Ibādat Khāna 'House of Worship'* at Fatehpur Sikri in 1575."

He had already repealed the jizya, a specific tax on non-Muslims that was collected to allow them to worship their own Hindu lords. This earned him pretty good reputation amongst Hindus and a title of being the most liberal Muslim ruler in India. On the other hand, a section of historians say that it was not repealed in all the regions. It was only a political measure that was part of the treaty between Akbar and the other Rajput rulers who got ready to bow before him. Few regions of the country were still paying Jizya during Akbar's reign. However, we cannot discard his favors to the Hindus, of course for a price.

In other words, the king who is known as a liberal face of the Islamic rulers is not spared from the taint of persecution of Hindus. As mentioned above, a huge section of Hindus also say that these were the political decisions of the great strategist to strengthen his roots in India which is quite visible in history. He gauged the fact that staying forever on this land was impossible till he established a tie with the Rajput rulers. This is the reason Mughals left their imprints on this country more than any other invader for the last 1000 years.

Before Akbar, Muslim invaders were constantly challenged by the Rajputs which was a reason that sooner or later they were pushed beyond the boundaries of Indian Subcontinent.

This sharp ruler who knew the nerve of the Rajputs joined hands with the kings who were ready to accept his suzerainty and marriage was a great method to realize that aim.

This solved two purposes. One, the Rajput rulers acted as

his weapons instead of challenging him. Second, the strategic move fragmented the Rajput society on ideological grounds. At one side there were rulers who accepted to rule under Akbar and enjoyed their kingdom, but on the other side there were rulers who wanted to stand for their dignity and decided to fight against him. As a result, the entire Rajputana got divided into pro and anti Akbar groups. This move of the sharp strategist sowed the seeds of enmity between the two ideologies. In a way, Divide and Rule policy is often associated with the British rulers but this Mughal ruler had used this tool for his reign of approximately fifty years.

It is evident in history, if we analyze the early years of this ruler that initially, similar to other Muslim invaders Akbar too was enthusiastically devoted to the cause of Islam and had a jihadist bent of mind that had compelled him to massacre Hindus in the name of the Divine.

Yes, the Siege of Chittorgarh fort, which was the fortress-capital of Mewar, is the biggest example of this statement.

Mewar had great commercial importance during those times as it lay on the shortest route from Agra to Gujarat and was also considered a key to hold the interior parts of Rajputana. Mewar also extended a route to southern India which was only a dream till now for the Muslim invaders. Also being situated near the western boundaries of India, all the foreign trade through the sea ports was difficult as the traders had to pass through the eye of Mewar rulers. Though during that period, most Rajput rulers had accepted Akbar's sovereignty except very few and on the top of this list was the city of Mewar. This Rajput clan is famous for its authority and valour. They never bowed or surrendered to any invader in the history of invasions into India. The descendents of Bappa Rawal, who pushed Mohammad bin Qasim from Sindh in the 7th century terrified the invaders for next 200 years, were expected to stand for themselves even during the reign of Akbar. Also the emperor was busy expanding in the other parts of India till then.

In 1567 AD, Akbar brought his attention to Chittor Fort to fulfill his political aspirations of the absolute rule on the Rajputana. Before this there have been several attempts to take over this fort but rulers like Rana Kumbha and others kicked the invaders away from Mewar. However, Mewar was important for Akbar. There are rumors that Akbar made many lucrative offers to Mewaris for accepting his sovereignty but every time he was refused and humiliated.

After this prolonged stretch between the Sisodias and Mughals, Mewar was losing its strength as Mughals managed to garner support of many Rajput rulers leaving the kingdoms like Mewar alone and fighting in isolation for the Indian heritage. This time King Udai Singh was sent to the hills of Mewar by the political strategists for a simple agenda of preparing for a bigger warfare later in order to protect the most desired kingdom of Mewar in the long run. Two Rajput warriors, Raja Jaimal and his brother in law, King Patta, a brave soldier of his time, took over the charge of the defense of his Chittor Fort in absence of Uday Singh. Jaimal Rathore was the ruler of Merta. He was the half-brother of a known Sage Meera and became the ruler of Merta after the death of his father, Rao Veeram Dev. His father was perceived as the strongest king of the east in his time.

Finally, the Mughals surrounded Chittorgarh and the siege continued for more than four months. The forces tried everything to get into the fort. They dug mines and attacked the fort's boundaries by continuous bombardment but the Rajputs were constantly reconstructing the fort's fences and filling up the mines again and again while preventing the Mughals from stepping into the fort.

Due to the availability of comparatively larger forces and cavalries along with advanced military resources like canons and gun power, Mughals managed to reach the fort's fences after a number of trials for a long period. It is said that Akbar himself had shot Jaimal with his gun called Sangram while he was busy constructing the fort's ruptured fences unknown to the fact that the man who was commanding the construction forces was general Jaimal himself. And finally there was a fierce battle that was fought inside the fort when 8,000 Rajputs fought with over 70,000 Mughals. General Jaimal, who had lost his limb by Akbar's attack fought with the same vigor and valor that Rajputs are famous for.

During the siege, the women and children immolated themselves in the fire of Jauhar before the men came out in the open for Saka. Saka is a ritual like Jauhar when warriors request their families to commit Jauhar and they march out in the battleground to attain a certain death while fighting with the enemy. This Jauhar is considered as the third Jauhar of Chittorgarh. The first one was initiated by Rani Padmini in 1303 AD and the second by Rani Karnavati in 1535 AD.

Self Immolation: Savior of Sanctity

The above chronology of Jauhars is challenged by the historical evidences, as the first Jauhar of the Muslim invasion was in 7th century when Raja Dahir's wife immolated herself to save herself from Muhammad bin Qasim, the first ever invader of

Muslim origin who attacked the Indian subcontinent.

In 712 AD, Muhammad bin Qasim with his army attacked kingdoms of western regions of the Indian subcontinent as discussed before. He laid siege to the capital of Dahir, the then Hindu king in a part of Sindh. After Dahir had been killed, the queen took over the commandments of the defense of the capital for several months. But after a certain period, the food supplies ran out and she had no choice, but to immolate herself along with other ladies for they refused to surrender to the Muslims. Finally, they lit pyres and committed mass *Jauhar*. The remaining men walked out to their death at the hands of the invading army as per the tradition of Saka. The incident is validated by Partha Chatterjee in his book called *Empire and Nation: Selected Essays*

After that and before also a series of Jauhars took place because it was a common practice for the women to preserve their dignity after they lost the battles with the enemies.

Shams ud-Din Iltutmish of the Delhi Sultanate attacked Gwalior in 1232 AD, which was then under control of the Rajputs. The Rajput women committed Jauhar instead of submitting to Iltutmish's army. The place where the women committed mass suicide is known as Jauhar-tal (or Johar kund, Jauhar Tank) in the northern end of the Gwalior fort.

Trudy Ring, Noelle Watson, Paul Schellinger (2012) in *Asia and Oceania: International Dictionary of Historic Places.*

In 1301, Alauddin Khilji of Delhi Sultanate besieged and conquered the Ranthambore fort. When faced with a certain defeat, the defending ruler Hammiradeva decided to fight to death with his soldiers, and his minister Jaja supervised the organization of a Jauhar. The queens, daughters, and other female relatives of Hammiradeva committed suicide in this Jauhar. It is also said that this Jauhar was based on sheer lies for the king never was defeated but his commanders mislead the ladies by sharing false information of his defeat. The local stories says that the Rana asked his generals to wave a black flag if he lost the battle to communicate to the ladies that they should immolate themselves to protect their dignity and wave a saffron flag if he wins. The commanders waved a black flag even though the king had won the battle.

In 1303 AD, Rani Padmini committed Jauhar along with all the Rajput ladies of the Chittorgarh Fort after the death of Rana Rawal Ratan Singh. This Jauhar is described as the first Jauhar of Chittorgarh when so many Hindu Rajput women including the very young, newly married, and pregnant women jumped into the fire to protect themselves from the dirty hands of Khilji.

In 1327 AD, the Hindu women of the Kampili kingdom of northern Karnataka committed Jauhar to escape the Delhi Sultanate armies of Muhammad bin Tughluq.

The women and children of the Chanderi fort committed *Jauhar*; the men dressed up in saffron garments had walked the ritual of *Saka* on 29th January, 1528 CE when Babur's forces attacked the fort of Chanderi during the reign of King Medini Rai who helped Rana Sanga in the battle of Khanua.

Rani Karnavati, the widow of Rana Sanga who died after the battle of Khanwa, committed Jauhar with other women on 8th March, 1535 when the army of Bahadur Shah Zafar attacked Chittorgarh. This Jauhar is also called as the second Jauhar of Chittorgarh.

And after that, stands the third Jauhar of Chittorgarh as mentioned above during the siege of the Chittorgarh fort by Akbar.

Rising pillars of smoke soon signalled the rite of Jauhar as the Rajputs killed their families and prepared to die in a supreme sacrifice. In a day filled with hand-to-hand struggles, virtually all the defenders died. The Mughal troops slaughtered another 20-25,000 ordinary persons, inhabitants of the town and peasants from the surrounding area on the grounds that they had actively helped in the resistance.

John F. Richards, *The Mughal Empire*

The list of such Jauhars and mass suicides is endless. Few of them accounted and many more stands unaccounted but the third Jauhar definitely placed a question mark on Akbar's heroic image in the Indian history.

The move will always be remembered as a black taint on Akbar's heroic and religiously tolerant portrait. It is written that on Akbar's orders, the heads of the surviving defenders and 30,000 non-combatants were erected as towers throughout the region. The booty of the royal palace was distributed among the Mughal nobles and army. The blood of Rajputs wrote the script of Akbar's jihadist ideology on the stones of Chittorgarh fort and the soil still smells of the patriotism of the martyrs who lost their lives to Akbar.

The young emperor remained in Chittorgarh for three days and then returned to Agra. To commemorate his victory, he installed the statues of Raja Jaimal and Patta on the gates of his fort. However, it is a subject of debate if that was to honor their bravery or to advertise his authority over Rajputs.

Historians also say that Akbar tried to buy Jaimal's loyalty by offering him the kingdom of Mewar that was under his sovereignty for ditching Rana Udai Singh II, but the dignified Rajput refused his offer and insulted him badly. He fought for his commitment till his last breath writing a tale of his victory on the Chittorgarh fort. Injured and amputated, he still gave a tough fight to the Mughals who were comparatively numerically superior to the Mewar army and carried advanced weapons of those times.

During the siege of Chittorgarh, thousands of innocent people including commoners were killed brutally at the behest of the emperor, which sounds like a lie when one learns History from Hindi movies but the fact is substantiated with evidence.

According to historians, the number of casualities account for some 8,000 Rajput soldiers were killed fighting 40,000 Mughals. The number of Mughals differs in history as different historians have quoted varied figures ranging from 40,000 to 80,000.

But it must be known to our future generations that 8,000 soldiers gave a tough fight to 80,000 Mughals. If only, the Rajput community or the Hindu community or the Indian community had not been disintegrated, Akbar would have had his last day in the battlefield of Chittorgarh. It was not the bravery of Mughals that made him rule the unconquered kingdom, but it is the silence and indolence of the Hindus, that still remains evident in modern era.

After Chittorgarh, Akbar planned to capture Ranthambore fort in 1568 AD. This was the most powerful fortress of India at that time, it was earlier seized by Alauddin Khilji in the 13th Century.

On February 8, 1568, Akbar began the siege of this impregnable fort. His army constituted over 50,000 men. His morale was boosted by his victories at the Battle of Thanesar and by the Siege of Chittorgarh. Now it was only the Ranthambore Fort which remained unconquered and he believed it was a threat to the Mughal Empire. This was because it was home to the great Hada Rajputs who were the sworn enemies of the Mughals and who never surrendered to anyone in the past. King Hammir Dev gave a tough fight to Allauddin Khilji. So winning over Hadda Rajputs was a symbolic declaration of Mughal power over Rajputana.

Akbar had first besieged Ranthambore Fort in the year 1558, but decided instead to capture Gwalior, northern Rajputana and Jaunpur, leaving the expedition as incomplete. This was the second attempt that he made with a foolproof strategy this time.

During the siege, the elite Mughal force of 5,000 captured an 8-mile circumference around Ranthambore Fort which was surrounded by the hilly rocks and a deep abyss. It was also perched on top of a steep rock cliff making it difficult to climb for an enemy. The emperor then led an army of more than 30,000 Mughals that brought with them some of the gigantic cannons ever built in the Mughal Empire. The fort was so constructed that it did not have a straight way of penetration. It was an epitome of an extremely intelligent architecture that adapted ways to deceive the attacker with multiple doors and caves. Only a well planned strategy could lead to such a victory and Akbar definitely deserved credit for his marvelous work as a military general. As planned, the forces set up the red imperial tent in front of the hill that led to the gateway into Ranthambore Fort. The camp was armed with massive cannons, three of which were more than 15 ft long. As per Akbar's orders, three nearby rocky outcrops were captured by his men and then the cannon batteries were placed on positions from where Akbar bombarded Ranthambore Fort.

As the siege continued the intensity of attacks grew higher. Akbar placed even bigger cannons and high velocity mortars on the two rocky outcrops facing the Fort. Akbar also ordered his men to start constructing covered ways so that the army could move forward. Within weeks the covered ways known as *sabats* allowed Akbar's men to gain control of territories just underneath the steep slope of the fort. By this time, the Mughals also built prefabricated walls to protect their gains around the fort and then placed highly accurate narrow barreled long-cannons that were about 20–25 ft in length.

As a result of such heavy bombardment, flames began to shoot out from the buildings within the fort's walls and the sky was blackened by smoke erupting out of the gunpowder. Such was the impact that war elephants within the fort went rogue. It could be imagined how suffocating it would have been for humans. It was during this stage that Akbar personally lead the forces near the gates of the fort. As a result, on March 21, 1568, Rai Surjan Hada opened the gate of Ranthambore Fort and allowed the Mughal Army to enter. He had already collected the statues of the Hindu deities from the temples when he expressed his agreement to Akbar's sovereignty. He knew that the army will plunder the temples and harm the idols, hence, he chose a peaceful surrender. Later, Akbar invited Rao Surjan Hada to his imperial camp and in the evening of that very day Rao Surjan Hada, the ruler of Ranthambore, submitted to the Mughal Emperor Akbar, after a fiercely fought campaign of immense strategic importance to the expansion of the Mughal Empire.

Akbar then appointed a commander of the Mughal garrison at Ranthambore Fort called Mehtar Khan and sent Rao Surjan Hada to Bundi.

No matter how civilized we get, survival of the fittest is the harsh reality of this civilized jungle of earth. Lack of military advancement and power due to missing integrity in Rajputs compelled many Rajput Rulers to surrender to these invaders against their will and bowing in front of the circumstances.

On the other side, in spite of this growing affluence of the Mughals, there were the sons of the soil who were still risking their life to protect their motherland. The son of Uday Singh II, Pratap Singh grew up as a well trained general and he continued to attack the Mughals. He managed to recapture most of the lost territories through his Guerrilla warfare making Mewar again a challenge for Akbar. Pratap was now Maharana Pratap for he was crowned as a successor of Uday Singh II after his death in 1572 AD.

Akbar sent a number of proposals entreating the Rana to accept his sovereignty like the other Rajput leaders in the region but Rana as expected refused to personally submit to Akbar. Hence an open war became inevitable between the Rana of Mewar and Mughals. This is the war that is known as Battle of Haldighati which is one of the fiercest battles in the Indian history.

'Rakta Talai', the Pond of Blood

Haldighati is a narrow mountain pass near Gogunda in Rajasthan. Maharana Pratap commanded a force of around 3,000 cavalry and 400 Bhil archers. These were the groups of outcastes and tribals who were trained by Maharana to fight for the motherland. The Mughals were led by Raja Man Singh of Amber, who commanded an army numbering around 5,000–10,000 men. The battle continued for more than six hours that resulted in bloodshed that seemed to be like a battle of several years. Rajputs fought against Rajputs for Mughals and tribals sacrificed their last breath for a Rajput Maharana; what an irony!

It is said that Pratap was seven and a half feet tall general who wore an armor of approximately 70 kilograms. His sword weighed 25 kilograms and spear weighed up to 60 kilograms. He moved like electric current, piercing the Mughal warriors into two pieces. In spite of having a larger army in front, Rajput warriors had almost won over the Mughals when suddenly the game changed. However, the victory of Akbar in Haldighati is disputed by many evidences.

Maharana and his horse Chetak got wounded while attacking Man Singh. It is said that Chetak hopped high grabbing the forehead of Man Singh's elephant which enabled Pratap to attack Man Singh. The warrior threw his spear with full force while piercing through Man Singh's mahout. This was a brave but strategically wrong move by Pratap because the Mughal army could now focus on him and Chetak. This shows an impulsive act of Rana which is understandable when one sees a Rajput brother fighting on behalf of an invader. But this emotional outrage had a price to pay. The Mughal army managed to surround the Rajput king from everywhere in those few seconds. During this challenging phase Jhala Man Singh, a loyal warrior of Rana, wore his crown to mislead the Mughal forces and convinced Pratap to find an escape route in order to survive and defeat the Mughals later and keep the battle on for the sovereignty of the motherland.

Battle of Haldighati is one of the fiercest battles of the Indian history. It is said that the rocks of the Haldighati that were pale yellow, which is the colour of turmeric, turned red with blood of Rajputs and Mughals in less than 3 hours. Since there was heavy rainfall that day this blood mingled into the clogged water only to be remembered as the river of blood post the battle. The place is restored as a historical site known as 'Rakta talai'. The ruins of Haldighati, statue of the royal horse Chetak and Rana could be seen in Chittorgarh but history could not do justice to these heroes who stood firm for the dignity of the motherland. We substituted these heroes with our persecutors in our history text books which are intoxicating our future generations even today. God must have cursed Hindus.

Though a part of Chittorgarh was conquered by Mughals during Uday Singh II's reign, Maharana Pratap managed to retain most of the Mewar regions with him by continuous strategy of Guerrilla warfare.

The Battle of Haldighati is referred as a hollow victory for the Mughals but actually it was an inconclusive battle. Mughals could not follow or find Pratap who managed to fling through a deep river; thanks to Chetak who jumped with his three legs crossing a river that was nearly 32 feet long. The horse died afterwards due to heart attack to write the history of loyalty of an animal for Rana Pratap which was missing in humans. Mughals captured Gogunda and nearby areas while Pratap could not be found by Mughal army. Later Pratap continued with his attacks on Mughals and recaptured the western regions of his dominion.

A section of historians also provided evidences recently claiming that Akbar never won Mewar. These evidences include a few government documents post the battle of Haldighati that was signed by Rana Pratap. Also the currency was embedded with Maharana's stamps during that phase. According to them,

Mughal Army could never defeat Maharana Pratap and the historical facts as usual were tempered either by the Mughals or the British. Had he won, these documents and currency would carry Mughal stamps and not Maharana's stamps.

Analyzed by any angle we cannot label Maharana as a defeated warrior because during his lifetime, Mughals could neither catch him, nor win him, nor find him nor kill him; what a soldier! He died his own death at the age of 56 while hunting a tiger and no invader or enemy could ever compel him to bow before them.

Had Man Singh, who was a Hindu Rajput along with many other Rajputs supported Maharana Pratap instead of a Muslim King Akbar, the history of India would have been different. But most of the Hindu Rajputs fought against their brother Rajputs, who fought alone for the preservation of his dignity, loyalty of the motherland and to his religion; adding another tale of our disloyalty to our own people. This is why the statement needs repetition after repetition that Hindus were invaded, looted, persecuted, and ruled by the others not because of others but because of their own flaws. Gods must have cursed us for we never learnt from our mistakes.

There were Rajput soldiers on both sides. At one stage, in the fierce struggle, Badayuni asked Asaf Khan how to distinguish between the friendly and enemy Rajputs. Asaf Khan replied, "Shoot at whomsoever you like; on whichever side they may be killed, it will be a gain to Islam."

Smith, *Akbar the Great Mogul*

"Hindus died in large numbers as soldiers for their Muslim masters in medieval India."

K.S. Lal, Kishori Saran. *Indian Muslims: Who Are They*

This has been the height of the persecution of Hindus due to the foolishness of our ancestors.

Till date we are repeating the same mistakes. Martyrs like Jaimal and Patta are hardly visible in the Indian history to inspire us for sacrifice. Maharana Pratap's valour is also questioned for his retreat from the battle of Haldighati where Mughals are granted the credit of victory. We make movies idealizing Akbar as a God of secularism in India overlooking the real facts where history was completely different. Akbar maintained the largest harem among the Muslim rulers having more than 5,000 women, it constituted majorly Rajput women. He would organize Mina Bazaar to be attended only by the women where men were not allowed. However, he would attend it himself and is often alleged to be molesting and misbehaving with the Hindu Rajput women on those occasions. He did everything that any other Muslim invader did. He killed, he massacred, he humiliated the Indian virtues, and he manhandled the women. But we fancy him as a hero of our history, painting a completely different picture of the emperor which is far away from the reality.

Had Bharmal joined hands with Rana Pratap Singh and Jodha was not married to Akbar, Rajput womb would not have brought Jahangir, Shahjahan, and Aurangzeb into this world. Rather more of Maharanas would have been born who would have kicked these invaders far away from our pious land and we would not have fought over a piece of land to build a temple of our own deity. Nor our ex-Hindu population would be standing against us being terrorists or as Pakistanis or as Bangladeshis killing their own brothers even today.

Akbar is also credited for the fact that he never compelled his women to convert to Islam or prevented them to follow their own religion. This fact too ends with a question mark. The biggest love story often mesmerized by Bollywood, the love affair of Jodha and Akbar is based on a myth. It has no substantial records in history rather a complete contrast of the same is available. History doubts even the existence of Jodhabai during Mughal rule. Few historians say that Jodhabai was actually married to Jahangir. Yes there was a Rajput queen who was a daughter of Raja Bharmal and was married to Akbar but her name is not certain. She is addressed with multiple names like Hira Kunwari, Harkha Bai, and Jodha Bai but her existence is accounted with the name of Mariam Uz Zamani, which was a Muslim title accredited to her by her son Jahangir, the successesor of Akbar. Her grave could also be found just a kilometer away from Akbar's grave screaming of the fact that the princess was converted to Islam which is why she was buried as per the Muslim funeral rituals and was not burnt on a pyre as per the Hindu funeral tradition. She was just like any other queen in Akbar's harem who only got importance after her son Jahangir held the throne. None of the sons of these Rajput princesses were allowed to follow Hindu practices, rather they continued with the holocaust of the Hindus extending the aspirations of their Muslim paternal genes. Jahangir was a son of a Rajput princess and Aurangzeb too was a grandson and great grandson of Rajputs but he is listed on top as one of the most brutal Muslim rulers who have been extremely cruel to the Hindus.

In bitter words, Hindu wombs were used to nurture the jihadists only to extend their ancestor's cruelty to the new Hindu generations.

Some parts of history were tempered by Muslims themselves

and some by the British to demean the Indian civilization as claimed by historians.

In spite of the above facts, Akbar was credited with the title of a great strategist and warrior who deserved to rule India because the Hindus allowed him to do so.

After him, Akbar and Mariam uz Zamani's son Jahangir was enthroned as an emperor to extend the tale of Mughal rule in India. Historians describe Jahangir as comparatively less cruel to the Hindus for he was a lover of royal luxuries and comforts and spent most of his life in recreations. But he too strongly endorsed the Muslim philosophies similar to his successor Shahjahan. Both father and son continued to extend the Mughal Empire as well as Islam in their capacity.

A section of Hindus claim that even the Taj Mahal in Agra which is also known as one the wonders of the world is based on a demolished Shiva temple. However, the historians do not certify the fact but it can't be totally discarded because it was normal for Muslim rulers to demolish temples for building their monuments.

Towers of Hindu Skulls

The biggest turnaround happened when Muhi-ud-Din Muhammad commonly known by the name of Aurangzeb became the sixth Mughal emperor and ruled over nearly the entire Indian subcontinent for a period of forty-nine years. Aurangzeb means the Ornament of the Throne and this is what his life revolved around. Power at any cost was his motto in life. He did not have any fascination for luxury, comfort or any other pleasure. All he enjoyed was fanaticism and power. He wanted to dominate other people, kingdoms and religions. Aurangzeb was one of the most prominent Mughal Emperor who hailed massacres and bloodshed mostly in the name of Islam.

Reminiscent of the shadows of Mohammad Ghori and Ghazni, he evolved with a title of Butshikan, the destroyer of idols and temples. He came out as a monster for the Hindus who lost a big section of their population either to Islam or to death.

Catherine Blanshard Asher in her book *Architecture of Mughal India – Part 1* entitled him as the last effective Mughal ruler.

This was because after Aurangzeb, the Mughal Empire saw its downfall. None of the Mughal descendents now could conduct the affairs of the kingdom like their ancestors. One more reason of this downfall was the extremism of Aurangzeb—the many battles, massacres and bloodshed and most importantly lack of political wisdom which hollowed the Mughal Empire and its resources. Hence, it was destined to collapse. He earned more enemies than friends. He lost a lot of wealth in his expeditions to enforce Islam and expand his empire. He is rated as one of the most cruel, merciless, and fundamentalist Muslim ruler in India who drowned Hindus in their own blood. There is no comparison to this monster in the entire Indian History.

Hussein, S M in *Structure of Politics Under Aurangzeb* mentions that he through his compilation of the Fatawa-e-Alamgiri was also one of the few rulers to have fully established Sharia law and Islamic economics throughout South Asia.

Historians say that his policies abandoned his predecessors' legacy of pluralism and religious tolerance. He re-imposed the Jizya tax that was removed by Akbar, Jahangir, and Shahjahan in the past. He took destruction of Hindu temples to another level and is known for the execution of the Maratha King Sambhaji and the ninth Sikh Guru Tegh Bahadur Ji with his brothers.

The reign of Aurangzeb witnessed one of the strongest campaigns of religious violence in the Mughal Empire's history. Aurangzeb re-introduced jizya (tax) on non-Muslims says Smith, Vincent in *The Oxford History of India: From the Earliest Times to the End of 1911*. He also says that Aurangzeb issued orders in 1669 to all his governors of provinces to "destroy with a willing hand the schools and temples of the infidels, and that they were strictly enjoined to put an entire stop to the teaching and practice of idolatrous forms of worship".

He led numerous campaigns against non-Muslims, forcibly converted Hindus to Islam and destroyed Hindu temples, say Ayalon and David in *Studies in Islamic History and Civilization*.

Some temples were destroyed entirely and some were converted into mosques after smashing the Hindu idols, ruining the Hindu scriptures and killing the priests. The extent of his cruelty could be imagined by a fact that the holy city of Krishna, Mathura was temporarily renamed as Islamabad in local official documents after plundering it completely.

He ordered for the amputations of limbs, killings of Brahmins, and other Hindus. He imposed heavy taxes on the non-Muslims. Failure to pay these taxes lead to their brutal killings along with family. Though this emperor carried the Hindu Rajput blood in his veins, he had no mercy on the maternal genes. He was an absolute and extremist Muslim who hated Hindus and their religion. He erected towers with the skulls of Hindu priests and would seek a large number of sacred threads that were to be taken off from the executed Brahmins every day, these Brahmins refused to accept Islam. Till the time he didn't get a specific number of these sacred threads taken off from those Hindus who were forcibly converted by eating meat or from the dead bodies of Brahmins, he would not have his meals. During his reign almost half of the Hindu population was forcibly converted to Islam. His fundamentalism was to the level of obsession which is substantiated by his actions. However, a section of historians also argue in his favor claiming that he was a very dedicated emperor who would not enjoy the comforts and luxuries of the royal family. He would sew the caps and write the copies of Quran to earn his living. They also say that he made donations for the reconstruction of the temples. Mahakaleshwar Temple of Ujjain was one of those temples. He was also a lover of Indian architecture, whereas we can find many facts substantiating his hatred for arts and Hindus. Some of them were for good - like prohibition of alcohol and gambling and some for radical reasons like banning the religious ceremonies in public, music, and dance.

History is controversial. Whatever we know and share is through the sources that lead us to diversified and multifarious directions. But we as readers have to form our own individual opinion of what could be true and what could be false?

Few Hindu rulers gave tough fight to these invaders time to time and during Aurangzeb's reign it was Shivaji. Chhatrapati Shivaji, the great Maratha ruler appeared as nightmare for Aurangzeb and acted as one of the major causes for the downfall of Mughal Empire by establishing the Maratha Empire.

As always we Hindus lost another chance where we could stop the series of persecution of the Hindus. Like all other sons of the motherland, Chhatrapati Shivaji also did not have the absolute majority of Hindu kingdoms. However, he managed to expand the Maratha Empire to the widest geographical measures.

We Hindus died for Mughals while fighting against

Hindus. We surrendered our motherland and allowed them to command us for power that was not based on dignity. We offered our daughters for their harems who were used to realize their political dreams. Marriage of Jodha and Akbar is one of the examples that would come into mind while analyzing these mistakes of our ancestors in the past. The story did not end on Jodha, after Jodha, Man Singh's daughter was also married to Akbar's Son Jahangir and many other princess followed her in the Mughal Harem. This is a reason why we were left with very few Maharanas and many more Aurangzeb's today.

Just one book is not enough to list how many temples were plundered, how many forts were attacked, how many daughters were sacrificed, how many women committed Jauhars, how many sacred threads were soaked in blood, how many heads were displayed into towers, how many pyres were lit on a daily basis and how many innocent souls are still screaming of their persecution.

In spite of immense efforts of manipulating history, these tales of cruelty and human bloodshed are so evident that anyone who goes through these facts would have tears in his eyes.

After Mughals also there were other Muslim rulers who ruled the Indian subcontinent.

Monster extends
to South

TIPU SULTAN, THE son of Haider Ali and the Sultan of Srirangapatnam is also portrayed as a religious liberal who supported pluralism but he too has few drops of the Hindu blood on his hands. Influenced by religious notions, he too is held responsible for plundering temples, converting Hindus into Islam, and even mass killings of men, women, and children.

"Tipu Sultan persecuted the Hindus, Christians with the Mappila Muslims and carried out forced conversions of Hindus and Christians" says Heathcote, T. A.

According to C. K. Kareem, Tipu Sultan issued an edict for the destruction of Hindu temples in Kerala that lead to the plunder of many temples while torturing the devotees and the priests. Tipu instigated Runmust Khan, the Nawab of Kurnool, to launch a surprise attack upon the Kodava Hindus who are also known as the Coorgs or Coorgis. This community of Hindus was besieged by the invading Muslim army of Runmust Khan that lead to the killings of 500 and migration of over 40,000 Kodavas who retreated to the forests to save their lives. The young men in Seringapatam were reported to be forcibly circumcised and incorporated into the Ahmedy Corps.

Thousands of Kodava Hindus were seized along with their king. They were held captive at Srirangapatna and forcibly converted to Islam. Those who resisted had to either die or at least were tortured. The British administrator link says that the number of these Hindus were not less than 70,000 and historian Lewis Rice arrives at the figure of 85,000, while Mir Kirmani accuses Tipu of torturing at least 80,000 including men, women and children.

In a letter to Runmust Khan, Tipu himself stated as under:

> "We proceeded with the utmost speed, and, at once, made prisoners of 40,000 occasion-seeking and sedition-exciting Coorgis, who alarmed at the approach of our victorious army, had slunk into woods, and concealed themselves in lofty mountains, inaccessible even to birds. Then carrying them away from their native country (the native place of sedition) we raised them to the honour of Islam, and incorporated them into our Ahmedy corps.

Miller, Roland E says in *Mappila Muslims of Kerala: a study in Islamic Trends,* "In 1788, Tipu reportedly ordered his governor in Calicut Sher Khan to begin the process of converting Hindus to Islam. In the month of July of that year, two hundred Brahmins were forcibly converted and made to eat beef."

According to Kamath, M. V. "The archaeological survey of India has listed three temples which were destroyed during the reign of Tipu Sultan. These were the Harihareshwar Temple at Harihar which was converted into a mosque, the Varahswami Temple in Srirangapatnam and the Odakaraya Temple in Hospet."

The text encrypted on a stone found at Seringapatam, which was situated in a conspicuous place in the fort screams of the persecution of Hindus by Tipu Sultan. The translation of the text is as follows.

"Oh Almighty God! dispose the whole body of infidels! Scatter their tribe, cause their feet to stagger! Overthrow their councils, change their state, destroy their very root! Cause death to be near them, cut off from them the means of sustenance! Shorten their days! Be their bodies the constant object of their cares (i.e., infest them with diseases), deprive their eyes of sight, make black their faces (i.e., bring shame)."

The above text clearly indicates the hatred Tipu Sultan had in his heart for the Hindus which also symbolize how the ideology of Muslim rulers revolved around the terms of *Ghazi, Jihad* and *Butkishan.* Their aim in life was to torture, convert or kill Hindus, to plunder their pilgrims and heritage.

There have been fewer persecution of Hindus in the South as compared to the North, but there is no direction in India that was spared by the Muslim invaders. Persecution of Hindus during the reign of Tipu Sultan is one amongst those. At one side Muslims continued sucking the Hindu blood and on the other side there were people who had an eye on the wealth and abundance of India.

The West was planning to catch this golden sparrow and establish their rule on this golden land. They had started sowing the western seeds into the Indian land which were to be grown into the toxic trees that would poison Hindus and their offsprings for ages.

Persecution by the Portuguese: Leave, Convert, or Die

THE CURSE CONTINUED. As mentioned previously, in the North, the Muslims had strengthened their grounds and on the other side, the Europeans were digging out their way into the Indian soil through the coastal areas. This was because after the collapse of the Roman Empire, the Europeans were bound to pay heavy tax duties to trade with the Indian subcontinent. Their dream came true when a European navigator, Vasco da Gama found a sea route to India on the historical day of May 20, 1498 AD

This was not just a route for Europeans to India but a way for Portuguese invaders to persecute Indians for a long period, extending the large arms of the monster of darkness. On one side, Hinduism was threatened by Islam and on the other side, by Christianity. India, the land that glittered to them like a fantasy world which was self reliant in every aspect and where everything required for survival and luxury was available in abundance. The spices, the vegetation, the gems, and the meat were always a fascination for the invaders coming from lands of environmental scarcities.

Portuguese interests on the west coast of India were largely determined by sailing conditions and they found a defensible island site with excellent harbor facilities on the Malabar Coast that included Goa and a part of South India. Adding to the horror, the site was already facing challenges from the Muslim invaders and entry of the Portuguese worsened the condition of Hindus leaving no way for the community to escape the holocaust.

The Portuguese first came to Calicut, the Kozhikode of today on the Malabar Coast. The story goes that the Portuguese invited native fishermen on board and bought some Indian items. It is said that one Portuguese accompanied the fishermen to the port and met a Tunisian Muslim, on whose advice, Gama sent a couple of his men to Ponnani to meet the ruler of Calicut, Zamorin. Well known for their sweet tongue, mannerisms, and manipulating tactics, they managed to convince Zamorin to support them. After a few denials, Zamorin agreed and allowed them to establish their factories in the Calicut area. It is to be noted that Portuguese were the first who brought the factories and printing press to India and not the British. In fact, it were the Portuguese who brought Christianity to India for the first time on such a massive scale. British simply extended it.

Like all our ancestors, another Hindu believer of the Indian philosophy of *Atithi Devo Bhava*, Guest is God; Zamorin once again opened the doors of this divine land for a new breed of invaders who came under the guise of traders, seeking shelter and opportunities on our banks. He was unaware of the fact that while signing a commercial treaty with them he was writing a chapter in the future of India with the Hindu blood. Our ancestors were either too naive to predict the intentions of the invaders or were extraordinarily overconfident and underestimated the approaching threat. This was a common trait amongst most of the Indian rulers. They repeated the same mistake again and again. The irony is that even in the 21st century our leaders follow the same tradition. It was fine to forgive but it was not fine at all to forget because 1000 years were enough to learn the crucial lessons. However, no surprise, till date we haven't learnt; the same scenario is still being repeated.

Portuguese initially traded with the Indians but they were nurturing the aspirations of colonizing India and Christianizing Hindus which amplified with time. Now they never wanted to return from this land which was a symbol of abundance. On the other side, the Arab merchants who were already doing a successful business in the area got paranoid about their survival. Portuguese were technologically advanced and intelligent, hence they became a challenge not only for Arabs but also the existing Indian merchants. As a result, a revolt rose between the two competitors.

Disturbed by the circumstances, Portuguese requested King Zamorin to resolve the matter in favour of the Portuguese traders but Zamorin chose not to intervene between the two foreign merchants. This was enough for Portuguese to be annoyed with the King and they revolted against Calicut.

Now an open battle was inevitable but Zamorin was a mighty King in possession of a huge army and it was difficult for a foreign invader to defeat him. They finally decided to seek support from the local rulers to strengthen themselves against Zamorin. They knew that Indians lacked integrity and it won't be impossible to find allies against the King. Hence, after presenting their proposal to many local rulers they finally formed an alliance with a comparatively smaller kingdom of Cochin. They signed a treaty with the ruler of Cochin and declared a war against Calicut in which Portuguese won. The battle was fought in 1504 AD from March to July in which Portuguese with the help of Cochin defeated the Calicut King Zamorin.

This victory boosted the morale of Portuguese and also of the other European communities to now see India as a land of opportunities. Now, along with Cochin many other Hindu empires started forming alliances with Portuguese for their short term benefits that resulted in the long term colonization of the area.

The incident reminds us of the same irony that we experienced between Prithviraj Chauhan, and Jaichand who refused to form an alliance with the fellow Hindu King against a foreign invader. The ruler of Cochin instead of joining hands with Zamorin stood by the Portuguese and supported a foreign invader to colonize his ancestral land for ages. They replaced nearly everything here, whether it was the culture, the surroundings, the heritage, and even history.

Doesn't this sound like a curse of the Lord as two local rulers sharing the same religion, geographical identity, and culture fought against each other allowing a foreigner to capture everything that was theirs and persecute their offsprings?

Also a strong army of Zamorin got defeated by the Portuguese who were not only foreigners ignorant of the local surroundings but were comparatively less in number. It was beyond anybody's imagination that Zamorin could ever be defeated by the Portuguese but it is history. Doesn't it hint about the curse on Hindus?

The governors of the state of India whether he was Gama,

Francisco de Almeida, Afonso de Albuquerque and the later governors, all of them focused on trade in India. This was made possible by forming alliances with the local rulers and building forts in the name of business which was all a part of their strategy to colonize the subcontinent in the long run. They carried an aim of enforcing Christianity on the land in the name of Lord and they were fully supported by the Christian Missionaries residing in the West.

It's a very sad reality of human history that religious missionaries have not only been the active participants in the human bloodshed for power, but they were also the driving forces behind the invaders. Whether it was in the name of Islam or in the name of Christianity, these so-called missionaries did exactly opposite of what was expected from them. It hasn't changed much till date as even today, religion is used as a triggering factor by few of the so called Protestants of God and the religion.

Finally, Goa became a Portuguese colony and the center of Christianization in the East. Christianization in Goa was largely limited to the four districts of Bardez, Mormugao, Salcette, and Tiswadi. Evangelization activities were divided in 1555 AD by the Portuguese viceroy of Goa, Pedro Mascarenhas who allotted Bardez to the Franciscans, Tiswadi to the Dominicans, and Salcette, together with fifteen southeastern villages of Tiswadi, including Chorão and Divar, to the Jesuits. The city of Velha Goa was shared among all, since all the religious orders had their headquarters there. Prior to that, the Franciscans alone Christianized Goa till 1542 AD. Other less active orders that maintained a presence in Goa were the Augustines, Carmelites, and Theatines.

Initially, Christianity was influencing the people. The

affluent lifestyle of the Portuguese attracted the attention of the locals. The first mass conversion took place among the Brahmins of Divar, and the Kshatriyas of Carambolim. In Bardez, Mangappa Shenoy of Pilerne was the first Hindu to convert to Christianity in 1555 AD, adopting the name Pero Ribeiro and thus becoming the first Christian of Bardez. His conversion was followed by that of his brother Panduranga and his uncle Balkrishna Shenoy who was the direct patrilineal ancestor of Goan historian José Gerson da Cunha. In Salcette, Raia was the first village to have been Christianized when its populace was converted *en masse* to Christianity in 1560 AD.

In 1534 AD, Goa was made a diocese and in 1557 AD an archdiocese. The Archbishop of Goa was the most important ecclesiastic of the East, and was from 1572 AD called the "Primate of the East". Though the Portuguese rulers implemented state policies encouraging and even rewarding conversions among Hindus, a large number of conversions took place by force.

This process of Christianization was simultaneously accompanied by Lusitanisation, as the Christian converts typically assumed a Portuguese semblance. The most visible aspect was the discarding of old Hindu names for new Christian Portuguese names. Hindu converts had to abandon their original names and were instructed and forced to adopt a new surname which was Portuguese. Consequently, the converts typically had to adopt the surnames of the Portuguese priest, governor, soldier or layman who stood as godfather for their baptism ceremony. Since in many cases, fathers and sons were not necessarily baptized in the presence of the same godfather, this would lead to them having different surnames. Thus, today it is difficult to find the lineage of those converts who are the descendents of the Hindu Brahmins, who must have been preaching Vedas during the Mauryan's rule and who must have fought as warriors for the Hindu Land during the Chalukya empires.

The biggest irony of the Hindus was that they gave up their heritage, their religion, their names, surnames, and everything but one evil that they still held on to was the caste based hierarchy along with their mother tongue.

The converts from the priestly Brahmin class were *Bamonns*. All Brahmin sub castes such as the Goud Saraswat Brahmins, Padyes, the Daivadnyas, and especially the goldsmiths and a few merchants, were sectioned into the Christian caste of *Bamonn* which still enjoys the highest rank in the converted community. The converts from the Kshatriya and Vaishya Vani castes became *Chardos* and those Vaishya who couldn't become *Chardos* formed a new caste *Gauddos*. Those converts from lower castes were grouped together as *Sudirs*, equivalent to Shudras. The *Bamonns*, *Chardos*, and *Gauddos* have been traditionally seen as the high castes in the Goan Catholic caste hierarchy.

These local converts, particularly the Brahmins, retained pride of caste and race. Caste consciousness among the native Christians was so intense that they even maintained separate Church confraternities dedicated to the perpetuation of the existing caste hierarchy. In church circles, the *Bamonns* and *Chardos* were rivals and frequently discriminated against each other. Caste discrimination even extended to the clergy. In such atrocities when we could not save our religion we managed to nurture the caste system. It means steps could have been taken to safeguard the religious practices too but may be caste was more important than the Hindu identity. It could be nothing but a curse.

Governor of Goa, D Constantine de Braganca issued an order on April 2, 1560, instructing that Brahmins should be thrown out of Goa and other areas under Portuguese control. They had a month's time to sell their property and migrate from there. Those found violating the viceregal order, it was declared, would have their properties seized.

Another order was issued, this time by Governor Antonio Morez Barreto, on February 7, 1575, decreeing that the estates of Brahmins whose 'presence was prejudicial to Christianity' would be confiscated and used for 'providing clothes to the New Christians'. The Hindus, who dared to oppose the religious persecution by the Portuguese administration or the Christian clergy, were punished, swiftly and mercilessly. Those who were fortunate got away with being banished from Portuguese territory. The less fortunate had their property seized and auctioned. The least fortunate either died or were forced to serve as slave labours. The wealth and the ruins of the chaos were transported from Indian shores to Portuguese coffers.

The Hindus, on a mass level, were manipulated and forced to accept Christianity, their scriptures were burnt, their rituals were banned, and their belief systems were declared as sins. Hundreds of temples were plundered; idols were dethroned only to use the looted land and wealth to construct Churches. Their names were changed and identity was completely transformed to foreign influence in a few centuries. Their religion, their skin color, and their identity were humiliated.

They were manipulated, tortured, and even killed in the name of faith. Shall we not call this persecution? Shall we not call it curse of Gods?

Till date in 21st century too, conversion is a reality in India and so is forced conversion.

Though a lot of Hindus accepted Christianity officially to save their interest and lives, their soul refused to give up their age old Hindu rituals and practices. This was seen as a threat and sacrilege by the Christian missionaries. On a special request of Francis Xavier, the Portuguese established the Goan inquisition Court in Goa to enquire about the status of the converts and punish them brutally if found guilty. They were tortured for crimes like singing their local hymns, wearing the Hindu attires, nurturing the basil plant at home, or even bathing in the morning as that was considered a Hindu practice and a sin for the Christians. The converts who indulged in such practices were called the crypto Christians who deserved to be punished according to the missionaries. Irrespective of gender, age or any other circumstances such converts were forced to give up all those practices immediately. These punishments were so harsh that the Goan inquisition is regarded by all contemporary portrayals as the most violent inquisition ever executed by the Portuguese Catholic Church. Its most virulent phase lasted from 1560 to 1812 AD.

The inquisition was set as a tribunal, headed by a judge who was sent to Goa from Portugal. He was assisted by two judicial henchmen and was answerable to no one except to Lisbon. The Inquisition Laws filled 230 pages that set the criteria to declare a crypto Christian as guilty and punished accordingly. The Inquisition was conducted in a palace which was known as the Big House. Its proceedings were always conducted behind closed shutters and closed doors. The screams of agony of the culprits could be heard in the streets, in the stillness of the night, as they were brutally interrogated, flogged, and slowly dismembered in front of their relatives. It is documented that they had to go through physical and mental torture. Their eyelids were sliced off, limbs were amputated, and skin was burnt. They were hanged and left alone in the jungle only to wait for their death. Pork was applied on their feet and burnt so that their cries horrified others too.

Conversion at knifepoint was the brutal reality of Christianity in Goa along with the Portuguese economic and political control over the Hindus, who were vassals of the Portuguese crown. This was not only in 15th and 16th century but even after independence when the missionaries forcibly converted many people.

Even during the end of Portuguese empire in Goa, the Hindus were given an ultimatum to convert, leave or be ready to die. This is what lead to the mass migration of the Hindus especially Brahmins from their ancestral land to find their place in the other parts of India. Even today we can find incidences where people tell us that how the missionaries are luring them or torturing them to accept Christianity.

Even today, the Portuguese ruled areas for instance Goa hardly shows any influence of the ancestral Hindu rulers Chalaukyas, the Cheras, or the Mauryans who ruled the region for thousands of years. If you visit Goa, you would see that most of the city is named after Portuguese leaders, the temples are converted into churches, the priests are converted into fathers of the Churches, and the Diyas are converted into candles. The holy basil plant is substituted with a cross in nearly seventy percent of the homes who from Hindus became the ex-Hindus

The Hindu idols showcased in the Museums narrate the brutal story behind them. The chopped nose, beheaded body and broken limbs of these idols clearly indicate how the idols were broken, Hindu temples were plundered, wealth was looted, and how temple ruins were used to build the Portuguese architecture on the Hindu land.

These attacks did not only hurt Hindu lives but their soul. When a place is colonized then the food, lifestyle, and thought patterns everything is influenced, but when there is a religious purpose to all this, then even the soul of a person is colonized. His own heritage is erased from the memory and future is conditioned in a way that he no longer is attached to his ancestors. His authentic history is snatched from his hands and the offsprings who know nothing about their own DNA relate with the foreigners who are far away from their original identity.

Portuguese ruled in India for many centuries. In fact, they were the last to leave the country; after India got independence, Portuguese sustained in Goa for several years. They refused to leave the region and finally left in 1954 after strict expeditions by the Indian army. They left behind a state that looked like a Portugal estate preserving the mummy of a saint who is alleged to have persecuted Indians in the name of religion. And right on the opposite site we see the consecrated Hindu idols in a museum. The entire story of Hindus from Goa could be related to the Hindus of Kashmir that will be discussed later in the book. They witnessed mass conversion, physical and mental torture; humiliation, massacres, and bloodshed in case they chose to retain their Hindu identity. Similar to the Kashmiri

Hindus, Goan Hindus too were converted, pushed out of their land, or were killed.

In the entire timeline of the invasions in India, what we constantly see is that the persecutors changed from time to time. Sometime they were from the West, sometime from Middle East, sometime from Britain but the persecuted community remained the same and that was the Hindu community. Many swords have tasted Hindu's blood after eating his food, taking shelter in his land , and drinking his water. Whose fault is this? Hindus must think.

The Greedy Dutch

HOWEVER, PORTUGUESE WERE not the only Europeans who had an eye on India. Dutch too were not far behind in this expedition. They too were busy sharpening their swords for plucking out a few feathers of the Golden bird that could feed their offsprings for ages.

Dutch presence on the Indian subcontinent lasted from 1605 to 1825 AD. Merchants of the Dutch East India Company first established themselves in Pulicat, as they were looking for textiles to exchange with the spices they traded in the East Indies. Dutch Suratte and Dutch Bengal were established in 1616 and 1627 AD respectively.

Apart from textiles, the items traded in Dutch India included precious stones, indigo, and silk across the Indian Peninsula, salt and opium in Dutch Bengal, and pepper in Dutch Malabar. The Dutch imported Indian slaves to the Spice Islands and the Cape Colony.

Dutch came with the same dreams that Portuguese and the British came with but they could not succeed in establishing themselves here. The Hindu religion had few kings who were capable enough to give a tough fight to such aspirations. One such king was Marthanda Varma, who defeated the Dutch army in the Battle of Colachel, or else before British we would have been colonized by the Dutch.

In the Battle of Colachel that took place in 1741, Marthanda Varma, the King of Travancore defeated the Dutch East India Company, resulting in the complete eclipse of Dutch power in Malabar.

As M. O. Koshy writes in *The Dutch Power in Kerala,* 'The defeat of the Dutch by Travancore is considered the earliest example of an organized power from Asia overcoming European military technology and tactics. The Dutch never recovered from the defeat and no longer posed a large colonial threat to India.'

The irony is that the story of heroes like Marthanda Varma who did their bit to protect this land and the Hindu religion is erased by the manipulative historians to completely alter the opinion of the future generations about the authentic Hindu history. But we must remember that if Hindu religion is alive even after such severe persecution it is because of known and unknown soldiers like Marthanda Varma.

The Brutish British

CURSE OF GODS continued further. In the northern India, the Muslim rulers continued with their mission of converting and persecuting the Hindu community from Kashmir to the Deccan peninsula while extending it further down south.

But after Aurangzeb, the last strong emperor of the Mughal Empire, the empire began to collapse. This became an advantage for other foreign invaders once again to colonize India and open more doors of her wealth to their not so sufficient homelands.

British had two major strengths; one was their advanced artillery and second was their shrewd politics. They did not have rules or any moral rights and wrongs similar to Muslim invaders, though their style of persecution was more of the sweet coated poison. They plundered less but looted more. They stole our scriptures and did not destroy them; their interest was their good at any cost. '*If we call Muslim invaders as wolves, British were the foxes*'. They simply wanted results as means were never important to them. Manipulation, diplomacy, and cheating, everything was fair for the British to establish their grounds on a land that had no strong fences.

Their policies and strategies were very much under the

carpet. They believed in manipulation and exploitation rather than beheading people right away but their hands too have the stains of Hindu's blood. They too destroyed our legacy, influenced conversions, and plundered our temples and idols; though it was lesser than the Muslim Invasions. However, they hit the spine of India in a different manner.

They initially came as traders similar to Portuguese. They wanted to enhance the commercial relations with India and wanted permission to establish their factories here. The first approval was given to the British by the Mughal emperor Jahangir whose son and grandson Shahjahan and Aurangzeb continued granting permissions, unaware of the fact that they were establishing British ground.

One persecutor handed over the game of persecution to another persecutor. The only common factor was the persecuted, the Hindu.

British did not come only to trade. If said in a harsh manner, they were the white skinned thieves who came as friends with black hearts. However, their aspirations surfaced in the next two hundred years when they sucked the remaining blood of the Hindu community and Indian Land.

Hidden in the skin of a commercial entity, known as the East India Company which was incorporated by the royal charter from Her Majesty Queen Elizabeth I, British came in 1600 AD. This was to extend the trading terms with India in silk and spices, and other profitable Indian commodities. The Company established 'factories' along the Indian coast, notably in Calcutta, Madras, and Bombay. They brought ammunitions and military with a justification that their business premises needed protection in the secluded coastal lands. They recruited soldiers in order to guard their assets and lives but they soon converted their means of protection into a mission of conquest.

The aura of the British, their affluent lifestyle, and their strength in war tactics was tempting to the local Indian rulers. Assuring them of their state's protection from the other states, British steadily intervened into the politics of the state and acquired the power to change the political game in India by bribing them of protection and later by force if they refused the offer. They displaced Nawabs and Maharajas for a price, emptied their treasuries as it pleased them, and took over their states through various tactics.

Thus, the ruling states were dragooned into signing up for the British protection for lofty returns. This steadily brought them under the debt and to pay those debts they handed over their territories to the British. They allowed Britishers to collect the revenues from the peasants. These peasants were not aware that the monster of darkness was hovering over them now. These revenues were no more revenues but extortion money in governance of the British. This brought a scenario, when the food producers started dying for being deprived of their own produce which was soaked in their sweat. Soon, heavy taxation, enslavement, biased policies, monopoly over markets, and heavy export of the raw material lead to famines in India. The already small bread of the Indians was also snatched by the British to be exported to England whereas Indians were dying of hunger in India. These famines were not a natural calamity but a created horror of the British rule. In 1866, at least a million and a half Indians died in the Orissa Famine which was followed by a series of famines in the entire country.

In a few decades, British indirectly gathered so much power

that they acquired the states of the monarchs who died without any heir and began a new chapter of persecution in India and the Hindus.

In 1843, Lord Dalhousie introduced a new expansionist policy that brought unrest to the classes and the masses of India. As per the Doctrine of Lapse, British began to annex the Indian states one by one giving different reasons; fair or unfair. They annexed Satara, Sambalpur, Jhansi, Nagpur, Jaipur, and others in North India. Later, the pension of few rulers was discontinued and the Queen of Jhansi was debarred from ruling the state in the absence of a biological heir.

British also imposed heavy taxations, policies that favored British industries and disfavored Indian industries, rules and regulations that weakened Indian's economic and social interest to the core.

Though, India was persecuted by the Muslim rulers for long but the immense potential still made it a glittering jewel for the world. British came to a land that shared a massive share in the world GDP with a figure of 23 per cent as documented and she was still a land of abundance and opportunities. That the Hindus were still sulking in their homeland is a different matter as government's revenues were collected from the Hindu pilgrims as Jizya.

As J.T. Sunderland stated:

'Nearly every kind of manufacture or product known to the civilized world—nearly every kind of creation of man's brain and hand, existing anywhere, and prized either for its utility or beauty—had long been produced in India. India was a far greater industrial and manufacturing nation than any in Europe or any other in Asia. Her world fame textile goods in cotton, wool, linen and silk, her exquisite jewellery and her precious stones cut in every lovely form were highly demanded in the civilized world. So were her pottery, porcelains, ceramics of every kind, quality, color, and beautiful shape, her fine works in metal, iron, steel, silver and gold.'

This has been the reputation of India since forever. But the GDP of 23 per cent, by the time the British departed India, had dropped to just over 3 per cent which shows that India was governed for the benefit of Britain that filled the British coffers by its depredations in India.

Dr. Shashi Tharoor quoted the British rule as the 'BrUtish rule' in India for the brutality and narcissistic strategies that the British used to persecute the Indian community. In other words, British came to take advantage of the Hindu land that was weakened by many persecutors already. They knew that India continued to restore her wealth despite the continuing plunder. Right from the time of Mohammad bin Qasim, Indians were only restoring her coffers to be looted by the next persecutor to arrive from a different land.

The Hindus were blessed with so many assets whether it was their climate, their fertile land, their heritage, their scriptures, and their civilization, but they could never reap the benefit of it completely. It was always scattered, looted, plundered and damaged. Doesn't this indicate that maybe Gods regretted their decision of bestowing the Hindu with such bliss?

Like all other invaders British looted a house which had an unlocked door, whose owner was sleeping, whose members were fighting with each other, and who never bothered to fight back with their full potential. They took away India's wealth, ruptured her economic and social strengths, shed the blood of the people and colonized not only the land but the minds of the natives who are still imprisoned in a belief that 'everything that is British is superior to everything that is Indian'.

They refrain from saree, cotton, ayurveda, dal rice and Hindi, and feel superior with western outfits, cosmetic medical treatments, pizzas, burgers and the English language.

As FJ Shore, the British administrator in India, opined: 'the halcyon days of India are over; she has been drained of a large proportion of the wealth she once possessed, and her energies have been cramped by a sordid system of misrule to which the interests of millions have been sacrificed for the benefit of the few… The gradual impoverishment of the people and country, under the mode of rule established by the British Government, has hastened their fall.'

Indian industry and the trade was destroyed. But the biggest wound that British gave to India was dividing the country forever by exploiting the greed of few politicians, who wanted the luxury of having a different country for themselves and their offspring to lead forever. They wanted to dominate the independent Indians even when they assumed to be independent. This time the tools were different. Instead of swords, artillery or spears, they used the political agendas, religious differences and caste issues. This curse still continues which will be discussed later in the book.

Before the British East India Company arrived, Bengal, Masulipatnam, Surat, and the Malabar ports of Calicut and Quilon had a thriving shipbuilding industry and Indian shipping ruled the Arabian Sea and the Bay of Bengal. The Indian Rulers possessed one of the best navies in those days. This was from the ancient times as Indus Valley Civilization too was found to have ruins of ports and ships. For instance the Marathas even ran a substantial fleet in the sixteenth century; the navy of Shivaji Bhonsle defended the west coast against the Portuguese threat. Even in south, the navy was strong under the King of Calicut, Zamorin. In every way, Indian shipbuilding industry was competitive enough to beat the global industry. But in 1757, the Company and the British ships exercised a monopoly on trade routes over Indian merchants. Duties were imposed on Indian merchant ships moving to and from not just foreign ports but also the Indian ports. This strangled the native shipping industry to the point of irrelevance in everything. They were only restricted to local trade of the low-value 'native' goods. Like every other strategic scenario, the manipulative and biased policies lead to a complete downfall of the shipping industry that further affected the entire trade and the financial solvency of the Indians.

As the Victorian commentator William Digby was to observe, 'the Mistress of the Seas of the Western world had killed the Mistress of the Seas of the East.'

The scenario was the same in the other industries for instance, the steel industry. In spite of being rated as probably the best in the world, it was handled in a biased manner so the steel produced by the Indian manufacturers was not approved by the government. This gave monopoly to the British manufacturers over the Indian steel producers.

The textile industry was smashed in a brutal manner. Indian textiles were world-renowned since the ancient times. Wearing Indian textiles was a status symbol in the west for its quality and finesse. The finishing by the Indian weavers was incomparable, whereas the British were trying to create a market for the machine made fabric in the West. The raw material was exported from India through the Indian ports and the finished products which were rather of inferior quality were sold in the Indian market. Apart from the white collar brutality, British were reported to physically torture the local weavers. As Dr. Shashi Tharoor mentions in his book, *An Era of Darkness: The British Empire in India,* the weaver's thumbs were amputated to prevent them from further rotating the weaving wheels and produce the textiles that India was once famous for. So much has been the extent of British greed that words like morality, humanity, justice, and even mercy were erased from their dictionary.

British are given the credit of bringing printing press to India, though it was first brought by the Portuguese during the 16th century, but British did extend it to another level. The publications including the newspapers, magazine and others were controlled by the British. The content went through censorship and if any information was found against the British government it was immediately banned. It was mostly governed by the British journalists and Indian journalists had to go through atrocities if they desired to exercise the freedom of expression as the British press did.

British also brought one thing to India that Indians probably can't do without today—it is the tea. Before the 17th century, British imported tea from China which was pretty expensive. Hence, they decided to exploit the fertile land of India to grow tea. They cut down the forests of the Nilgiris and Assam. They also ravaged the forests of Coorg to grow coffee. Besides this, they brought exotic species like eucalyptus, pine, and wattle to produce viscose, which was sent to the United Kingdom to be used into fabric production. All these plants were devastating for the fertility of the soil. For instance, eucalyptus thirstily drinks up the ground water; thanks to their plantations, the British converted the once lush tropical rainforests of the Nilgiris into an almost dry area. The soil that was producing basil, Aloe vera, and other blissful herbs was used to grow drugs like opium during the British Raj.

Not only the resources but human beings were exported as commodities. To get cheap labour in their factories, the British decided to take the Indians away from India. This was either by cheating them, when they were given fake assurances of being taken to a land of opportunities and abundance or by forcing them at gunpoint. In 1825, the first massive migration of Indian workers took place from Madras to Mauritius. In 1835, Mauritius received 19,000 migrant indentured labourers from India. Workers continued to be shipped to Mauritius till 1922. Apart from these, there were many ships that sailed with the Indians to work as slaves in fields of remote areas, who were never able to meet their loved ones again. These labourers are still living in the foreign lands knowing nothing about their background except that they were Hindus from India.

The story goes that these people were poor labourers and farmers from villages of India who were told that they would be taken to a closeby village called 'Shri Ram Desh' for a better future. Carrying few belongings and the Hindu scripture Ramayan, these people were trafficked to an unknown land by the British. Nearly three lakh indentured labourers were taken to British colonies during the 200 years of British Raj. These labourers were not only cheated, but also extreme atrocities were done to them by the British and that too at a completely unknown place.

In a nutshell, heavy taxations, enslavement, famines, and discriminatory policies against Indians were disturbing the commoners along with the rulers for long. Now it was difficult to tolerate as the pressure was building throughout the country. Many Indians still remained quiet, but some of them reached a stage, where they were prepared to die for their dignity.

India was suffering. In the land of agricultural bliss, people were dying of hunger by the British created famines, western laws and policies paralyzed the economy, and most importantly, humiliation by the British as a result of their strong racist behavior was suffocating Indians. As a result few Indians were awakening and realizing the curse they were going through. They realized that something was wrong and that they needed to revolt against it.

The frustration against the British was cooking among Indians from royals to ordinary farmers, but it surfaced during 1857 when soldiers revolted against the British for their attempt to violate their religious beliefs. The deployment of the new breech-loading Enfield rifle was filled with the cartridge that was made of pork and beef, it hurt the Hindu sentiments to an intolerable level. When Hindu troops learned that the tip of the Enfield cartridge had to be bitten off to prepare it for firing, a number of soldiers refused to accept the ammunition for religious reasons. They also blamed the British of deliberately violating their religious sentiments.

Not only eating beef is considered a sin as per Hindu religion, but it also became a reason for him to be discarded from his community. The Hindus held strong beliefs about this aspect of their religion that ignited fire all over the country. Prior to the incident also, Indian soldiers were treated inferior to the

British and higher ranks were given to the English and not the Indians. Hence, the cartridge incident only gave a platform to the already brewing frustrations in the Indian minds.

The revolt first took place in 1857 in Barrackpore of Bengal when Mangal Pandey, a British soldier of Indian origin killed British officers in a parade on 29th March. Later, it had spread to the entire north India. Followed by Barrackpore, soldiers at Meerut Army Cantonment followed the footsteps of Mangal Pandey. After this many states joined the ongoing revolt. Banaras, Allahabad, Aligarh, Kota, and Indore, all followed their footsteps.

Along with soldiers, the local rulers also jumped into the revolt to gain control over the lost kingdoms or to preserve the existing ones. However, the well planned strategy, advanced artillery, and strong military generals like Havelock on the British side, suppressed the revolt by all means. The local rulers died, escaped, or surrendered to the British. In comparison to the British, Indian strategy was highly localized and restricted to north India which gave the power to the British government on a silver platter.

Most importantly, many rulers from India openly supported the British instead of the local rulers who chose to fight for their identity as an Indian and as a Hindu.

Veer Savarkar defined 1857 mutiny as the first war of independence that officially offered the destiny of India to the Queen's hands.

Finally, in 1858, the British government took charge of India officially ensuring on paper that this rule will completely surrender to the Indian benefit and humanity. But it was just a piece of paper that Queen Victoria signed as the reality was way different. The brutality of the whites against the browns took an intense turn from here.

The local political institutions were abolished and a foreign government took over the command of legal and social justice of the Indians. These people were hardly aware or sensitive to the Indian sentiments and customary trends. In spite of agreeing on paper, Indians were debarred from the Civil services as only a small percentage of the jobs quota was allotted to Indians, that too of the lowest ranks, irrespective of one's caliber. Even if they were graduates from the best of the international institutions, they were certainly not in the priority list for the higher echelons of government ranks. And in case a brown candidate occupied a position of his caliber, he had to endure the rants of racism from his British colleagues.

Allegedly, British also widened caste fault lines in India. When the British first came, to be able to understand the Indian culture and the social and communal background of the people, they needed to read the scriptures. These scriptures were written in Sanskrit. They needed people who could translate the scriptures for them and that community was the Brahmins. Brahmins were anyway one of the most influential classes of those times. Hence, British had a special place for the upper classes especially Brahmins, of course for their own interest and benefit. The irony here was that Brahmins once again exploited the opportunity for their own benefit and not for the religion as a whole as mentioned by Dr Tharoor justifying the curse of Gods.

This further widened the gap between the castes and somewhere a section of Brahmins exploited the opportunity to get a good position compared to other castes. Before the British came to India, different communities from diverse backgrounds mingled with each other as the line of discrimination was not as harsh as the British made it to be. They strictly defined the hierarchical placement of the castes that were further divided into sub castes and sub-sub castes. Many castes that British could not categorize were tagged as the scheduled or backward classes. This was the seed of the poisonous tree of the reservation issue in India that took a fearsome form in the 1991 Mandal Comission when students even committed suicides over this burning issue.

As per the British this was to assist the policymakers to draw the policies for social development. However, the development that we saw was solely for the British. Yes, it did create very deep pits between the communities that were earlier not so deep, but now the communities identified themselves only as a restricted community with hardly any affiliation for the state.

Even after the persecution by the Muslim rulers somewhere Indian's philosophy of 'forgive and forget' helped them to merge with the Muslims, but the British came and refreshed the old scars. Similar to caste prejudice, the British also deepened the religion based discriminations. Since British officially and unofficially treated Hindus and Muslims differently through their policies and procedures, both became another reason for further persecution. And we all know how this difference further amputated the arms of Mother India and fragmentized the country into three separate nations in the long run that still continue to be the enemies of each other. Many Hindus as well as non-Hindus were killed in the partition.

British 'Divide and Rule' policy did not stop here. They used all means to execute their strategy. Wherever there was a crack, it was deepened and widened. But we cannot deny that we had the cracks because of our faults. These cracks were exploited because we were cursed.

This was not all. British also separated the nation on linguistic identities which now transformed into regional differences. It is agreed that India was not one nation even before the British but the common people were not strictly divided on paper. They had freedom to move to another kingdom without much difficulty. But now this power was snatched away by the British governance.

The flexibility in the laws and policies was missing in the British Raj. In India, before the British, the rules were flexible and sensitive to the circumstances. In case of extreme emergencies, the taxes were waived off, loans were provided on human grounds and in case of marriage, special benefits were granted with the goodwill of the monarch or the local body. But the British pen was insensitive to human emotions. Irrespective of birth or death in the family, heavy taxes were imposed, making their life miserable. Whatever the circumstances, the common man was condemned. His life crushed under the polished boot of an insensitive foreign government that had taken over the power to decide India's destiny.

The British defend themselves by arguing that they came to India with an intention of enlightened despotism for the benefit of Indians, whereas the reality and facts scream of the hypocrisy of this statement. They say that Indians were incapable of governing themselves. The descendents of the great Mauryans, the Guptas, and the Chanakya who can still teach any policymaker to design the government policies were incapable of governing themselves according to the British. But somewhere they were true. If we were capable of governing ourselves we would not have been captured by the Muslims in the last 1000 years or by the British. It was the curse of Gods that all our scriptures got blurred and we lost the vision that we inherited.

Every mistake has a price. The atrocities by the British continued to grow and they amplified after the 1857 mutiny.

As per the records revealed by Dr. Shashi Tharoor, in his book, *An Era of Darkness*, "the suppression of the 1857 'mutiny' was conducted with extreme brutality, with hundreds of rebels being blown to bits from the mouths of cannons or hanged from public gibbets, women, and children massacred".

'Most of the time,' says the historian Jon Wilson, 'the actions of British imperial administrators were driven by irrational passions rather than calculated plans.'

Dr Tharoor also says that "brutality was an early feature of the military campaigns of the East India Company. When the Vellore mutiny occurred in 1806, sparked by changes in the uniforms of the Company's Indian sepoys that were found offensive by Hindus and Muslims, the British put it down with ruthless ferocity. Three hundred mutineers were tied together, lined up against the wall of a fives court and shot at a range of thirty yards; this happened without even a summary trial or an opportunity to explain themselves. After a more formal court-martial process of the rest, six mutineers were blown away from the mouths of cannons, five were shot by firing squad, eight were hanged and five transported to a penal colony. During the Revolt of 1857, thousands of mutineers were killed by similar means, as were large numbers of civilians of both sexes. General James George Smith Neill, in Allahabad and Kanpur, was particularly bloodthirsty, as was Sir

Hugh Rose in Jhansi, where some 5,000 civilians were massacred, with no 'maudlin clemency' shown to the inhabitants of the rebel city of the brave queen Rani Lakshmibai. When Delhi was retaken, the savagery was pitiless: in one neighbourhood alone, Kucha Chelan, some 1,400 unarmed citizens were massacred. 'The orders went out to shoot every soul,' recorded one young officer. 'It was literally murder.' So many civilians were killed that an eye witness reported 'dead bodies in every street, rotting in the burning sun'. Refugees sheltering in mosques were plucked out and executed. Mass hangings were the norm. Delhi, the Mughal capital, a rich and bustling city of half a million inhabitants was left a desolate ruin."

"Some of these killings might be sought to be explained, if not excused, by the heat of battle, particularly in putting down a rebellion. But some reprisals were in cold blood. Atrocities also took place under civilian rule, on official orders and against civilian victims. In 1872, in Malerkotla, Punjab, some 65 Namdhari Sikhs were blown to bits from the mouths of cannons; in Peshawar's Qissa Khwani Bazaar in 1930, 400 Indians were butchered; and innumerable smaller incidents of beatings, floggings, racial abuse and assaults, shootings, hangings and transportation of Indians for a varied list of offences peckle the bloody history of British colonialism."

"Such examples of brutality from the days of the East India Company or the early days of Crown rule tend to lay themselves open to the defence that those were other times, when other mores applied. But they continued even in the twentieth century. The brutal force used to repress the Quit India movement in 1942 involved tactics that, in the words of a British governor, if 'dragged out in the cold light of the day, nobody could defend'. Gang rape by the police was not uncommon: 73 women were violated by police in a bid to terrorize the satyagrahis, prisoners were forced to lie naked on blocks of ice till they lost consciousness, and thousands were beaten in jail. Even strafing of civilian protestors from the air was authorized. At the beginning of the century, Ruskin declared that 'every mutiny, every danger, every terror, and every crime, occurring under, or paralyzing, our Indian legislation, arises directly out of our national desire to live on the loot of India'. Reprisals against Indians who were challenging British exploitation continued he pointed out, had no moral basis. Still, they continued to be exacted."

General Dyer targeted Hindus on many occasions. He issued the orders specifically against Hindus when they tried to rebel against the Christian missionaries who were brought to India specially for converting Hindus into Christians.

As Dr. Shashi Tharoor quotes Will Durant's words, Hindus using the street in which the woman missionary had been beaten should crawl on their bellies; if they tried to rise to all fours, they were struck by the butts of soldiers' guns. He arrested 500 professors and students and compelled all students to present themselves daily for roll-calls, though this required that many of them should walk sixteen miles a day. He had hundreds of citizens, and some school boys, quite innocent of any crime, flogged in the public square. He built an open cage, unprotected from the sun, for the confinement of arrested persons; other prisoners he bound together with ropes, and kept in open trucks for fifteen hours. He had lime poured upon the naked bodies of saints, and then exposed them to the sun's rays that the lime might harden and crack their skin. He cut off the electric and water supplies from Indian houses and ordered all electric fans possessed by Indians to be surrendered, and given *gratis* to the British. Finally he sent airplanes to drop bombs upon men and women working in the fields."

This happened because though a few Hindus were fastening their belts against the monster of darkness, not all Hindus retaliated against the British. Few of them tried rather harder to secure a place for themselves in the British lobby. It was a curse of Gods that we got used to for ages which is why their moral was high and they continued to do so.

'Guest Was Not God'

Apart from the above-listed atrocites mentioned by Dr. Shashi Tharoor, in his book, *An Era of Darkness*, who can forget the most brutal massacre of Jallianwala Bagh in the British history of Indian rule in1919. After making so many sacrifices in the World War I, a huge contribution in men and material, blood and treasure to the British side in the world war, Indians expected that they would be rewarded with peace and the rights of self-governance to an extent, as they had been promised. But those hopes shattered when the British government backed off from its promises. Finally, this instigated chaos and revolts in India. They showed their disagreement in different ways. Insecure of the rebellion, the British government passed orders according to which Indians were supposed to be arrested if they gather together as they would suspect these gatherings to be a threat to peace in the country. Not even three men could stand together on the street. In this scenario, some 10,000–15,000 people from outlying districts gathered in the city the same day to celebrate the Hindu and Sikh festival of Baisakhi. These people were the innocent commoners, women, children and even pregnant women and infants. They had assembled in an enclosed walled garden that had only five narrow passages used for both exit and entry. This was known as the Jallianwala Bagh which was a popular spot for public events in Amritsar.

When General Dyer, the British Commander that Indian History will never ever forget, learned of this meeting, he did not seek to find out what it was about, but used it as an opportunity to crush the Indians as mosquitoes. He promptly took a detachment of soldiers in armored cars equipped with machine guns as if they were going to the borders to kill dangerous terrorists. They blocked the passageways of the garden by their armored vehicles so people would not find exit from their death. Without giving a single warning to the crowd to disperse or clarify their objective behind the gathering, Dyer ordered his troops, standing behind the brick walls surrounding the Bagh, to open fire from some 150 yards away. The crowd, of thousands of unarmed and non-violent people started screaming and pressing in panic against the closed gate, but as per Dyer's orders his men continued to fire the bullets till the entire ammunition was exhausted and a garden decorated with colorful flags turned into a cemetery. The music was drowned by the bullet firing and the folk songs with cries of innocent commoners. They fired mercilessly and continuously. By the time the troops had finished firing, they had used 1,650 rounds, killed at least 379 people and wounded 1,137. Few historians say that these figures are much lesser than the real numbers. 'Barely a bullet was wasted' was a statement that Dyer wrote in one of his reports to the British government while narrating this cruel incident to them.

These bullets still exist on the Indian soul, for it was the reward of our tolerance, all embracing culture, unconditional acceptance, and the principle of *'Atithi Devo Bhava'*, 'Guest is God'. If the soul exists after death, an innocent child of the village woman, who had died in this horror episode of the British rule, would have surely asked that day; why this guest killed us. And no scholar would have been able to answer his question till date. Even the future generation will always ask the same question, how would you justify these principles, while having the marks of these bullets on your land.

May be it was a curse of Gods for not having a clear perspective of what was taught to us.

These people who came to trade in our country with a polished tongue and white collar behaved as if there was no human evolution till date, as if it was a jungle. The irony is that even in the jungle an animal only kills what is needed to satisfy his hunger. But British swallowed so many Indians and they haven't burped till date.

As Dr Tharoor says, "No other 'punishment' in the name of law and order had similar casualties: The Peterloo Massacre had claimed about 11 lives. Across the Atlantic, British soldiers provoked into firing on Boston Commons had killed five men and were accused of deliberate massacre. In response to the self-proclaimed Easter Rebellion of 1916 in Dublin, the British had executed sixteen Irishmen." Jallianwala confirmed how little the British valued Indian lives.

Dyer forbade his soldiers to give any aid to the injured. He ordered all Indians to stay off the streets of Amritsar for twenty-four hours. No relatives or friends could pour the last drop of water into their mouth. They were left to yearn and wait for their death. The majority of those who were killed were Sikhs and Hindus who came to perform the dance of joy, Bhangra, on the ever blossoming tunes of Punjabi folk songs. Soon, the yellow colour of Baisakhi turned into the authentic red colour of their own blood that came out of their heart that was big enough to greet everyone in their home with utmost affection. The music, the spirit, and the celebration transformed into the cries of those who died or who waited for their death in pain.

Apart from Jallianwala Bagh, British hands were colored with Indian blood many times during the Raj. Few are accounted and many are lost. And if they did not kill they instigated the others to kill.

Finally, a section of Indians stood up for their country and geared up the ongoing freedom movement in India. A section of freedom fighters believed in nonviolence including Mahatma Gandhi and Pandit Jawaharlal Nehru and the other section believed in fighting by all means to push the British away from their homelands. Contribution of martyrs like Bhagat Singh, Sukhdev and Rajguru, who were executed for their dignified fight for the freedom and the aggressive approach of Subhas Chandra Bose hollowed the British foundation in India. In 1942, when Quit India movement was going on, and Congress leaders were jailed, Subhas Chandra Bose established the Indian National Army, Azad Hind Fauj to fight with the British Raj.

Their consistent rebellions were pinching the British by now. Mahatma Gandhi's contribution and Jawaharlal Nehru's contribution is praised by all the books that talk about the freedom struggle. While preserving utmost respect for them, people's attention should be drawn to a fact that somewhere the Indian independence is not a fruit of only nonviolence and Satyagrahas. Many lives were offered into the sacrificial fire of the freedom struggle and we cannot afford to overlook that.

How can we forget the struggle of the martyrs who were hanged or shot by the British? Thousands of soldiers lost their lives to the world wars, thousands were killed on streets during protests, many were executed by the British, and many offered their blood to organizations like Azad Hind Fauj. There was a military aspect to the freedom struggle in India that can never be denied. Leaders like Subhas Chandra Bose's slogan of 'Give me blood and I will give you freedom' indicate that freedom only by nonviolence is a sheer myth. It was a story of blood, massacres, swords, torture, bullets, blasts, and rebellion.

It is also argued that India was granted freedom in 1943 when Subhas Chandra Bose was supposed to be the first Prime Minister of India. But the game of thrones was a reality in 1947 also. There is a lot to the story than what we know; little surfaced in 2018 by exposing the documents concerning the death of Subhas Chandra Bose, which will be discussed later in the book.

Apart from this, there are many myths that prevail with the British image. Besides political unity and democracy, British also get credit for bringing the great Railways, the technological advancement, the printing press, tea, and the English language, which according to the British became a foundation for the Indians to grow further globally. Yes, British build the fantastic railway tracks. They brought industries and technologies. Most importantly, British did bring the English language as India possesses a massive English speaking community worldwide. But as there is a disguise behind every blessing, there is blessing behind every disguise.

The British infrastructure was either for the convenience of the British living in India or was an emblem of their domination over India in the history.

The railways were used to transport the raw material to England that was robbed from India. Also India was a huge market for the machine made British produce that paralyzed the handmade industry. Lord Dalhousie underscored 'the important role that India could play as a market for British manufacturers and as a supplier of agricultural raw materials'. With the coming of railways, not only raw materials but the laborers could be transported to and from where they were needed for the British industries established in India. Those regions that were abundant in agricultural resources would be accessible to the British. The fields and mines could be tapped to send material to mills of England. The British investors were given extraordinarily high rates of returns at the cost of Indians who paid exorbitant taxes. The cost of construction of the railways charged Indians at least nine times higher than it had cost in any other country around the world. In return, the tax payer Indian was deprived of all significant residual benefits. Indians were not even allowed to travel in the British compartments that openly put signs of 'Dogs and Indians not allowed.'

Political unity was not a new concept for India. As it was mentioned in the sacred Hindu texts like Ramayana and Mahabharata, the Indian subcontinent was referred by a collective title called 'Bharat Varsha' that shows 'Oneness of the nation' in the past. Of course, we need to be blamed for not being able to preserve it during the medieval period. But the Mauryans and the Gupta Empire had integrated the Indian subcontinent under their flags in ancient India.

The English language was introduced to Indians by default because they had to communicate with the ones they came to rule. Apart from this, the intentions of colonizing India would have remained a desire if Indian minds were not colonized. English is for sure a great language and with due respect we honour all the languages in the world, but the British intention was to colonize the Indian mindset so that the western thoughts could be implanted into the Indian minds and the Swadeshi honor be suppressed to keep them away from their age-old civilization. The irony is they succeeded to an extent that was beyond even their imagination. Today the Indian mind is completely colonized and English language has a big role to play in it.

The aspirations of bringing Christianity to the country by converting Hindus could not be fulfilled without promoting the English language. English played a big role in converting a major percentage of Hindus into Christians. The Hindus, who were going to Gurukuls and learning Sanskrit, reading Vedas and other Hindu scriptures that were fully equipped in science, mathematics, economics, astronomy and all other disciplines, chose the convents where Christianity and the British philosophies altered their minds forever.

Today we ask British to apologize for what they did to India. But shall we not seek apology from this land that nurtured us and our ancestors for not being able to protect it. Despite the prolonged persecution, the Hindu unfortunately never woke up from the sleep of Kumbhakarana (a demon known for endless sleep). The sedatives lasted for more than a thousand years. The same mistakes and the same weaknesses are hanging around the Hindu's neck like snakes till date. The curse of Gods continued.

It is only now that it seems this curse is beginning to fade away, but the bitter fact is that even after 70 years of independence, the Hindu hasn't learnt his lessons, which is a curse and the reason behind this curse.

Power Hunger
of Politicians: India
into Pieces

BRITISH SENSED THE differences among the Hindus and Muslims. They exploited the opportunity and fed these differences through their dirty politics. Their pampering of the Muslims to use them as pieces on the chessboard of Indian politics divided India forever. Their biases for the Muslim leaders, their policies, rules and regulations kept the seesaw tilting towards the Muslim side.

Hindus, the believers of the polytheistic religion, had almost embraced Muslims as one other community like Jains and the Budhdhists, but the bonding was never strong enough to deceive the British sword of 'divide and rule'.

Disagreement between the two communal representatives soon converted into the Hindu-Muslim riots that were common during the freedom struggle. Earlier the Indians were fighting against the British, but the cunning policies of the British turned the table completely when Hindus and Muslims started fighting with each other leading to the massive Hindu and Sikh killings. The irony was that British were fuelling this enemity between the two. The Sikhs were considered a part of the Hindus. Hence, they too had to go through the same atrocities that Hindus went through.

Whether we talk about the riots before the Independence, or during partition, Hindus lost a major section of population to either the British pen or to the Muslim sword. Those who refused to convert to Islam had to go through atrocities that still go into ears like acid.

The biggest contribution of the British was their support to the Muslim leaders to create Pakistan. This incident could be perceived as neutralizing a virus that was induced in the Indian blood, and for which, Hindus could not find the antidote.

The revenge of the British, greed of the Muslims, ignorance of the Hindus, and shrewd politics of few prominent leaders resulted in the map of India being ripped apart into two pieces. One was given to Muslims as Pakistan and one to the Hindus as Hindustan, India.

This seems to be nothing, but the curse of Gods is that even after sacrificing our soldiers and resources in the World War I, the World War II, and the freedom struggle when we earned our independence, we couldn't prevent our population from being divided into two different parts that too with an abyss filled with blood.

As quoted earlier, British always played their game on the chessboard of Hindu-Muslim Divide. When Allan Octavian Hume formed the Indian National Congress and invited the Indians from all faiths, the British unhappy with Allan's liberal attitude, instigated a Muslim noble, Nawab Khwaja Salimullah of Decca to start a rival organization for his Muslim brothers with the name of Muslim League.

On the other side, Lord Curzon's decision of partitioning Bengal and supporting the Nawab also watered the seed of

Divide and Rule between the Hindus and Muslims. British, in fact, openly admitted of their wish to divide Hindus and Muslims.

The Lieutenant Governor of Bengal, Sir Bampfylde Fuller, said publicly that *of his two wives (meaning the Muslim and Hindu sections of his province) the Mohammedan was the favourite.*

As Henry Nevinson, senior English journalist said,

"I have almost invariably found English officers and officials on the side of the Mohammedans where there is any rivalry of race or religion at all. And in Eastern Bengal this national inclination is now encouraged by the Government's open resolve to retain the Mohammedan support of the Partition by any means in its power. It was against the Hindus only that all the petty persecution of officialdom was directed. It was they who were excluded from Government posts; it was Hindu schools from which Government patronage was withdrawn. When Mohammedans rioted, the punitive police ransacked Hindu houses, and companies of little Gurkhas were quartered on Hindu populations. It was the Hindus who in one place were forbidden to sit on the riverbank. Of course, the plea was that only the Hindus were opposed to the Government's policy of dividing them from the rest of their race, so that they alone needed suppression."

These seeds turned into a full grown tree when Mohammad Ali Jinnah decided to play the politics of separatism, of course, resting his backbone on the British who instigated and supported him till the time he realized their dream. Suddenly, the fight for independence between the British and the Indians turned into a fight between the Hindus and Muslims.

Jinnah, who failed in gaining the full majority in 1937 elections chose to play the Muslim card for regaining the prominence that he aspired for. He took advantage of the religion based politics to realize his individual goal of letting the Hindu leaders down and separate the entire Muslim population from the Hindus.

As Dr Tharoor says, "two years in the political wilderness after the electoral setbacks of 1937 had already transformed the League. Congress rule in many provinces had unwittingly increased Muslim concern, even alarm, about the implications of democratic majoritarian rule in a country so overwhelmingly Hindu. Many Muslims began to see themselves as a political and economic minority, and the League spoke to their insecurities."

"Jinnah had begun to come to the conclusion that the only effective answer to the Congress's political strength would be separation—the partition of the country to create an independent state in the Muslim- majority areas of the northwest and east. This demand would be enshrined in the League's Lahore Resolution of 23 March 1940 calling for the creation of Pakistan. Nehru and his fellow Congress leaders were largely oblivious of the change of thinking amongst many League members, manifest in an increasingly populist political strategy."

"In October 1939, Jinnah persuaded Lord Linlithgow, the viceroy, to enlist the League as an interlocutor equal to the Congress and as the sole representative of India's Muslims, a position to which its electoral results did not yet entitle it. The viceroy, anxious to prevent Congress–League unity on the war issue, consented."

Later, the Congress-turned-League leader openly admitted that he wants to defend the stake of Muslims from the

Hindu dominion. He argued that their food, their beliefs, their treatment of women and everything is different from the Hindus. Hence, drawing a line between the two extreme communities is the only practical solution for peace. He openly threatened the Congress with war in case the country was not divided. He said that Muslims either wanted "a divided India or the destroyed India".

Suddenly, the conservative and liberal Muslims began to match their opinion for their material interest was politically attached to the community's interest. The ever delicate Hindu-Muslim bond broke and the ambassadors of '*Ganga – Jamuni Tehzeeb*' fell apart. Thousands of Muslims came onto the grounds to demand a separate country called Pakistan. These crowds transformed into mobs beating and killing the Hindu population. Thousands of people were killed in mere three days and the stories of these killings are horrific. Hindus were brought out of homes, shops, and temples only to be smashed by the people who were living in harmony with them for many years.

These were the same people who grew up with them, went to school with them, and celebrated their festivals with them. The volcanic eruption of the riots compelled Nehru and the other leaders to come to terms with Jinnah assuming that the settlement will calm down the aggressive Muslim mob and save many lives, little did they know of the scariest and bloodiest future of the Hindus post the partition that awaited them.

"He agreed to Mountbatten's proposal for a referendum in the North-west frontier provinces and Muslim majority district Sylhet, gave in on a Congress counter proposal for a similar approach in regard to Hindu-majority districts of Sindh. He also agreed to dominion status for India within the

British Commonwealth, rather than the full independence the Congress had long stood for." Dr Tharoor wrote.

The historic date arrived. Jinnah with his Muslim ideologies managed to divide India and added a new country to the world map in the name of Pakistan, made possible only by the biased support of the British. This was not an ending. This was a beginning of the new chapter of persecution of Hindus.

As a result, crores of Hindus and Muslims were displaced from their land when the decision makers were raising a toast for their victory and bright political future. In a day's time, many Hindus found themselves in the Muslim territory and were bound to face the atrocities for one sin and that was their identity of being a Hindu.

Indian government going with Mahatma Gandhi's decision, which was strongly opposed by Sardar Patel, allowed the Muslims in the Indian Territory to remain here if they wished to. The same was supposed to be a criterion for the Hindus in Pakistan but the outcome was horrible.

The Hindus in Pakistan were forced to accept Islam in case they wanted to live in Pakistan. The choice for them was either their land or their religion. Those who chose their religion had to leave their house, property, and everything there and run towards the railway stations that were loaded with people, who were making a choice between India and Pakistan. In a day's time, the Hindu blood began flowing like a river.

And if this was not enough, the exit doors were blocked by the fundamentalists running around with swords to kill them, irrespective of gender, age, colour or caste. Being a Hindu was enough to allow them to scratch the bodies of men, women, daughters, and children.

Simple killing was not enough for women. The daughters and sisters were raped to show their dominance over Hindus and Sikhs. Women were openly stripped off on their way to the railways stations or in the trains for their sole fault of being born into a Hindu family. It is reported that parents themselves killed their daughters to save them from Muslims. They handed over bottles of poison to young girls so that they could save their dignity if a vulture attacked them. Many girls committed suicide, but few unfortunate ones couldn't even get a chance to have that poison because the vultures snatched that away from them before violating their sanctity.

Story of those who were left in Pakistan by chance also did not have a happy ending. They were forced to marry Muslims to save their lives and bodies that were tempting for the vultures, who were justifying their sins in the name of revenge and religion. They were raped and then married to the man who raped them. How many Seemas became Salmas and Ashas became Ayeshas, nobody knows till date. They had to stay away from their families forever. Few of them, even when found were disowned by the families as their religion was contaminated during the riots according to the Hindus; just a mean act of ours towards our own daughters. Their skulls must be present somewhere in the wells, the rivers, or soil of Pakistan with their own story of persecution of Hindus. The British left such pyres of emotions, humanity, dignity, and morality that are still burning.

We could do nothing for them. We killed them, failed to rescue them, beheaded them, gave them poison and then disowned them. Why would Gods not curse Hindus?

Millions of Hindus were burned in this fire and this is an irony of our times.

The Hindus, who migrated from Pakistan had to re-establish themselves in the new regions. They went through thirst, hunger, torture, insecurity, and nightmares of the past. Living in the refugee camps, people were looking for their loved ones among those who were alive or dead. Women got widowed, children became orphans, and parents became childless in just a few days. So much blood couldn't satisfy the thirst of the monster of darkness. It was just the beginning and what followed is published in newspapers as common news in the Indian as well as international newspapers as Indo-Pak affairs.

Till date we are spending a huge amount of money in dealing with the continuous attacks on the border. In spite of making endless attempts to keep peace with the neighbor, we are only sacrificing our people to their artillery. The population of Hindus declined during the partition and the trend continued forever. Hindus are fighting terrorism in various forms till date. The line that was drawn by the British changed the destiny of Hindus forever.

And, we also hear that British bestowed India with Political unity.

It is often debated who was more responsible for the partition of India. Whether it was Jinnah and Mountbatten or were there more people in the background who are worshipped by the Indians? What was the real reason that drivers of the freedom movement of India drove it in two different directions all together as if India was their personal inheritance? Many scholars even blamed Nehru and other leaders of the Congress for the Partition of India. A section of historians say that Mahatma Gandhi had opined that if Jinnah was offered the Prime Minister's position, he might have changed his mind for the partition, but Nehru did not agree. Although, it is still a subject of debate what would have been the outcome if Jinnah was the first Prime Minister of India.

The Hindu's interest was at stake in all scenarios. Even Nehru and Mahatma Gandhi could not protect the interest of Hindus after independence. Mahatma Gandhi decided to allow the Muslims and Hindus to choose if they wanted to stay in India or Pakistan. The result of it was that the Muslims of India stayed in India, but Hindus who stayed across the border were either converted or were killed. Today, population of Muslims has grown to 20 per cent of the Indian population, whereas population of Hindus in Pakistan has declined to barely 2 per cent of Pakistan's population. The statistics speak for itself. It is difficult to forget the genocide of 1947, but the irony is that we could not learn our lessons from it. We continued to make the same mistakes since then. We kept on forgiving and our generations continued to suffer. We did not teach a lesson to the opponent and they took us for granted. How could we not learn from so much loss? This seems to be a curse of Gods.

The division amplified into monstrous affairs between the two countries that are often discussed as the Indo-Pak Affairs; the ever burning and ever sensational issue of the Indian Media. Continuity of terrorism, deceit, enmity, extremism and revenge is still leading to the suffering of the Hindu on a grand scale. The Hindus and the converted Hindus are fighting for the decisions that were imposed on them during the last 1000 years; what a scenario this is! Our government, our people, our policies and our attitude did not change. We made the same mistakes; one after the other.

Indian Independence:
Truth or Myth?

DID INDIA REALLY get independence that day? Was it peddled by unconditional non-violence? Was it real independence or was it just on paper; fake, hypocritical, and meaningless? For Hindus, it sure seems that independence was another chapter of persecution, this time by its own people.

There are a lot of perspectives to this statement. Many patriots say that India never attained freedom. It was simply the transfer of power from British to people who had the Indian blood but the British mind. They only managed to get few papers signed by Lord Mountbatten on behalf of the British government agreeing to carry forward the British legacy but in different attire.

Majority of the British companies remained in India after 15th August, 1947. Only East India Company went away so the loot was on even after that. These companies still exist in India and are a huge source of revenue for the British till date.

The constitution of India that is accepted as the Bible of independent India was a replica of the constitution created by the British. Apart from very few amendments, we are still governed by the same constitution, where even the punctuation remained the same leave alone the content. We are still seeing the country through the British eyes and still applying the British formulas to solve Indian problems.

In fact, the Common Civil Code that was articulated by Dr. Bhim Rao Ambedkar to enforce the reforming measures for the social development in India was also converted into the Hindu Civil Code while excusing Muslims from the Indian Law. This allowed Muslims to practice few of the Islamic laws even if they are contrary to the constitution of the country. This resulted in the continuity of norms like triple talaq, polygamy, gender biases and few others.

The education system remained the same. As British recommended educating Indians the British way, Macaulay drafted a British code of conduct for the Indian education system which is still followed religiously. None of the Indians could dare to take strict action either to discard the persecutor's perception of education or to enforce the rich and ethnic knowledge based upon Indian texts that would enhance the Indian civilization. This lead to the creation of a generation with colonized mind, it sowed the idea in a child's mind since birth that *what is British is superior and what is Indian is inferior*. Children who speak in English get better opportunities; they feel superior in wearing the foreign brands, eating the continental food, and adapting the western lifestyle.

Another group of historians says that in 1946, British passed a bill named India's Independence Act to relieve India for they did not have the resources to finance their troops to maintain their hold in India. It was the British, who already decided that they will withdraw from India. Independence was a deal that took place between the British and few Indian leaders because British wanted to ensure that their interest is taken care off even when India attains freedom on paper.

The most important and burning controversy related to the freedom of India is the actual date of attaining it. The real date of freedom is debated by few historians and scholars. It is said that it was in 1943, on 21st of October, when India attained freedom for the first time under the guidelines of Subhas Chandra Bose, who was supposed to be the first Prime Minister of India. He even unfurled the Indian flag in the Northeast with his army and planned to unfurl the same in Delhi, but because of a conspiracy, the Delhi plan did not succeed. However, he was accepted as a Prime Minister by twelve countries including USSR. Even the currency was generated with his name that can be seen at Kranti Mandir Netaji Subhas Chandra Bose Museum at Red Fort.

For seventy years, we were kept in the dark. These facts surfaced when Major General Gagan Deep Bakshi SM, VSM exposed some burning facts in his book, 'Bose: An Indian Samurai' published by Knowledge World Publication. General GD Bakshi quotes from a conversation between former British Prime Minister Clement Attlee and the then Governor of West Bengal Justice P.B. Chakraborty.

In 1956, Clement Attlee had come to India and stayed in Kolkata as a guest of the then governor. Remember, Clement Richard Attlee was the man, who was leader of the Labour Party and British Prime Minister between 1945 and 1951. He signed off on the decision to grant Independence to India.

Chakraborthy was at that time the Chief Justice of the Calcutta High Court and was also serving as the acting Governor of West Bengal. He wrote a letter to the publisher of

R.C. Majumdar's book, *The History of Bengal*. In this letter, the Chief Justice wrote, "When I was acting Governor, Lord Attlee, who had given us independence by withdrawing British rule from India, spent two days in the Governor's palace at Calcutta during his tour of India. At that time, I had a prolonged discussion with him regarding the real factors that had led the British to quit India."

Chakraborty added, "My direct question to Attlee was that since Gandhi's Quit India movement had tapered off quite some time ago and in 1947 no such new compelling situation had arisen that would necessitate a hasty British departure, why they had to leave?"

"In his reply, Attlee cited several reasons, the principal among them being the erosion of loyalty to the British crown among the Indian army and navy personnel as a result of the military activities of Netaji," Justice Chakraborty said.

Chakraborty also added, "towards the end of our discussion I asked Attlee what was the extent of Gandhi's influence upon the British decision to quit India. Hearing this question, Attlee's lips became twisted in a sarcastic smile as he slowly chewed out the word, m-i-n-i-m-a-l!"

This startling conversation was first published by the Institute of Historical Review by author Ranjan Borra in 1982, in his piece on Subhas Chandra Bose, the Indian National Army and the war of India's liberation.

To understand the significance of Attlee's assertion, we should look back in time to 1945 when the Second World War had ended. United States ally Britain had won and Hitler's Germany had been vanquished. In India, officers of Netaji Bose's Indian National Army were put on trial for treason, torture, and murder. This series of court martial came to be known as the Red Fort Trials.

Indians serving in the British armed forces were outraged by the Red Fort Trials. As a result, in February 1946, almost 20,000 sailors of the Royal Indian Navy serving on 78 ships mutinied against the Empire. They went around Mumbai with portraits of Netaji and forced the British to shout Jai Hind and other INA slogans. The rebels brought down the Union Jack on their ships and refused to obey their British masters. This mutiny was followed by similar rebellions in the Royal Indian Air Force and also in the British Indian Army units in Jabalpur. The British were terrified and were also reluctant to fight.

Military intelligence reports in 1946 indicated that the Indian soldiers were outraged and could not be relied upon to obey their British officers. There were only 40,000 British troops in India at that time and they were eager to go home. It is under these circumstances that the British decided to grant independence to India.

Netaji's family alleges the then political leaders for spying on them and hiding the mysteries behind his life and death. It was only in 2018 that the government released documents related to Netaji in the museum on the direction of Honorable Shri Narendra Modi and with kind cooperation of Honorable Mamta Bannerji, when public could see the reality behind the mystery.

The mystery of Netaji's death is not yet resolved, but many other facts are enough to make us feel ashamed of what we are doing with the freedom we attained because of the sacrifices of these people. How thankless we have been that we couldn't even honour them with due credit? Not only Netaji's death but many facts were kept secret. Why Netaji who first installed the national flag in the Northeast was not accepted as a prime minister by the Indian politicians when twelve countries accepted him? Why his army could not reach Delhi and install the flag there? Wasn't the freedom that Netaji Subhas Chandra Bose attained more dignified than what Nehru managed to get by negotiating with British on their terms? Bose's independence was of a united India and the Gandhi-Nehru victory was of a divided India, which one was better?

Azad Hind Fauj was an aggressive movement with people from all religions as well as women who believed in commanding and demanding for our rights and not negotiating with the British government.

This is the reason that on 21st of October 2018, Prime Minister of India, Shri Narendra Modi unfurled the national flag on the Red Fort symbolically validating the authenticity of this fact. He also inaugurated Netaji's Museum in the Red Fort on January 23rd, which is the date of Netaji Subhas Chandra Bose's birthday. The museum showcases vast number of evidences that sing the glory of Netaji's patriotism and his supreme contribution in the freedom movement of India.

The height of shame was that he was called a 'war criminal' by few politicians who wanted to reap the benefits of the contribution of leaders like him. We should be ashamed of either defaming martyrs like that or forgetting them. Netaji Subhas Chandra Bose was not the only victim of these conspiracies. Shaheed Bhagat Singh was called a 'terrorist' before him. A 23-year-old freedom fighter, who sacrificed his life for this country being called a terrorist instead of a patriot is a black taint on India's integrity.

Isn't this a big question that if 1943's independence would

have been carried forward, perhaps India would never have been divided. So much bloodshed wouldn't have taken place; so many women would have been saved from rapes, so many children would not have been orphans. What was the mystery behind this, who conspired, who benefitted are the burning questions. And there are no answers. Why we Indians especially Hindus don't get up and seek answers? Why don't we raise our finger to the ones who were involved in the conspiracies? But as always we were sleeping. We never bothered. People sacrificed their blood and lives for us, but we were sleeping. Losing a leader like Bose, was it not a curse of Gods? Doing this injustice to his name and fame, was this not a curse for the Hindus? It was not only a curse but a reason to be cursed further and live in a miserable condition for decades.

'The Hindu needs to do penance to free them from this curse'.

Apart from the above, there are many controversies related to the independence of India.

Few scholars also say that Bhagat Singh, Sukhdev, and Rajguru could have been saved if leaders like Mahatma Gandhi and Nehru truly desired so but these young sons of Mother India died even before the announced time of the execution.

Gandhiji declared that 'Pakistan will be created on his dead body'. He strongly opposed the idea of dividing India. But Nehru and Jinnah went ahead with the division staking the lives of so many Indians and also sidelining Mahatma Gandhi. Why did they do so? And why Gandhi who was able to convince Dr B R Ambedkar to drop his idea of a separate country for the underprivileged Indians, Subhas Chandra Bose to resign from his position on moral grounds and Sardar Patel to spare the

Prime Minister's position in spite of winning the majority vote of 12 as compared to Nehru who won only 2 votes, could not convince Nehru and Jinnah to drop the idea of a divided India? Why didn't he opt for a hunger strike to convince these two leaders who pushed the millions of people into misfortune for ages? Why this leader surrendered to his own people who grew up under his own shadow?

In an interview with Senior Journalist Pushpendra Kulshrestha, Shri Chandra Kumar Bose, the grand nephew of Netaji Subhas Chandra Bose, had stated that after the independence, Gandhiji said that Congress should be dissolved because it was not a political party but a platform to fight for freedom. Indian National Congress was dead in 1950.

Netaji was the President of Congress, but he left it for Nehru and left the country long ago for freedom struggle. He knew that Congress leadership then would not be able to acquire the absolute freedom. Negotiations and roundtables can't bring absolute freedom and he was so right, as India was divided. Neither Gandhi nor Bose wanted partition, but Nehru and Jinnah supported it for their political interests. Bose quit the party and Gandhi was cornered. Hence, as told by Chandra Kumar Bose, Gandhiji regretted his decision. Disclosing this in an online interview, the grand nephew of Subhas Chandra Bose said that in a discussion with his father, Amiya Nath Bose, brother of Subhas Chandra Bose, Gandhiji made the statement that 'I backed the wrong horse' and 'I should have backed Subhas Chandra Bose'.

Who was the wrong horse according to Gandhi? Did he imply Jinnah and Nehru while making the above statement?

And Hindus haven't learnt their lessons from this too. We

continue to back the wrong horses. Descendents of people who betrayed India ruled the country even after Independence; the irony is that the voters of the democratic India elected them, that's why they governed the country as ministers. These are the descendents of people who were involved in the killing of martyrs like the Queen of Jhansi and many others. The entire nation knows who they are. But we continue to avoid mentioning their names.

India's obsession with self destruction: Mistakes after Independence

HISTORY DOESN'T FORGIVE! It always demands a price from the present and the future generations for the mistakes committed by their ancestors. Few mistakes grow from seeds to a full grown cactus that pinches and make the generations bleed forever. They have complex cascading effect on a nation's future that can never be compensated by any means. Here are few historical blunders committed by our ancestors, knowingly or unknowingly, leaving us and our offsprings to wonder what was wrong with us?

Were we cursed by someone or by Gods? Because these mistakes changed the course of independent India's history and cast a monster's shadow over its future. These costly mistakes will continue to haunt India for generations and our offsprings will have to pay a price for it, until an incarnation appears. This does not only highlight the inadequacies of India's decision-making ability and the incompetent leadership but also compel us to doubt the integrity of the stakeholders and hints of the conspiracies hidden behind.

Inclusion of Kashmir in India

There can be no better example of hitting the axe on one's own foot than India's clumsy handling of the Kashmir issue. It is a saga of naivety, narrow vision, inept leadership, and may be the hidden agendas that make us wonder…Why?

After partition, the princely state of Kashmir was a tempting land to occupy for Pakistan. By hook or crook the new born Muslim country wanted to enhance its boundaries. They decided to win over Kashmir as they shared the common boundaries. After a series of failed attempts to convince the King Hari Singh of Kashmir for its inclusion into Pakistan, the country began a series of terrorist activities in Kashmir.

As a result, Raja Hari Singh wrote to the Indian government and requested to include Kashmir within the Indian boundaries on 26th October 1947. This may be because Kashmir was originally a Hindu state ruled by a Hindu monarch for ages. Indian Prime Minister after considering the entire matter gave his consent to welcome Kashmir to India, similar to all other states. He officially signed the documents and happily accepted the Indian status for the people of Jammu and Kashmir. Governor General Mountbatten also agreed to the merger. Terms and conditions for Jammu and Kashmir were similar to all the other states that became a part of India with the consent of the respective kings.

No special status or condition was requested for Jammu and Kashmir in the documents nor were they granted. The entire Jammu and Kashmir became a part of India right after signing this document. This also included the area that was illegally captured by the Pakistani forces. Even after this, Pakistan never gave up the greed for the state of Kashmir. Pakistan, as a greedy nation, wanted to loot a land that was neither given to them by

Mountbatten nor Raja Hari Singh, nor the people of Kashmir.

India and Pakistan were divided and were given their respective resources as per the agreements, but Jinnah while exploiting Kashmir's shared boundaries with Pakistan began another chapter of persecution of Hindus. Thousands of Kashmiri Hindu's lives were drawn into a never ending circle of holocaust. Blood mingled with the pure water of the rivers and the valley of Kashmir still echoes of the cries of Kashmiri Hindus. Raja Hari Singh, to save his state and people from Pakistani dacoits took this rational decision because Pakistan was never a choice for the Kashmir rulers. But to Jinnah, the hunger for the Hindu blood did not satiate after killing millions of them before and during partition. He sowed the seeds for the never ending terrorist activities in Kashmir.

Indian army taught a tough lesson to the Pakistani's but the Prime Minister of India, Shri Jawahar Lal Nehru, presented the matter to the United Nations on 31st December, 1947. This was to invite UN's intervention into the matter and pressurize Pakistan to withdraw their forces from Indian territories. This was a surprising move as Indian forces did not need any intervention as they dominated the Pakistani forces on the border and were sure of their victory.

Ceasefire was declared on 1st January, 1949, between India and Pakistan. Gods only knows why Nehru did that. Prior to this, in 1948 also Indian forces pushed the Pakistani militants from the boundaries of Kashmir when they made subsequent effort to acquire this land.

Indian forces were sure to capture the Pakistan occupied Kashmir in a short span of time, then why Nehru made the blunder of taking the matter to United Nations, making it disputed forever.

It was not at all required because India was capable of handling the matter and teaching an unforgettable lesson to Pakistan that would have put a full stop on terrorism in Kashmir.

Today, India is paying a huge cost for this one blunder by the then prime minister. It will always remain a mystery why Nehru deliberately prevented the Indian forces from pushing the Pakistani forces forever from Kashmir and ensuring peace and harmony there. He became a reason for the persecution of Kashmiri Hindus in independent India forever. Today this community which is limited to only a few lakhs in the world is struggling to visit their homeland. They lost everything, life, family, land to the terrorist activities from Pakistan and added to the list of persecuted community of Hindus. India will never be able to compensate for this mistake of Nehru.

Later, in the assembly of Jammu and Kashmir, Kashmir was given the maximum seats when Jammu had a higher population. 43 seats out of 75 were allocated to Kashmir alone, which could be seen as an injustice to the other two areas housing the majority of Hindu population. As a result, Kashmiri Hindus were swept off the Jammu and Kashmir valley with time as Kashmir had Mulsim majority who dominated the area and its political spectrum. This dominance also indirectly strengthened the terrorist groups in India and Pakistan who target Hindus till date.

Indo-Chinese friendship: Indian delusions

Ignoring Chinese Threats and Neglecting the Military lessons of the year 1962 is also another blunder that Indian government committed. Our slogans for nonviolence, peace, and guest is God were crushed by the neighbor when Indian leaders were busy believing Chinese dialogue *'Hindi Cheeni Bhai Bhai'*,

Indians and Chinese are brothers.

Indian delusions had lulled the government into believing that its assertions and banalities of peaceful co-existence with the neighbor would be reciprocated by the world. Unfortunately, this has not been the case, since forever. It was often stated that a peace-loving nation like India did not need the military at all which was a repetitive mistake of India in the past and in the present, from Mohammad bin Qasim's time to the British invasion. Negligence on the defense front and weak intelligence support brought India into trouble again. Their unconditional nonviolence and brotherhood seemed fancy terms in Gandhiji's speeches but have no relevance in the real world.

In spite of constant signs of China's aggressive intentions for years, the Indian leadership decided to keep its eyes shut in the fond hope that the problem would resolve itself and the opponent would melt respecting our principles of nonviolent resistance. But the reality hit hard and China shattered the Indian illusions. The country was caught totally unprepared to an extent that troops were rushed to snowbound areas with summer clothing and outdated rifles. Despite numerous sagas of gallantry, the country suffered terrible embarrassment. India had to taste defeat. With the national morale and pride kept within, India was forced to appeal to all nations for military aid, which is an example of our psychological malfunctioning of repeating the same mistake again and again; with no count of the number of times.

1965 War and Tashkent Treaty: Persecution by the International commune

This time it seemed that the entire world propagated against Hindus. When Pakistan designed to infiltrate forces into Jammu and Kashmir in 1965 to precipitate an insurgency against Indian rule and India retaliated by launching a full-scale military attack on West Pakistan capturing a vast area of the opponent's geographical boundaries, India was compelled by the international community to return it and sign a ceasefire agreement, even after thousands of casualties, huge financial loss, and artilleries.

'India,' as McGarr Paul stated, 'had the upper hand over Pakistan when the ceasefire was declared'.

Apart from the cease-fire after the Indo-Pak War of 1965, a Russian-sponsored agreement was also signed between India and Pakistan on 10th January 1966. Under the agreement, India agreed to return the strategic Haji Pir pass to Pakistan, which it had captured in August 1965 against heavy odds and at a huge human cost. The pass connects Poonch and Uri sectors in Jammu and Kashmir and reduces the distance between the two sectors to 15 km whereas the alternate route entails a travel of over 200 km. All India got in return was a false promise by Pakistan to abjure war, which they had no intention to fulfill.

It was the same war for which the Prime Minister of India Sh Lal Bahadur Shastri requested Indians to sacrifice a meal as United States refused to export wheat to India. Indians were requested to cut down their expenses to save the money for war. This indicated that Shastriji had no intention to allow Pakistan to raise weapons against Indians ever in future. But because of the curse, we were stuck in the hands of circumstances and forced to return whatever we won after sacrificing our blood.

Later, Lal Bahadur Shastri died in mysterious circumstances that are not yet resolved.

Anil Shastri, Lal Bahadur Shastriji's son said in an interview on television that his face was blue and there were white spots on his forehead. His mother spoke to doctors at the time and they said that these circumstances are not observed in case of a heart disease. And because of this there is a doubt in everybody's mind even today.

Shastriji did not have a history of a heart disease or cholesterol. His personal physician was surprised of his death because of heart stroke. He wanted to investigate Shastri's body for a clue behind his death, but he was denied. Later, on special recommendation of Shastriji's wife Lalita Devi, he was allowed. Even after constant requests by her and his personal physician why was his body not sent for postmortem.

Anil Shastri also said that his accommodation in Tashkent was not taken care off. There was no bell in his room or a telephone that he could call for help. His doctor's room was far away through a veranda and there was no jug of water available. There was only a flask available and that took time to open in case of emergencies.

All these circumstances clearly indicate that his death was conspired and not natural.

11th January, 1966, was a night of conspiracies, mysteries, and misfortunes for Indians. As Kuldeep Nayyar, the senior journalist and author, exposed the circumstances in which Shastriji died, it seemed a preplanned murder mystery that India has not solved as yet.

Who was behind his murder? Who benefitted from his death, who prevented the requested postmortem and who kept quiet are the burning questions till date. Even in an ordinary killing, a dead body is sent for postmortem then why a Prime Minister's body did not go for postmortem in spite of being warned of the mysterious marks on his dead body? A man who taught a lesson to Pakistan, who exemplified the true Hindu spirit of being a fighter for his dignity to the world, who was an authentic Indian and a Hindu by his belief system, his actions and his lifestyle was disposed off so casually?

Where Brahmanism was a reality of India, we also had Brahmins like Lal Bahadur Shastri whose slogan was *Jai Jawan, Jai Kissan'*, 'Hail the warrior and Hail the farmer'. Now he had vanished and no one raised his voice? No one bothered to enquire. Why? A Prime Minister, who was about to finish the Indo-Pak rivalry by capturing entire Pakistan and installing the Indian flag in Lahore, within two hours bid farewell to this world in mysterious circumstances and we did not even know what happened to him? Isn't this a curse on Hindus?

Shastriji was not the first or the last patriot who was lost by the motherland. Before him we lost many sons and after him too. Why was there this continuity of conspiracies even in independent India.

It is clearly evident that India's sacrifice for global peace went down the drains. Neither Pakistan stopped making attempts to acquire Kashmir nor did the Muslim extremists stop the terrorist activities against Hindus. India had to face the direct and indirect wars with Pakistan for different regions again, losing soldiers, most of whom were Hindus or the ones who stand in support of the Hindus or secular beliefs.

Pakistan never gave up its dream of acquiring Kashmir. We kept on forgiving them since 1947, but they always returned just like Mohammad Ghori who attempted to defeat Prithviraj Chauhan, but was defeated sixteen times. What we must remember is that the seventeenth time he did succeed in defeating Prithviraj Chauhan. Hence, Gandhiji's philosophy of offering the other cheek to someone who slaps you on one cheek, never found any substance when it came to strategic matters with opponents like Mohammad Ghori or Pakistan.

We have nothing against Pakistan as a country, but definitely we are against the mindset the country carries since its creation. Having almost 100 per cent population of those whose ancestors were Hindus, the country holds poisonous feeling towards Hindus giving no reason for us to forgive and forget because forgiving and forgetting means more persecution and sacrifice of Hindu lives.

Anyway the series of blunders did not end here. We can imagine the curse of Gods by how India allowed Pakistan and the world to persecute us forgetting the millions of lessons.

In the 1971 war, after offering so many soldiers to the war, after becoming responsible for women becoming widows, seeing the pain of soldiers who lost their limbs in the war and of orphans who lost their father, we went ahead showing another example of our foolishness; foolishness or something else?

In spite of a decisive victory over Pakistan when over 96,000 Pak soldiers were taken Prisoners of War, India signed another document that laughs at government's illness and cries for the misfortune of the people, who are nothing but cursed. On 2nd July 1972 at Shimla, an agreement was signed between the two countries, according to which both the countries agreed to exchange all prisoners of war, respect the line of control in Jammu and Kashmir and refrain from the use of threat or force. Additionally, Bhutto gave a solemn verbal undertaking to accept LOC as the de facto border. India released all Pak POWs, in good faith. However, that they never stuck to their word is another story.

Pakistan, on the other hand, released only 617 Indian POWs while holding back 54 PoWs who are still suffering in Pakistani jails. The Indian Government has admitted this fact a number of times, but has failed to secure their release. India failed to use the leverage of 96,000 Pak POWs, to discipline Pakistan. A rare opportunity was thus wasted for nothing, disrespecting the sacrifice of our forces. The establishing of permanent peace in the subcontinent merely remained on paper, but what was unforgiving was that India failed to ensure release of all Indian POWs, which was a criminal omission by all accounts. The naivety of the Indian delegation can be seen from the fact that it allowed Pakistan to bluff its way through at Shimla. The Indian leadership was fooled into believing Pakistan's sincerity. Unquestionably, everybody knew that Pakistan never intended to abide by its promises, both written and verbal. Fruits of a hard-fought victory in the battlefield were wasted on the negotiating table by the ham-handed leadership.

Again no one knows what went wrong with the government to make such a move. Was there something behind this that we need to figure out or was it the curse of Gods? Or perhaps it was both.

The Nuclear reluctance: Peace or inferiority complex

Subsequent to the Chinese Nuclear Test at Lop Nur in 1964, India showed rare courage in carrying out its first nuclear test on 18th May, 1974 at Pokharan. Outside the five permanent members of the UN Security Council, India was the only nation to prove its nuclear capability. The whole country was ecstatic and every Indian felt proud of its scientific prowess. But Indians had not contended with their Government's inclination for converting opportunity into adversity and squandering hard-earned gains. In spite of so many bruises on its philosophy of unconditional nonviolence, India again attempted to convince the world that it had no nuclear ambitions for its peace loving notions. Strangely, it termed the Pokharan test as a 'peaceful nuclear explosion'—a term unheard of till then. The Defence Minister went to the extent of claiming that the Indian nuclear experiment was 'only for mining, oil, and gas prospecting, for finding underground sources of water, for diverting rivers, for scientific and technological knowledge.' It was another axe on India's foot by its own leaders who were experts in it. India chose not to be counted as a member of the exclusive nuclear club. Instead of showcasing its nuclear strength to the world, it went into an overdrive to show a placard to the world indicating her self-imposed cessation on further testing; sounds such a mockery.

It lost out on all the advantages provided to it by its scientists. It suffered sanctions and yet failed to gain recognition as a nuclear power while missing a golden opportunity. *'Na maya mili na Ram'*, the hindi phrase is apt here which means 'neither got the material nor the divine'.

This blunder boosted the morale of small countries like Pakistan who threaten India time and again and continue the series of holocaust of Indians with majority of Hindus.

Isn't that a curse of Gods?

The Kandahar Hijacking: Internal Security loopholes

The hijacking of an Indian Airlines aircraft to Kandahar by Pakistani terrorists in December 1999 continued to boost the morale of terrorist groups. The hijacking revealed how ill-prepared India was to face up to the challenges of international terrorism. According to an article published in Hindustan Times, 'India lost face and got reduced to begging for co-operation from the very regimes that were actively undermining its internal security'.

We were simply not prepared. We were not equipped to even protect our people, let alone fight. The eight-day long ordeal ended only after India's National Security Advisor brazenly announced that an agreement had been reached for the release of all the hostages in exchange for three Kashmiri militants including Maulana Masood Azhar.

Sadly, the Prime Minister claimed credit for forcing the hijackers to climb down on their demands. The worst was yet to follow. India's Foreign Minister decided to accompany the released militants to Kandahar as if seeing off the honoured political guests. Kandahar Hijacking was a prime example of Indian government's poor crisis-management skills and extreme complacency in security matters that allowed the hijackers to take off from Amritsar airport after a 39-minute halt for refueling, thereby letting the problem get out of control.

India's much-vaunted decision-making and lenient approach towards defense apparatus could not protect the country's interest against the audacity of a bunch of motivated fanatics. It was a comprehensive failure of monumental proportions and it was not beyond expectations. India's slack and amateurish functioning made the country earn the tag of a soft nation which was not appreciated by the world but was targeted. To repeat, in the real world; survival of the fittest is an unchallenged reality that we Indians often forget.

Illegal Immigration and Passage of IMDT Act: Anyone could be the Indian guest

It is a standard practice all over the world that the burden of proving one's status as a bonafide citizen of a country falls on the accused. It is accepted in India as well under the Foreigners Act, 1946. But Indian Government made an exception for Assam and continued its tradition of inviting adversities to the country for reasons that only our profound politicians were aware of. In one of the most short-sighted and anti-national moves, India passed the Illegal Migrants - Determination by Tribunals (IMDT) Act of 1984 for Assam. It shifted the onus of proving the illegal status of a suspected immigrant on to the accuser, which was a tall and virtually impossible order.

As a result, detection and deportation of illegal immigrants became impossible. Whenever demands were raised for repealing the Act, the Congress, the Left Front, and the United Minorities Front, as they always do, resist strongly. As expected, vote bank politics played its part and illegal immigrants became the most loyal vote bank of the Congress. Every protest against the Act was pacified by the so called minority supporters thereby imparting communal colour to the issue of national security.

The government's 'pardon' of all Bangladeshis who had come in before 1985 was another unconstitutional act that aggravated the problem. The Act was struck down as unconstitutional by the Supreme Court on July 13, 2005, more than 20 years after its enactment. The Apex Court was of the view that the influx of Bangladeshi nationals into Assam posed a threat to the integrity and security of the country, especially the northeastern province. Unfortunately, immense damage had already been done to the demography of Assam and the local people of Assam had been reduced to minority status in certain districts. Illegal immigrants became so powerful that no party can hope to come to power without their support. Nearly 30 Islamic groups are thriving in the area to further their Islamist and Pan-Bangladesh agenda which is directly against Hindus. This includes torturing, converting and even killing Hindus. It is unbelievable that a nation's leadership can stoop so low for their hunger of votes and political power that they could endanger even national security for their nasty motives. Even today the immigration of Rohingya Muslims and state governments favoring them is another example of staking national security for few votes. What's more, we put the tag of humanity on the ugly political moves of these anti-nationalists in nationalist's attire. It is also an example that we never learn from our mistakes. We are cursed by Gods.

Division of States: Vote bank politics

Lack of integrity has been the reason that we went through persecution for centuries, but our obsession with disintegrating the country on variety of basis continued. We still demand for further division of country on regional, cultural, and linguistic differences. Continuing with our obsession for division, a social activist named Potti Sreeramulu took to hunger strike demanding a separate state for Telugu speaking population. Though Potti's demand was not rational, expecting a threat to the political power, the ruling party allocated a separate state to the Telugu speaking population. As a result, many states till date are demanding a separate status based on their linguistic backgrounds. Few of them have already come into existence. This is how we nurtured the British dog of 'Divide and Rule' which is still barking and biting the national integrity of the country.

Coco Island: Political Extravaganza

An island called Coco Island was gifted to Myanmar in 1948 by the Indian Prime Minister, Jawahar Lal Nehru. Myanmar further gave the island on lease to China that facilitated the opponent country to monitor the Indian Navy's activities, which remain a threat to our national safety from China. This was like gifting your loaded gun to an enemy to shoot you and your loved ones; wow India!

Gwadar Port: Foundation of CPEC (China–Pakistan Economic Corridor)

Sultanate of Oman offered Gwadar Port to India for $1 million, but Indian government rejected the offer. We had to because how could we give up our age old tradition of self persecution. Following this, Pakistan bought it for triple the price. This port could have been a strategic advantage to Indian navy as Chinese naval activities could be observed from there and Pakistan could have been out of the picture. Currently, China is building CPEC on the same port challenging the national security of India forever.

Refusal of a Hindu state: After all who cared for Hindus?

In 1952, the King of Nepal Tribhuvan Vikram Shah wanted Nepal to be merged into India but Prime Minister Nehru rejected the offer with a reason that this will affect their relations with the other countries.

"Shortly after independence, the then Nepal Prime Minister Matrika Prasad Koirala had conveyed his country's wish to join India to Pandit Jawaharlal Nehru," former RSS Chief KS Sudarshan had said in 2008 while addressing a function. He also said that it was Independent India's first Prime Minister Jawaharlal Nehru who rejected the offer.

It is still a million dollar question that why a mutual merger of two countries would have affected the relations with the other countries. Was it because Nepal was a Hindu country and would have annoyed the Muslim community in India and other countries?

Common Civil Code Biases: 'Common but not common'

The rules and regulations of the Constitution of India were drafted on the assumption of equality amongst people from all religions. Dr Ambedkar constructed a Common Civil Code with reforming measures concerning marriage, property, divorce, and other issues. These regulations were meant to be followed by all the religions including Muslims, but the common civil code was handed over to Hindus and all other communities including the Sikhs and Jains. Only one community was exempted from it. It was not imposed on Muslims, who got the luxury of following their own Islamic and Sharia laws disowning the Indian constitution completely.

Shah Bano Begum Case: another example of Appeasement Politics

Shah Bano, a Muslim woman was divorced by her husband without giving any compensation leading her to the Supreme Court. Supreme Court considering Shah Bano's argument and analyzing the circumstances related to the divorce passed the judgment in favour of the woman. This agonized the Muslim community that appealed to the Indian government to withdraw this judgment.

The Muslim politicians mounted a campaign for the verdict's nullification. The Indian Parliament reversed the judgement under pressure from Islamic orthodoxy.

Jindal, T.P. (1995). Ayodhya Imbroglio

As a result, extending a chapter of appeasement politics, Rajiv Gandhi invited a special session in the parliament to intervene into the matter and enforced another act called the Muslim Women (Protection of Rights on Divorce) Act, 1986, according to which Shah Bano received only 3 months compensation from the man who divorced her. This did not only act against Muslim women, but also hurt the sanctity of the country's belief in the court. If a Hindu is bound to obey the Supreme Court, Muslims too should obey. This is the example of persecution of Hindus because it allowed Muslims to have their own laws in a democratic country.

Bhopal Gas Tragedy: Indians are born to suffer

Warren Anderson, owner of Union Carbide, left the country after the Bhopal gas tragedy that led to millions of death and casualties in India. This was of course not without the government's support.

Several reports have suggested that the government of PM Rajiv Gandhi was pressured by the US to let Anderson go.

Senior Congress leader Arjun Singh, who was then the chief minister of MP, wrote in his autobiography A *Grain of Sand in the Hourglass of Time*, 'Had we removed the landline phone from his room, Anderson would not have escaped. He possibly made calls to contacts in the US to help him leave India'. The US embassy reportedly mounted pressure on the Indian government, which released Anderson on a personal bond of 25,000.

Till date the innocent people of Bhopal are suffering from the aftermath of this tragedy, where Indian coffers are providing the compensation to these victims instead of the company that was responsible for the accident, nor did the American government take responsibility for the same.

Who was responsible for Warren's exit, was it the US government or our own leaders stabbed our back? Curse of Gods!

The Kargil War was another opportunity to end the Tom and Jerry game with Pakistan but India refrained from war considering the economic conditions of the country. Even after the parliament attacks in Delhi, Indian government did not show any aggressive retaliatory action which projected a very passive image of the government. This continued to boost Pakistan's morale and it continued with its evil practices. There have been many occasions where India found opportunities to end the game of rivalry with Pakistan, but Indians deliberately chose to either keep quiet or kept wasting its resources in either dialogues or in war that resulted in no conclusion. This can't be without a curse. How can a country be so negligent of her past, present, and future?

Separatist Movement in Punjab: An attack on the Hindu's Backbone

The separatist movement in Punjab is also alleged to be a political propaganda that lead to the persecution of Hindus. Sikhs have been a community that has highly blended with the Hindus, since forever. They always stood by us through thick and thin. Many of the Sikh Gurus died for the Hindus in the past.

Shri Guru Teg Bahadur sacrificed his life for the protection of Kashmiri Hindus. He refused to accept Islam in the reign of

Aurangzeb, the icon of brutality.

But political games of independent India reached a stage when they perceived Hindus as their enemies at a certain point. However, soon reality began to sink in and things normalized, but both Sikhs and Hindus had to go through atrocities propagated by the shrewd politicians. This was right after 'Operation Blue Star' when the then Prime Minister, Smt Indira Gandhi was killed in retaliation by her own Sikh bodyguards. This lead to the bloodshed of Sikhs, and Hindus were blamed for the same. It was rumored that Hindus in retaliation were killing the Sikhs, but the real stories told by many surviving Sikhs reveal that it was the Hindu families in neighborhoods who protected them from the unknown mob. As a matter of fact, Hindus and Sikhs lived in great harmony before that.

Even marriages happened between the two communities. Muslims considered Sikhs as part of the Hindus, which is why Sikhs had to go through atrocities during the Hindu-Muslim riots. There was no way that Sikhs and Hindus could be thirsty for each other's blood. It is said that the so called Hindu mobs came and killed Sikhs, but there is hardly any proof of the fact. They were clear cut massacres as told by few journalists in those days. Their statements are substantiated by the fact that there are not many records of the FIRs launched. Not many participants of the mobs were proven to be the culprits. It seemed to be all in the air. It is said that it was a politically generated mob that was bought by money. They targeted Sikhs while blaming Hindus to separate them forever to break India's backbone. Right from promoting Bhindranwale by the ruling party to curb the rising dominance of the Akali Dal in Punjab to the extent of declaring him a terrorist when he shifted the gun from Akalis to the ruling party.

Sh Subramanian Swamy, the politician and former cabinet minister has clearly told in his interviews that 'Operation Blue Star was Indira Gandhi's biggest mistake and the entire Khalistan issue was a political propaganda to weaken Hindus by separating them from Sikhs'. He even called Bhindranwale a seer instead of a terrorist. Swamy says that the seer raised voice against the social evils and did not demand Khalistan. It was an issue that was a branded political agenda to attack the Sikhs who were the strength of Hindus.

Till date there has not been many arrests of the people from mobs but the Hindu was blamed. The Hindu's fault was not being able to identify their enemies roaming around their parliament. On the contrary, they continued to stay in darkness and gave them plenty of opportunities to persecute them further; what an irony.

Bofors Scam: Curruption to the Core

A huge compromise was made on the country's security in 'Bofors Scam'. Rajiv Gandhi and few associates were accused of making big kickbacks of nearly USD 9 millions through an Italian middleman named as Octavio Quattrocchi.

While the case was being investigated, Rajiv Gandhi was assassinated for unrelated reasons by the LTTE. However, on 22 October 1999 (when National Democratic Alliance government led by the Bharatiya Janata Party was in power) the Central Bureau of Investigation (CBI) filed the first chargesheet against Quattrocchi, Win Chadha, Rajiv Gandhi, the defence secretary S K Bhatnagar and a number of others.

The hard earned money of Indian tax payers went into the pockets of anti-nationals; the most crucial defense budget was embezzled by those who were supposed to be the saviors of the motherland. They not only staked the country's security but also played with sentiments of the defense forces, who stake their lives for the country. It was such disrespect to their lives and the media's mouth was sealed with the gum of political powers.

Apart from these, our political leaders have been noticed exercising the Extra Constitutional powers in the so-called independent India. In a way, after invaders, few of our own countrymen ruled the country as monarchs in a so-called democratic fashion. It is difficult to say how far the moves like Nas-bandi, Emergency, and Shah Banu case were justified. How would these leaders justify a series of scams that attacked India's backbone since Independence? 2G Scam, Chara Ghotalas, Iraqi Oil Scam are only few in the list.

So many scams happened, but the Supreme Court and media both were crawling to resolve the matter. They went on for decades and decades. People were looting India and making innocent Indians pay the price of their mistakes and blunders. The monster came and painted India's face with so many taints but everyone was quiet. No leader stood against them and if someone tried, he was killed. Female Feticide was never curbed. Innocent girls were killed in the womb itself misusing the advanced technologies like ultrasound. They were burnt for dowry and were raped in public. This has been the extent of indolence, sins, conspiracies, fraud, and cheating. People who were Indians by birth were no less of the persecutors than Muslims and British. For petty individual gains the country's dignity, security, wellbeing and honour was kept on stake. Gods must have cursed Hindus. And why would he not curse Hindus when the Hindu cursed himself. He is so used to be tolerating it that he doesn't even take it as a curse anymore.

Apart from this, Independent India has a long list of mistakes committed by leaders that lead to our sufferings. But we all are responsible for their mistakes because we were the ones who chose them, may be because we are cursed by Gods.

The Surviving Persecutors: Terror and Horror

REPETITIVE MISTAKES AGAIN and again strengthened the monster of darkness to pluck more feathers of the golden sparrow. It took various forms, shapes, and images but the curse continued.

After loot, torture, and atrocities of 1000 years, routine socio-economic challenges of a developing country were expected. Rapidly escalating population graph, majority of illiterate people, poor education apparatus, insufficient infrastructure, inability to provide nutrition, health, sanitation, and unemployment were few of them. But it was more than that; sequence of bloodshed continued as the monster's thirst of Hindu blood was not satiated.

The curse extended in the form of severe External and Internal Security threats gauging the country's vulnerable leadership, which continued for a long time. The after-effects of the age old mistakes of our ancestors are visible till date in multiple ways. Somewhere a Mohammad bin Qasim and Mohammad Ghori are targeting India from the west and the east till date and we need to be prepared to prevent history from repeating itself.

Externally, Pakistan has been a constant threat for Hindus for the religious and political rivalry of more than seven decades. On the other side, China has always been eager to dominate this country. Both the countries have attacked India in the past and caused great damage to the nation.

China, though, does not have a religious reason behind its aggression, but in a country where the majority of population is Hindu, the maximum damage will be caused to the Hindus if the opponent targets land, especially with the growing friendship between China and Pakistan, who is solely driven by its hatred against Hindus. Gazwa-e-Hind and mission to be a 'Ghazi', has been accelerating the terrorist activities financed by Pakistan directly or indirectly, whether it is to capture Kashmir, planting bombs in the Capital, a biological weapon or any other means. The aim to eliminate the Hindu religion from India has been the motive behind all these activities through all the terrorist groups with different names. The growing friendship between China and Pakistan is also a warning signal to India, where two opponents may unite and encircle a major part of North and East India and realize Pakistan's mission of eliminating the Hindu religion.

And, if these threats are not enough, we have the bigger challenge of internal terrorism, there are many terrorist groups living in the Shadow of Mother India waiting to stab her back. The reason is the same. Yes, Gazwa-e-Hind which accelerates these terrorist activities financed by Pakistan. This Islamic mission is the biggest threat to India since independence. Enemies outside could be tackled but it's difficult to identify the ones at home. From north, west, south, and east, Indian boundaries are not spared by the terrorist groups. Out of these, western frontiers of India have been the hyper sensitive areas for 1000 years. And the equation remained the same even in independent India. Political impotency in the past for 70 years in dealing with this monstrous curse on India resulted in the development of the full grown network of terrorist groups that target Hindus and humanity. In India, there was never a single decade when the Hindu was not targeted as if a monster is asking for 'Bali', sacrifice of a human life.

In August 2008, National Security Advisor M K Narayanan has said that there are as many as 800 terrorist cells operating in the country. As of 2013, 205 of the country's 608 districts were affected by terrorist activity. Out of these, the most dominant threat has been from the Islamic terrorism, which is noticed to be growing every decade.

Media reports have alleged and implicated terrorism in India to be sponsored by Pakistan, but Pakistan always denied Indian allegations and blamed India for terrorism funding against Pakistan. However, this was a sheer lie as we all know. This could be revealed if we listen to the speeches of many Pakistani leaders who are often seen instigating the Kashmiri Muslims to continue killing the Hindus in the name of freedom struggle and jihad. Many of the innocent Hindus became the victims and the incidents are countless. We do not want to mention the figures and data here as everyone knows that there has been a continuity of blasts, killings, massacres, bloodshed, kidnappings, rapes, and hatred in Kashmir and against the Hindus. However, it is never highlighted from a Hindu's perspective.

The Hindu is under a relentless threat and we can't deny this fact. Talking intellectually on television about peace and harmony does not bring peace. Peace can't be begged or acquired as a favour. If that was the case, there wouldn't have been riots during partition as Mahatma Gandhi accepted the Partition on Muslim's terms. There wouldn't have been the war in 1965 even after financially helping Pakistan. We returned their land and Indian forces backed off from the warfront for a peace treaty in Tashkent, but after that also there was a war in 1971 when we returned 96,000 soldiers to Pakistan, but they still did not stop. Terrorist attacks have been a daily routine in Kashmir, there was Kargil war, and recently there was Pulwama attack when we lost a number of soldiers. This list is long and never ending; sometimes on a big or on a small scale.

The obvious lesson must be learnt now as it's high time. One has to compel people to maintain harmony by showing the power to retaliate. Only then, peace is maintained. To repeat, the Hindu religion never preached unconditional non-violence. Our Gods and Goddess carry a flower and blessing in one hand, but the other hand carries weapons and the head of the monster. We believed in sacrificing blood or beheading the enemy for the rights reasons. The Hindu religion believes in following the righteous and peaceful path, but also keeps its weapons sharpened in case someone violates morality and humanity.

The lessons from the 1000 years of darkness that says that weak entities have no rights to ask for as nobody will spare them. Only those who retaliated did survive in history or in history books. India needs to exhibit its power to the world. Only then others will bestow us with the right to live with peace, harmony and dignity.

For so many years government continued to initiate dialogues with Pakistan, release terrorists after kidnappings and hijacking, preach to the world about peace and nonviolence.

This only lead to a scenario where these terrorist groups have now strengthened their network. They are much more in number and far more powerful. They openly threatened us, tortured us, and killed our people mercilessly. But we continued to stay passive. Isn't that a curse of Gods?

Somewhere we have nurtured terrorism and terrorists. Article 35A in Kashmir, appeasement politics of our government, negligence on the defense front, and lethargic police apparatus have been feeding milk to these snakes that turned into huge anacondas today.

Defense Appratus: We haven't learnt, we haven't learnt, and we haven't learnt!

IN THE LONG and dark period of 1000 years, the biggest weakness of India was its weak artillery and technology. Indian kings had to surrender to Babur for he brought gunpowder to India for the first time. Similarly, they surrendered to Portuguese and British for they brought more advanced weapons with a refined war strategy. When Indians were depending only on manmade weapons like the swords, bows, and spears, these people found advanced methods of commanding the battlegrounds.

Indian defense apparatus has not been one of the most modernized and suitable weapon systems. Obsolete equipments, poor human resource management, lack of dynamism in policy making, and political dependency are the challenging factors for the Indian defense industry.

India needs to gear up on its defense front because that is the primary need for the sustenance and security of any country. Indian defense forces have managed to maintain respectable position for themselves on the global front, but it must be admitted that there is a lot of scope for improvement that we must take care of, so the past mistakes do not repeat in future and take the country in the reverse gear. Mere patriotism is not enough to save the nation!

Our defense budget was pretty less than it was required. Our soldiers were left on their bravery and patriotism with limited artillery so far. The current government has been observed taking necessary measures to alter the dynamics of the defense arena but we are still very far. Now in this case, what is our responsibility? Can we do something about it? Yes. We surely can. Big decision of voting for the right candidate to small decisions like voicing out one's opinion in public and media and making small choices of contributing to the right cause, even if for a small purchase will affect a country's defense budget. The irony is we often overlook our responsibility towards both country and religion. This could only be a curse.

But we are obsessed with the colonial imprints of liking the foreign brands, foreign culture, and foreign lifestyle and giving away a lot of our money to the other countries. From toothpaste, shaving creams, soap, clothes, food, drink, to cars, mobiles, and computers, most of the things that we use are manufactured by foreign brands and contributes into foreign government's funds as taxes. These taxes enhance their defense budget where Indian defense is struggling with the difference widening between rupees and dollars to buy imported advanced equipments and fighter planes.

China is a very big example in this context. So much money has been going from the Indian pocket to the Chinese government who is using it for projects that are directly and indirectly threatening the country. China–Pakistan Economic Corridor is a visible example.

When we are focusing on enhancing our economy which is

surely a must for the prosperity of the country, it can't be at the cost of our defense apparatus. We must recall that economy of India was strong in the ancient times too. Right from the Indus valley civilization, India's economy was always prospering. During the reign of Mauryans, the Guptas, and even when Qasim came to India, the economy was strong.

When British came to India, it had the highest GDP in the world, 23 per cent. In fact, why would foreigners come here if we did not have economic potential? It was only because of our weak defense and their strong attacks, Indians were persecuted; be it for our insufficient artillery or our inferior approach that never let us stand for ourselves.

The practical truth is that there is no peace without power and this power has to be exhibited so people refrain from violating our peace. For 70 years India wasted its time in dialogues for peace with Pakistan. Millions of deaths, casualties, billions of rupees for help, constant invitations to their prime ministers, and opportunities to their talent, but result was 26/11, Pulwama, blast in the Parliament and the list goes on till date with a series of attacks.

Indian government also backed off from the membership of the Nuclear Club to please China but China in return attacked India compelling us to lose a number of soldiers.

Our misinterpretation of Sanatan Dharma brought us here. We got lost into the darkness of fatalism in the name of destiny and cowardice in the name of non-violence. But Sanatan Dharma is not this. The earliest societies and communities in all their wisdom and going by the needs of those times created the four Varnas (Brahmins, Kshatriyas, Vaishyas, and Shudras) as per the Hindu texts. We Hindus related it to our birth based identity but it was to symbolize the multiple roles a human has to play during his lifetime. He should be knowledgeable like a Brahmin, prosper and gather wealth like a Vaishya, serve like a Shudra, and when it is required he should fight like a Kshatriya, the warrior. Only then life will be balanced. We are not here to gather wealth so one day a Qasim, a Ghori, or a Clive snatches it from us. It is our duty to protect it too.

The Indian Persecutors: Threat to future

Vote Bank Politics

POLITICIANS EXTENDED THE British rule of Divide and Rule for their political interests in different forms in independent India. The attire changed, but the core of these political games was British. They decided to divide the country the same way as British did. They played community cards. Some played the minority card, some the caste card, and some the women card and that's how the British mindset ruled the democratic and independent India even after independence.

Minority Card

People now divided the country on minority and majority scales. Yesterday's Muslims became minorities and Hindus became majorities and continued to fight the political battle in parliaments and outside. Hindu-Muslim rivalry changed into majority and minority rivalry on strategic level. Muslims often show their insecurity being a minority in spite of owning the maximum rights. Political leaders give special privilege to Muslims over Hindus in spite of knowing that they are not the minorities but the 2nd largest majority in India. This continued practice of politicians trying to buy the Muslim voters is known as the Appeasement Politics, which is a reality in India. The population of Muslims in India is more than the Muslims of many Muslim countries and they hold quite a strong position in the country.

When the real Minorities who are hardly 1 per cent, 2 per cent, and 3 per cent in the country like Parsis, Sikhs, Jains, Buddhists do not feel insecure and contribute to the prosperity of the country then why Muslims often are seen raising this issue and politicians are seen pleasing them with strategic moves that are often against the Hindus. They are treated somehow as the spoilt child of the Indian mother. Neither Parsis, Jains, Buddhists, nor Sikhs raise security concerns, nor they are given any special privileges, but few politicians continuously sow the seeds of insecurity in the Muslim's minds. They continue to play the game of politics using this community as a weapon. This is not very different from what was done by Jinnah to create Pakistan. We know what was the outcome of bending in front of this man in 1947.

The Hindus accepted Muslim people even after so much persecution. And this is proven by the fact that Muslims have ruled in the highest of positions in the government, judiciary, bureaucracy, and all other commanding positions. The biggest irony is that they are elected by the Indians and not just Muslims. The Hindus pay taxes and those taxes are used for the development of Muslims. The Hindu forces not only protect Hindus but also the Muslims and other communities then why even after learning a lesson from Jinnah we are allowing these politicians to divide India again and again. The politicians continue to sow the seeds of differences amongst a special community and we all dance to their tunes as puppets.

On the other side, the Hindu's interest is never taken care of, though it's called as a majority community. Only in India and in Nepal, Hindus forms a majority but on a global scale Hindus are lesser than Muslims. So should Muslims be called as minority or majority?

But this game is still on in India. We take a stand for Rohingya Muslims who could be accommodated by Pakistan and other Muslim countries, but not for our Kashmiri Hindus, who are suffering and still waiting to return to their homeland. The Hindus of Sindh in Pakistan are also bound to live there and face the atrocities by the Pakistanis. We allowed such governments to persecute Hindus because Hindus have no sense of voting.

Caste Cards

This cancer never spared India. Similar to minority and majority politics, caste becomes another weapon for the corrupt leaders to divide India. To woo a community for specific rights and reservations in educational institutions and government jobs, we sow the seeds of difference. Not only the politicians but people are equally involved in it. The percentage and number of castes in the list of scheduled caste, schedule tribes, and other backward classes kept on increasing after independence. We allowed politicians to use us as their personal vote bank. We, ignoring the real value of our vote, elect a leader because he belongs to a particular community and has promised us reservations. We do not think if he is capable to lead the country or not? We do not bother if he has a criminal record or he is corrupt or he is simply playing with our future to secure his political career. So many centuries of persecution have passed but caste differences are not completely eliminated from the society. They only transformed into categories.

Previously, there were only upper caste and lower caste. Now they are identified by general category, OBC, and scheduled castes. What has changed? Nothing! People are still stuck in those limitations and narrow mentality that prevent them from practicing their rights and duties from the national perspective. In fact, due to this vote back politics the gap between the castes is deepening day by day. All categories still hold a grudge for the other secretly, which is why the corrupt politicians succeed in maligning the people. In the end, the Hindu's interest is crushed by a Hindu because we are still scattered though living in the same country. We Hindus even when our religion was at stake, life was at stake, country was at stake, refused to give up on such caste based hierarchical differentiations in the Hindu community, which has been the fundamental reason that we have been persecuted for one thousand years and even now it is on.

Newspapers and online media often showcase stories of the persecution of a Dalit by the upper caste. So many Dalit women were raped, so many Dalit men were beaten by the upper caste mobs and children were left to suffer or get into the trash looking for their survival. This is another reason why Gods must have cursed the Hindus. We left a major chunk of our community in vulnerable circumstances that made them a soft target for the conversion missionaries.

If we decode our scriptures, caste was just to identify the community. It was meant to differentiate the communities based on their professions so that the skills are polished further to produce better services and lifestyle in the society. It was never meant to discriminate people. It was never ever a hierarchy. Nobody was on top and nobody was at bottom. Castes were based on Karma, actions and not Janma, birth. It means that one's caste was determined by what he does with his life, which lifestyle he follows, how much knowledge he gathers and what profession he chooses. And not by where and to whom he was born. But we completely twisted the idea as per our convenience which lead to a dilapidated foundation of the community of Hindus.

Regional and Language Cards

Regional and linguistic differences: Many of the states based upon their geographical boundaries and their language are demanding a separate state or country. In the name of freedom, we often try to divide the country further.

There are multiple 'aspirant' states in India that are looking to attain independence from the status-quo. This shows that we have learnt nothing from our past. We still perceive ourselves within a small limited community and not as a nation.

There have been demands to create separate states. Harit Pradesh (Western Uttar Pradesh), Purvanchal (Eastern Uttar Pradesh), Assam (Bodoland), Saurashtra, Gorkhaland (Northern West Bengal), Kongu Nadu (Southern Tamil Nadu). These are only few. There are more groups based upon linguistic grounds or cultural grounds who are demanding for separate entities. How long will this mindset continue amongst us. Our land is divided and our religion is persecuted even today. Only the weapons changed.

Uttaranchal from UP, Chhattisgarh from MP, Telangana from Andhra Pradesh, Jharkhand from Bihar, Ladakh from Jammu and Kashmir have already been created.

How ironical is a fact that in spite of lesson after lesson, losing 50 per cent of our population to this persecution and ongoing threats to the country, we are repeating the same mistakes to invite the same troubles again and again. In the world of globalization, we again want to crouch within a community, a region, a language or a caste. We haven't grown an inch, we haven't learnt a single lesson, and we haven't improved our mindset at all. Such a shame! This is only because Gods must have cursed us for he does not find us worthy of this land.

Apart from the above, votes were literally bought either in cash or in kind. Right from paying money to voters to vote for a particular party, they were gifted blankets and even alcoholic drinks. At the same time, the Indian voter staked his long term future for petty gains. The entire politics revolved around wooing the voter with promises to fulfill their demands, reasonable or unreasonable. The idea was to win at any cost. *They were promised not what they need but what they wanted.* Hence, the standard of integrity of politicians and people continued to decline. The height of everything is that even those demands were not fulfilled with honesty. Free medical clinics, free laptops, free rations, electricity bill waiver, loan waiver could be considered noble attempts, but most of them gave birth to more and more scams for they happened more on paper than on the surface.

Religious Exodus of Hindus: The Biggest Challenge

THERE ARE MASSIVE conversions taking place internationally and within India. Hindus are brainwashed, lured for material benefits, or threatened to accept other religions. Islamic Jihadis and Christian missionaries both are working aggressively for this cause.

The Dalit Hindus are tempted with the financial, educational, and employment opportunities offered by the Church and accept Christianity. On the other side, Islamic missionaries do this by hook or by crook. Incidents of killings in the name of conversions are reported on regular basis. For expanding Islam and to reduce the number of Hindu wombs, the Jihadis are exploiting all tactics. One strange strategy, which has been actively reported in the past few years is 'love jihad'. Use of emotional and moral tactics for converting women is a reality in India which is spreading its roots under the surface.

Conversion is a cause for alarm for Hindus as in front of our eyes, we have seen so many countries become Islamic countries for their *hyper secular notions*. So many states in India became Muslim dominant states in the past few decades and the conversions are still on. This is not about violating one's freedom of choosing his idea of God, form of God, and worship rituals. A Hindu can choose his way of relating to his master but it should be natural and not out of compulsion, threat or manipulation. But these conversions are still on in India, which is rapidly reducing the Hindu population.

A Hindu must be worried about it but he is not. It must be a curse of Gods.

The tired Hindu Shoulder: Superficial Secularism

'INDIA IS A Secular Country'. This one statement is engraved into our minds since childhood. We all are equal and we should embrace all the religions. But what is secularism exactly? What is religion? And what is Dharma? And the burning question is that why secularism is only a Hindu's liability in India? Hindu governments are seen pleasing the Muslims for their vote bank politics. Hindus are constantly seen pleasing the other communities and seeking approval of the Muslims.

Being a Hindu itself is exemplary of being secular. A fundamentalist Hindu is a secular person because Hinduism does not differentiate people on religious beliefs. We believe in one God but also in polytheism i.e. God may manifest in any form. We also believe in all living beings are his creations. Forget about differentiating humans, we don't even differentiate between animals and plants. We even pray to stones, plants, nature, water, air, and everything that constitutes life. A Hindu does not need to prove himself to be secular to embrace other communities because we don't impose our Gods and our beliefs on others. Then why do Hindus try to act hyper secular just to please the other communities. Why can't they proudly be a

Hindu and embrace others if they want to.

After so much of bloodshed, holocaust, conversions, partition, riots, terrorism, the Hindu's shoulder is tired of carrying the burden of this word called 'Secularism' because it has lost its sanctity. And this is only because it seems to be a one-sided phenomenon in India especially when it comes to Muslims.

A Hindu, if he speaks for his own religion, is seen as a fundamentalist where non-hindus are not restricted to endorse their religious sentiments. Anybody can challenge the Hindu rituals and religious values, which is impossible to do in the other religions.

Everybody can openly debate why women should go to a particular temple? God is not limited to a particular temple and it is not required to hurt the religious sentiments of a shrine that is built on the belief of celibacy. But everybody will stand against the Hindu sentiments including the Hindus, but no one dares to challenge the prohibition of Muslim women who can't go to the mosque since ages. We don't question Christianity on why is there no female pope in churches all around the world. Hinduism is the only religion that could be twisted, altered, questioned, criticized, and manipulated; in fact by its own people, what an irony!

When so many women are facing rapes, domestic violence, gender biases, female foeticide, triple talaq, halala, polygamy, lack of education and other challenges, is it feasible to fight for their entry in a particular temple or should we divert these energies in fighting with the other evils? But here the target is soft, one who will never raise his voice, but will be submissive to the voices raised against his religion.

Hindu's Jagrans and Kirtans have to obey the rules of not using loudspeakers but the same could not be applicable to the mosques. Even the police does not dare to intervene in the mosque's morning activity that uses loudspeakers.

The judiciary of India has also been biased against Hindus which is exemplified in many occasions, be it the entry of women in the Sabarimala temple, the Dahi Handi issue, and many other verdicts on religious matters. Supreme Court immediately intervened in the smallest of the religious decisions of the Hindus, but when it came to the core issues like building the Rama Mandir in Ayodhya which was against the Muslim's interest, the same Supreme Court took ages to come to a conclusion. Why so? And even when the judgment came recently on 9th November 2019, it was criticized. A balanced judgment that gave justice to a plundered temple to be restored again and five acres of land to a mosque that was built on a plundered temple of a Hindu land was also condemned by the so called leftists. A case that was pending for nearly seven decades is also criticized for being solved. The irony is that not only Muslims but the so-called liberal Hindus too are criticizing and condemning the decision. The curse of one thousand years of persecution seems to be waning away with this little light piercing the darkness, but the Hindu is still not ready to open his eyes because he is so fond of the darkness and persecution; his obsession with self persecution.

After attaining freedom in 1947, how many temples have been rebuilt that were plundered by the invaders. Not even 1 per cent. The Ram Mandir issue was pending in the court for ages. Even in independent India, restoring a plundered temple is so difficult. Neither the Hindu demanded it nor did the

Muslims ever stand by the Hindus for the same.

On the contrary, a section of Muslims protest against the reconstruction of the Hindu temples till date. They don't stand for the religious sentiments of their Hindu brothers. They defend their religion and comment upon Hinduism openly and Hindus zip their mouth to prevent themselves from saying a single word against them or to defend their religion. Is it wrong to stand for one's own religion? If secularism really exists then why our Muslim brothers and sisters do not stand for our ancestral heritage to be reconstructed on our own land? Why are we bound to carry the burden of the invaders graves in so many places including the capital city Delhi?

Recently when the government made efforts to welcome back the Hindu brothers in Muslim countries along with the five other communities including Parsis, Sikhs, Christians, Buddhists to India through the Citizenship Amendment Act, the Muslims and leftists came to the roads and initiated riots to oppose them. Wow, if Muslims from the Muslim countries come to India for seeking refuge that is commendable but if the Hindus come to their own country to save themselves from fierce persecution they get offended. Why? The Rohingyas don't find refuge in the Muslim countries but they must be accepted by Hindus. But if Hindus embrace their Hindu people it is against secularism. Shame on those Indians; be they Hindus or Muslims who stand against this move which should have been done decades ago. Muslims from Tibet got citizenship in Kashmir for being Muslims but Hindus were kept away. They were thrown out, killed, raped or made to sweep their floors and clean their toilets. Are we alive? Can't we see? Minorities especially Muslims flourished in India as India took special care of them, but look at the condition of Hindus in Pakistan. See how many of them occupy the major ranks. How many became prime ministers, presidents or beaurucrats? Forget about the higher ranks they did not even get the basic education. They could not even survive. They are rather reduced to a meager percentage becoming food for the hungry wolves. And we shouldn't even allow them to come back home? The riots on CAA when the public property was damaged seems to be the trailer of what happened with the Hindus in the past. And we still haven't fastened our seat belts for the upcoming upheaval.

The journalists are simply interested in their hot news, politicians in power, and businessmen in money even if it deepens the communal pits; pit that increases the distance amongst Indians on religious beliefs. We had caste system which was anti-human so we are dealing with it, then why can't we deal with the imprints of invaders the same way? Soaked in our ancestral blood, the names of the invaders are still hovering over our streets. Aurangzeb Road, Akbar Road, Shahjahan Road, and many other roads named after those who infused the Hindu land with Hindu blood remind us of our failure to safeguard our motherland and stand for our religion in the last 1000 years, but till date it brings severe chaos when an attempt is made to change this scenario. A lot of voices rose against these much obvious decisions. Even when the names of these barbaric invaders were to be substituted with the names of the noble Muslims, then also there was mayhem. APJ Abdul Kalam Road had to go through these hypocrite voices before it was finally done. This is something beyond anybody's understanding. Do we intentionally want Aurangzeb to motivate Indians in 21st century? If not, then why?

This is an example of 'Superficial Secularism' which is also known as 'Pseudo Secularism'. People, just to sound politically correct, choose to be incorrect or far from reality. Ironically, when someone points his finger towards Hinduism, he is referred to as opinionated, but if a Hindu does the same, he is called fundamentalist; no matter if he is wrong or right.

Somehow this secularism is doing great damage to India because our definition of secularism is so hypocritical and meaningless that it is only giving us terrorism, murders, humiliation, economical liability, and apprehensions of a dark future. Why don't the liberal Muslims do something about that?

There are teachings against the other religions that are openly conducted in some institutions that prompt the fundamentalists to kill those who are infidels according to the values taught to them in that environment; hence it does give rise to terrorism. It not only spoils their life but also harms the entire humanity time and again. Why can't they address such activities and put a full stop to all these that instigate intolerance towards the other religions in the name of God? Shouldn't they challenge these belief systems that they say are false on television screens but are openly destructing the global peace.

It's not that Hindu customs did not have the evil social practices. There were and there are a lot, but a section of Hindus always tried to oppose them to overcome the evils in few texts as they were found inhuman. Then why can't the liberal sections of the Muslims and Christians also do the same. They are often noticed defending the respective religions stating that humanity is supreme and there is nothing above that. But refrain from taking actions against such practices whenever it is required. They either defend themselves or stay quiet. Why terms like Ghazwa-e-Hind, Butshikan, and Ghazi are glorified by the Islamic heroes? Why should they be given this freedom of practicing the evils that are ruining innocent lives? Why only the Hindus are burdened with secularism?

Why Muslims are scared of Sardar Patel statues? Was he not their leader? Did he get freedom for only Hindus and not for Muslims? Why are they scared of Hindu God's statues when Hindu Gods believe in pluralism? They preach to us to accept everyone irrespective of religion unlike religions that preach to slaughter someone who doesn't believe in their idea of God. How logical is that? New Zealand, Australia, and Germany, every country has erased and are erasing the imprints of their painful past, then why in India we cannot do that?

Why our provinces are still a home to the graves of those who sucked our blood till their last breath?

Besides this, the above discussed fundamentalism and misinterpretation of few religions empower the people to manipulate concepts like triple talaq, cow slaughter, halala, extremism, polygamy in marriage. As a result, what is born are the threats like Ghazwa-e-Hind severe social differences and other terrorist activities in the name of religion.

These parasites that are left untreated are still adding to the hollowness of India as a nation. Whenever the government attempted to address these issues somewhere the fundamentalist laws and rules prevented that from happening. These laws intersected the Indian constitution and discarded the common code of conduct. Why a particular religion's laws are above the constitution of India? When all the other communities follow the common code of conduct including Hindus, Sikhs, Parsis, and Jains then why only a selected community was given the special privilege to follow their own laws discarding the constitution of India?

Ghazwa-e-Hind: What does the Indian Muslim have to say about this? Is a Hindu aware of this Islamic mission? Is he ready to face it? Does he even know how vigorously it is going on in India behind the so-called liberal statements of liberal Muslims?

Ghazwa-e-Hind or the battle of India is an Islamic term mentioned in some Hadiths in particular predicting a final and last battle in India and as a result, a conquest of the whole Indian subcontinent by Muslim warriors.

The term has recently become a subject of vast criticism in media for being used by militant groups to justify their activities in the Indian subcontinent.

Conquering India, converting all Hindus into Muslims, killing those who protest against it, installing the green flag and removing the saffron from this land of seers and penance is a mission that is titled as 'Ghazwa-e-Hind'

The above mission is the main reason for the never ending terrorist activities from outside and within India, forced conversions; killings in the name of religion and mob violence, but people deliberately shut their eyes to an undeniable reality.

A particular community had the luxury of a separate state with separate constitution, separate rules, and everything for almost seven decades in Kashmir. They were not governed by a minister but a prime minister of their own to indicate that it is a country on its own and not a part of the nation. This special privilege was Article 35A and 370 which has been recently repealed by the current government.

What was Article 35A?

It was a special favour to the state of Jammu and Kashmir that allowed its legislature to define permanent residents of the state. The government of Kashmir enjoyed the absolute right to decide who will stay in Kashmir and who will not? It was inserted through the Constitution (Application to Jammu and Kashmir) Order, 1954, that was issued by President Rajendra Prasad under Article 370, on the advice of the Nehru-led Union Government. When the J&K Constitution was adopted in 1956, it defined a permanent resident as someone who was a state subject on May 14, 1954, or who has been a resident of the state for 10 years.

TEXT OF ARTICLE 35A

"Saving of laws with respect to permanent residents and their rights—Notwithstanding anything contained in this Constitution, no existing law in force in the State of Jammu and Kashmir, and no law hereafter enacted by the Legislature of the State:

    (a) Defining the classes of persons who are, or shall be, permanent residents of the State of Jammu and Kashmir; or

    (b) Conferring on such permanent residents any special rights and privileges or imposing upon other persons any restrictions as respects—

        (i) Employment under the State Government;

        (ii) Acquisition of immovable property in the State;

        (iii) Settlement in the State; or

        (iv) Right to scholarships and such other forms of aid as the State Government may provide,

Shall be void on the ground that it is inconsistent with or takes away or abridges any rights conferred on the other citizens of India by any provision of this part.

These special privileges to the Muslims and the state of Kashmir extended the curse on Kashmiri Hindus who had to go through so many adversities.

As a result, the Kashmiri Hindus were attacked as a wolf attacks a deer. The story of Kashmiri Hindus is a painful example of the persecution of Hindus in the last 1000 years. The irony is that it continued in independent India. In 1990, which is not even three decades ago, there was an exodus of this community when they had to leave their age old civilization, property, homeland, and retreat barefoot to start their lives all over again.

They had to say goodbye to their beautiful valley to save their daughters from rapes and murders. They had to go through the atrocities and find shelter in other parts of the country. A Kashmiri Hindu portrays the true example of the Hindu spirit as even after so much loss and atrocities they did not turn out to be terrorists. They focused on reestablishing their lives by education and professional achievements. The entire country was quiet for so long. Nothing was done to rehabilitate this community until the current government focused on their cries by repealing Article 35A that became a reason for Muslim dominance in Kashmir. Why were Hindus quiet until then? Who stopped them from raising their voice for their own countrymen who were displaced from their own land and the government was still trying to please those who endorsed the persecutors? Does it sound natural or seems to be the curse of Gods?

However, the political geography of Jammu and Kashmir has been changed by the Modi government. Home Minister Amit Shah, in the Rajya Sabha announced the central government's decision to repeal Article 370 and Article 35A of the Indian Constitution, which were hollowing the country like a parasite since decades. The government also announced the reorganization of the state which will now have two union territories - Jammu & Kashmir and Ladakh for simplifying the social and economic development of both.

This was such an easy move as there was a provision in the constitution of India to reverse and undo the above sanctions to Jammu and Kashmir which was boosting terrorist's morale for decades. It was mentioned that the above regulations will be temporary in nature and could be withdrawn by the President whenever required. Thanks to the then President.

However, it is still a burning question that why the Indian government deliberately kept quiet for the last 70 years. Why the previous governments did not consider repealing these illicit laws in the past? Why the Indian government gave wings to this separatist attitude of Muslims? Why they were given this special privilege when all the other religions are following the common code of conduct since forever?

What happened to Kashmiri Hindus could be the future reality of all the Hindus; the fact that every secular Hindu must know is that secularism can't be held on a Hindu's shoulder alone, other religions should equally carry that weight, only then it may survive in the long run. We must be afraid of the fact that one day entire India could be a Kashmir and all Hindus could become Kashmiri Pundits if the Hindus keep sleeping.

Why are we still nurturing ideologies of Babur, Genghis

Khan, Aurangzeb and Khiljis to enable them to plunder our temples, burn our scriptures, rape our sisters and kill our children once again?

The so called liberals argue that Muslims had similar atrocities as Hindus during partition and after that. What must be asked to them is a question that why there are less than 2 per cent Hindus in Pakistan and why there are more than 20 per cent Muslims in India living the best of life being ministers, presidents, bureaucrats, doctors, engineers, and even film stars? Can you name some Hindus who became the Prime Ministers and Presidents of Pakistan?

But even after such absolute acceptance by the Hindus they could not accept Hindus. They still endorse terms like Ghazwa-e-Hind, Nizam-e-Mustafa, scream *'Bharat tere tukde honge Inshallah Inshallah'* meaning India, you will be fragmented into pieces, *'Afzal ham sharminda hain tere katil ab tak zinda hain'* meaning Afzal (terrorist) we are embarrassed as your killers (Indian government and Supreme Court) are still alive. An Indian Muslim and a so-called liberal Hindu is screaming these lines favoring terrorists but they have all the problems in saying 'Jai Hind'. That this is not even considered a contempt of court is another joke.

Can this scenario be imagined in Pakistan when a Hindu is screaming *'Pakistan tere tukde honge Jai Shri Ram Jai Shri Ram'* meaning Pakistan you will be fragmented into pieces, Jai Shri Ram Jai Shri Ram'. No! Not at all! It is only in India when even a terrorist is defended saying that he turned into a terrorist for his poor background. A country where half of its population resides under poverty line can we excuse a terrorist for his poor background? Does that allow half of India to turn into terrorists?

What kind of message these liberals are giving to the youth?

Everything seems so messed up but one thing is loud and clear that the Hindu needs to fasten his seatbelts. So much is happening around him but he is still sleeping behind the veil of superficial secularism under a blanket of nonviolence.

Why the intellectual Muslims shut their eyes on these matters? They do not come forward and raise their voice against it? Why there is so much hypocrisy? Why Muslims do not stand by their Hindu brothers and justify their demand for restoring the age old cultural heritage, be it temples or the other archeological sites? Why can't they spare cows from their cuisines knowing what they mean to the Hindus? Why can't they go to Hindu temples if Hindus could go to mosques. Why they can't follow the common code of conduct like all other religions? Why can't they paint those sign boards with the name of invaders with the colour black showing that they are a part of this nation and not against it. Why don't they do all this to set the right examples for their future generations and make them understand that 'nation comes first to them as well'?

All these are burning questions that smolder in every Hindu's heart and should reverberate into Muslim's hearts too. After all, they are not alien to this country. They are very much a part of this land and belong to the same ancestors that Hindus belong to.

The Ex-Hindu: Who are you fighting with?

THE EX-HINDUS, still in captivity of invaders, are living and dying to enforce the ideologies of those who snatched their ancestral identity. Ex-Hindus are similar to that baby elephant that is tied with rope by the mahout so he doesn't move. This elephant, when fully grown up and is much more powerful to break that rope in one go, he still doesn't. This is because he is unaware of the fact that time has changed and the master cannot command him anymore. He no more has to be in his control. He continues to sit where his master made him sit far back, unknown of his probable freedom.

This is the irony of the Muslims who were converted forcefully in the past, but now when we are free, we do not want to give up what was compelled and imposed on us. There are neither Arabs, nor Mughals, nor British, but we still find ourselves in the captivity of their belief system, philosophically aware but literally unaware of our freedom.

Muslims should have more problems with that because it is they who were completely deprived of their roots forcibly. Their ancestors could not protect their culture and could not save their freedom of religious beliefs. In a way, they should be more active in erasing the imprints of the invaders on streets, books, history, and even on Indian minds. They should rather actively restore their lost civilization, but they are so captivated by the footprints of the injustice done to their ancestors by Muslim invaders that they are still manipulated by the ignorant and selfish people in the name of religion.

We feel more pity on the Muslims of India than Hindus because their foundation was shaken more than the Hindus; their culture, ancestral heritage, and their religion that gave them freedom and tolerance. Their repute worldwide is completely snatched by the invaders to an extent that God knows how many generations of ex-Hindus will suffer from this and will they be able to realize what happened to them even after reading the history books is also a million dollar question.

Women have to go through social ailments like triple talaq and halala. There have been cases where women are exploited for this practice and their relatives abused them sexually in the name of religious beliefs. Many of these women are of Hindu origin that were pushed into these circumstances. How can we as Hindus or as ex-Hindus or as Muslims let such sick rituals stay in the spiritual texts that are meant to violate the human ethics.

The beliefs that were imposed on them out of fear, pain, animosity, and helplessness, what is the need to be captivated by them now when there are no Ghoris and Qasims is a big question. Aurangzeb, Genghis Khan, Ghazini, and Nadir Shah, all have gone. Now they are free from these evils then why can't they evolve out of them. Why don't they free themselves from that mental prison? Why don't they open the temples that their ancestors built with love and devotion? Why don't they free their daughters, who were suppressed under the laws of those chauvinist men who manipulated a religion's name for their personal agendas? Why don't they free themselves from the rigidity of foreign invaders when their own people have given them fundamental freedom to live the way they want with equality, justice, and freedom? It's high time that they come out and break the barricades after all religion is for people's well being.

You should decide if it is the belief system that is becoming a cause of massive killings, injustice, bloodshed, fundamentalism, intolerance, then what is the point of holding on to them? We should believe in one God who just wants us to live in harmony and he belongs to all, but we must choose a religion that is tolerant to all, benefits all and bestows humanity with prosperity; it doesn't matter what the name is, Sanatan Dharma, Christianity, or Islam.

God doesn't need anything from us. He doesn't need protection nor does he need any dominance. He is dominant by his very existence. Don't allow people to manipulate his name to justify their dirty motives. He is an ultimate giver why would he want us to destroy his world? We must accept that anyone who resides in Hind is either a Hindu or an ex-Hindu. Their ancestors were Hindus, their blood is Hindu, their roots are Hindu, and it's a widespread fact not an illusion. Why they don't ever bother to introspect, look back into their history, differentiate reality from illusions, and break free from these ties and return to their roots? If they do belong to Hind, then the values that were forced on them on knifepoint should be cross checked once to see if beneficial for humanity or not?

They are not even aware of their true history and are so easily manipulated by few selfish groups. Do they even know that Raja Dahir who was a Hindu king gave shelter to Prophet Mohammad's family when Mohammad bin Qasim was after their lives? He killed them and they rather praise Qasim. The first mosque in India was built on a land donated to them by a Hindu King and still a Hindu is a terrorist and fundamentalist to them.

Author and social activist of Pakistani origin Tarek Fatah confirms the above facts about Raja Dahir's support to Prophet Mohammad's family and first mosque in India. He said this in his various speeches and many interviews given to renowned television channels.

The Captivated Indian Mind: Modern & most dangerous Weapon of Persecutors

THE BIGGEST AND easiest persecution is the persecution of one's intellect. When you capture somebody's mind, you need no weapons to persecute him further. His mind itself will lead him into the direction you want him to go. The Hindu intellect has been persecuted since ages and the irony is that we still can't understand and keep falling into this trap. Sometimes it's addressed as Intellectual Terrorism and sometimes as brainwashing. Intellectual terrorism because it hinders the valid actions against the terrorist activities and in favour of the country's security with so-called intellectual arguments. Brainwashing because it conditions the generation's brains to act and react in a way a particular section desires. Hindus often have to deal with media and social media biases because even after a history of scariest holocausts, a Hindu is tagged of being an extremist and really compels one to wonder, if we Indians need psychiatric medicines?

So many Hindus and activists are killed in the name of religion and no one knows, but if Muslims are killed everybody knows. So many temples have lost their idols as they are stolen, but if somebody throws one stone on a church it becomes a headline saying that minorities are under threat in India.

Corporatism has captured us. Our views have changed as someone else has hijacked our minds to an extent that we strongly endorse a mindset that everything foreign is good no matter how inferior it is for our lives; whether it is a foreign drink, foreign fashion, foreign medicines, foreign language, or foreign culture. We choose to eat a burger that has much lesser nutritive value then our *Idly* and *Poha*. We consider English language as a status symbol while leaving Sanskrit on an outdated shelf of an old government library. We value foreign multivitamin tablets more than our cow's milk. We value foreign style of dining instead of the Indian way of dining, we value tea instead of our buttermilk, and there is a long list to follow. We are not aware of the fact that whatever is Swadeshi has much deeper scientific reasons then the commercially driven foreign influence that has raised the index of diabetes, depression, and many other issues in the country.

Till the time it was just us, it's fine but we are also projecting these ill psychologies to our future generations depriving them of their gracious history. We are the culprits to cut their ties with an age old civilization that they have inherited which is their fundamental right and which is beneficial for them. The poor children are drawn into river tides that are washing off the heritage that they were blessed with. In the name of a Hindu, we barely have the hypocritical attire with a sacred thread and a tilak mark. It is hollow and meaningless. We are saying that we are proud to be a Hindu but our pride has to be substantiated by the actions that are lacking.

Even water is bought by paying our money to the foreign brands because we are made to believe that our water is polluted.

We are made to believe that foreign brands are better than the Indian brands to an extent that even the goods that are only available in India are bought by Indians after a foreign tag. This is the extent of our dependency on foreign approval.

Chinese products are a big threat to India. Here we continue to buy Chinese products and pay our money to Chinese government where they are using this money to build CPEC with Pakistan and helping its defense apparatus directly or indirectly. This money, if spent on Swadeshi products would enhance our defense budget and strengthen our security apparatus. It will create employment for our youth and will help stabilze the economy. These factors are often perceived as a boring lecture by our upcoming generations but they have a deep and intense signification in their future.

Persecution of History: Contaminating the Roots

The irony is that we can't even know what happened exactly in history because all we have is an extremely biased perspective of the historians of non-Hindu origin and the inferior documentation and historical evidences that can't be relied upon. The stories of our heroes were either erased or squeezed into a tiny paragraph into the history books where the invader's narratives are amplified and praised. As a result, we perceive Akbar and Shahjahan as our heroes and we don't even know about Marthanda Varma and the winning Hindu dynasties and their kingdoms that ruled for hundreds of years.

Can you name one king from any of these Indian kingdoms? Mauryas, Satavahanas, Guptas, Pandyas, Cholas, Pallavas, Chalukyas, Ahoms? Can you name the capital of these kingdoms?

Do you know how long they ruled? How vast were their

empires? Have you even heard of all these names? Ask any average educated Indian to name the kings of Mughal period that ruled for only 250 years. 99 out of 100 will name them in the sequence—Babur, Humayun, Akbar, Jahangir, Shah Jahan and Aurangzeb. Now, if you ask them to name the kings of the above dynasties which ruled India for much larger period of time and during whose reign India was the most prosperous country in the world, would they know? For instance, Mauryas ruled for 550 years, Satavahanas ruled for 500 years, Guptas ruled for 400 years, Pandyas ruled for 800 years, Cholas ruled for 1000 years, Pallavas ruled for 600 years, Chalukyas ruled for 600 years, Ahom Dynasty of Northeast ruled for 650 years but we say Mughals 'the great'. None of our children know even one great king from each dynasty; forget about the entire list of kings in chronological order. That is how ill-informed almost everyone is in India and the same is transferred to our future generations. People know that Hindus created the present day caste system but no one knows that it was intended to enhance the professional expertise of the people and not to discriminate it.

Some say the British got us civilization, then what was Indus Valley Civilization, when people from the west did not even have the basic sense of textiles and they learnt it all from India. Others believe India did not have scientific thinking and forget that we discovered the solar system and its functions when west was struggling for their survival. There are still others, who say India may have been rich in parts more than a millennia ago, but was the poorest country for over a millennia which was because we allowed others to capture our land and rob our wealth and civilization.

Isn't this a curse of Gods when someone who is sailing

in the Ganges is dying out of thirst? We are forgetting what we taught to the world. We know the jazz, salsa, and hip hop but Bharatnatyam, Kathak, and Manipuri are struggling to survive. Is there even a comparison between these? We are cursed because we are deprived of this pride and honour in spite of having this in our DNA. And this is the reason that our children look for honour in behaving like British or Europeans by speaking English and wearing foreign brands. They don't know the real India and its intellectual wealth because our scriptures were burnt and stolen by the outsiders and ignored by our own people.

Our forefathers are not alive to share what they faced though a little we come to know from our grandparents who heard a part of it from their great grandparents and so on.

Even after 75 years of independence, school textbooks are dominated by the Muslim invaders and half truths about the freedom movement. They highlight the role played by the non-violent movement, while the role of the Indian National Congress is dismissed in few cursory paragraphs. There were so many sacrifices that martyrs and their families made and our children owe no thanks to them as their name is simply erased from the historical documents.

The Hindu needs to realize how important it is to revisit Indian history and acknowledge the glory of our intellectual wealth, narratives of the kingdoms, relevance of Indian civilization today and the immense contribution of leaders like Netaji who helped India win its freedom.

Concoctions in History resulted into an education system that is based on fallacious and biased content, hence we lost stories of proud contributors like Marthanda Varma and King

Hemu in the Battle of Panipat, who was a Hindu king who acquired the throne of Delhi but was killed in the reign of Akbar. Bairam Khan's army injured his eye and later killed him when he was not carrying any weapons and was blind.

Many soldiers of the Hindu origin were on the cusp of changing what has now been written as India's history, but the lack of integrity and unity got them killed by the invaders, then by the historians, and now by us who do not even make efforts to keep them alive in our history. We allowed people to mess with our truth and fool us for ages making us ashamed of our past.

Why Raja Dahir was completely eliminated from the Indian history, when he was the most important part of the medieval period. The education minister Maulana Azad is alleged by some historians to have deleted the great contributions of this great king from the history text books to keep our generations away from their own historical facts, so that the Muslim barbaric invaders shadow the Indian history forever. Only God knows how many soldiers like Dahir are unknown to us who sacrificed their life for securing Goddess India.

This could be nothing but a curse.

Archaeological Persecution: Persecutors all around

Wherever there was Muslim rule, Hindu heritage was burnt to ashes. The archaeological heritage has been destroyed, never to be restored again. Even independent India is busy in preserving the heritage of the persecution phase, which should actually be a nightmare for the residents of this nation whether they are Hindus or Muslims or Christians of the Hindu origin. When we say Muslims or Christians from the Hindu origin it means the hundred percent population of Muslims as well as

Christians because no Muslim or Christian in India belongs to a foreign DNA and if they are, they are very few in numbers.

We preserve the Mughal architecture, the British architecture, even the invader's graves, but we do not bother much about preserving or restoring the heritage of ancient India that was created by our own ancestors more than a millennia ago. This can only happen in our country. If we learn from Germany, Hitler has been a leader of global relevance, though he is an icon of barbarism. But Germany chose not to remember a persecutor. The name of Hitler is being erased from the streets, the discussions, and the books. No one wants to remember him and they have followed it religiously. Even the law supports the deletion of this chapter from the history of Germany. But what are we doing? We not only failed to erase the name of these barbaric invaders from history, but we are even holding on to the objects that remind us of their deeds today. The height of everything is that we want to preserve them for our future exemplifying our so-called liberal mindset. Or shall we call the persecuted mindset that has lost its sensitivity to see things as they are for they are cursed by God.

There are so many historical monuments of ancient India that are ignored by the government even today. The archaeological departments don't even keep them in their agenda. Even the transport routes are not properly developed nor the maintenance is been taken care off. The buildings are dilapidating continuously, but neither the state nor the centre bothers because the Hindu is still in the Kumbhakarana's sleep. Sometimes the so-called backward local villagers make small efforts as per their capacity to preserve what their ancestors left but we the so-called educated free citizens do not even know if such a heritage exists while letting our taxes continue to be spent on the graves of the murderers and rapists of our ancestors. Thankfully, our ancestors made them so well that in spite of such negligence they are still present to remind us of what we owe to our heritage, but they may not survive forever if we do not wake up.

If we travel through the whole of India we will find so many such Hindu temples, monuments, and other archaeological sites which are neglected. There is so much content engraved on the pillars and walls of these sites to speak of our past, but no one even bothers to translate it in Hindi or English so people could understand it. The thousands of our scriptures are preserved in Sanskrit and we did not even bother to get those translated into Hindi or English. The British took the Vedas and translated them, read them, and learnt from them, but we are still keeping them in the corner as if what Muslims destroyed and what British stole were not enough.

We must learn from the British. Even the artifacts, the idols, the archaeological structures they had taken from India, are not only transported carefully from here, but they are kept in the British Museum in London with so much care to speak of their victory over such a rich cultural land. But we neither realize what we have nor do we want to take care of what speaks of our victory over the world.

We see the mosques, monuments, buildings built during the Muslim rule everyday, but we don't see much of the physical space created by the great Marathas, the Rajputs, and the Sikhs in the Medieval Period. And even the few that remain are much lesser in ratio as compared to Muslims and also British architecture. Even in Delhi, the capital of India, these monuments occupy the most premium locations. Even the British do not occupy as much geographical and historical space as is occupied by the Muslims. It could be nothing but a curse.

Holocaust of literature: Stealing the biggest inheritence

If we closely analyze, the text books that we teach our students are designed to make them hate ourselves and our very existence. These books whisper so many contaminating messages into their ears in such a subtle way that we cannot even imagine. Few of them might not be written but we see them everywhere around us. For instance, everything foreign is good, educated means speaking in English, western culture resembles high society lifestyle, Mughals were the Great Mughals, Akbar was a secular king, and many other fallacious and biased factual information that they don't find our culture as an inheritance to be proud of. They feel Hindu temples mean superstitions, Sanskrit means an old language, and Indian values are hypocritical. It is a huge conspiracy. It is true that as any other commune, Hinduism too has its own flaws which is the reason we have been persecuted to this level, but there is a brighter side to this narrative also that is often shadowed by a so-called leftist school of thought. For instance, the Gupta period was referred to as a very prosperous and harmonious period by the scholars of those times. We can rely on their write-ups because they were not even from this country that they would be biased towards the Hindu emperors. Many of them were of foreign origin, still we discard their opinion and throw dirt on our positive historical facts without even substantiating our comments with evidences. And this is only done when it is about praising a Hindu's contributions. It does not happen with any other community; still they are called minorities who feel insecure in this country. This is propaganda to contaminate our history and its interpretation in the minds of our future generation so that we feel ashamed of our past and continue with the distorted narrative that leads us to more and more persecution. How can we afford to confuse our children who are innocent and vulnerable ? In any dignified country such text books would be burned to ashes but we are buying these lies with our hard-earned money and paying the teachers to intoxicate our future.

Isn't it our duty to preserve our language, culture, family, community, state, and religion? If we don't do this and keep on sleeping generation after generation, there is no way we can save our heritage from the hands of the monster of darkness and get rid of this curse.

The irony is that even today when we are a free country for the last seventy years we have no proper documentation of the declining population of Hindus and evaporating Hindu values. We don't even discuss and we don't act.

In a nutshell our physical, mental, traditional and even individual space is in danger and something serious needs to be done.

We must be awakened before we melt into the oceans along with our heritage. It is said that we can awaken the one who is sleeping, but who can awaken the one who is deliberating pretending to sleep to simply ignore what is going on around.

We should monitor the condition and demographics of Hindus to know what is going on and act accordingly. We should establish a system of maintaining the state wise and region wise reports.

The sad part of the narrative is that it's only a Hindu who allows others to persecute him to such an extent and even today a Hindu himself is persecuting a fellow Hindu. The converted Muslims and Christians of the Hindu origin fight for anti-hindu campaigns. For example, Bangladeshi Hindus who were persecuted in their own land came to West Bengal as refugees. After that, instead of standing for their religion they stood against it by screaming in favour of Marxists. The Kashmiri Muslims, who were converted at gunpoint by threats of raping their daughters and sisters, stood for the ones who forced such belief systems on them. The Muslims in Pakistan are also the ones who have their roots in Hinduism, still they are ready to disappear from the world map for their outrage against Hindus. This is such a drastic virus that is infused into the blood of Hindus that it is paralyzing the Hindu intellect, preventing them from even opening the blindfold that is taking them to the path of complete destruction.

The problem is not that a part of Hindus accepted other religions and followed their practices because they still could claim to be Hindus. Hindu texts do not disown a person for worshiping a different deity being a polytheistic religion. As per Hinduism, one can create any image of the Lord and pray in whichever way he wants. He can also choose not to worship at all but the problem arises when they nurture the anti-hindu psychology by claiming that their idea of God is superior to the Hindu idea of God and their practices are superior to Hindu practices. It doesn't even stop here, they further call Hindus as infidels and make all efforts to make them quit what they believe in and accept what they think is the right way of worship. And these efforts could sometimes be human or inhuman.

Hindu temples are barely funded by the government. Rather the funds are collected from temples as taxes and spent on the Madarsas and other religious institutions as subsidies.

We can't burn crackers and play loud music in Bhajans and Kirtans but Muslims can have loud Azaan and can slaugher the animals publicly for their religion. Media is controlled by foreign sources that do not let the persecution of Hindu stories come out in public. The stories are suppressed under the surface and our Hindu brothers are murdered and women are raped and persecuted. If seen carefully, there is a complete media blackout on these issues, unintentionally or intentionally. This is never allowed to surface or shared. This gunpowder is being spread under the ground for Hindus in jet speed and the Hindu is busy with many other things that will have no meaning if this gunpowder is inflamed just with one trigger.

If the persecution of Hindus is compared with Jews, the statistical figures of the persecuted Hindus would be much higher.

A Hindu never has to prove that he is secular because it is the only religion that allows polytheism. A believer of Hinduism can worship as many gods as he wants, in whichever form, in whichever way, and at whichever place, which also includes the Muslim God and the Christian God, if that's how God is categorized as fundamentalists. He will still be embraced by the Hindu community as a Hindu. Then why does he always have to prove his secularism when the pseudo monotheistic religions are openly practicing things that can't be called secular at all. They are not allowing their children to marry Hindu girls without conversion. Why only a Hindu should carry this burden of fallacious secularism?

It is a secular religion from its very origin. Honestly, the shoulder of a Hindu is smashed now and bleeding while carrying the burden of hypocritical secularism. And he cannot even see this blood. It's very important to offload this burden now. It's important to heal this wound so it doesn't intoxicate the entire system. And this burden could only be shared by the other communities including Muslims and Christians.

Why can't we extract the pieces of our idols and *vigrahas* from the staircases of the mosques and finally give them a Bhu Samadhi and Jal Samadhi for consoling the sentiments of Hindus.

Why can't the Muslim brothers stand for the extraction of those pure objects of worship for their Hindu Brothers to prove their secularism? May be that positive energy is humiliated everyday under the feet of Muslims which is why neither they are happy nor are we. Why doesn't the government intervene? Why doesn't the archaeological department intervene?

Many temples are lying ignored. They are not maintained in countries like Pakistan, Bangladesh, in a few countries of the Middle East and also in the remote corners of India. These temples were energized once by our ancestors and now they exist on the ruins of Hinduism. Maybe those energies are blocked causing us distress since ages. We must energize such places once again and allow them to emanate positive vibrations and power to the devotees. This would help bring out Satvik energy spreading the message of peace and harmony once again.

Despite finding evidences of the use of advanced technologies during the Mahabharata and Ramayana, despite discovering the scientific approach of the Vedas, despite witnessing the refined and detailed architecture exemplifying the talent of the Hindu ancestors thousand and million years ago, Hindus are often projected as backward people belonging to the country of snake charmers. This is the level of persecution of Hindus.

Do our children even know that they have to preserve our religion, and why? The Satvik tendencies, the Vedas, classical music, spiritual knowledge, scientific solutions, and socio economic fundamentals have to be preserved. We tell them to study, get into IIT, secure an H1B visa, buy hi-tech cars and use foreign brands, but not about what really is a part of their existence and well being. Isn't that a curse?

The Half Blind Watchdog: Persecution by the Media

Indian media too is biased against the Hindus. This too is for the unconditional silence of the Hindus. Being the majority community of India and the highest population of tax payers, Hindu grievances find little space in the media; may be because the news does not create sensation for Hindus, as he does nothing more than being the audience for the injustice to his community. Left-liberal's obsession with minorities leads to a negligence of vital debates on the uniform civil code or the grim realities of Islamic terrorism. It is seen fashionable to speak against Hindus and in favour of Muslims. Especially the English language media particularly, is ignorant, elitist, and turns a blind eye to the Hindu issues. It is often caricatured as a stereotype communication platform that is immune to the Hindu's persecution and hyper sensitive to selective minorities endorsing their *pseudo secularism*. It has become a habit to abuse Hindus and to stand in favour of Muslims and other minorities sitting in the air conditioned studios of television channels wearing western attires. So the westernized English media reflects the liberal view that is far from religious, rather it defines religious views as extreme. However, they do not see the same when it comes to minority religions.

The murder of a Bajrang Dal activist in Moodbidri was restricted to short articles on the internet and the killing of RSS workers in Kerala or mob violence in Malda to a YouTube video. If a Muslim is even beaten it becomes main news. It is often claimed by the Hindu activists that the media simply does not report on crimes committed by other communities or by the Left as vigorously as it does on crimes committed by alleged Hindu activists.

There are many incidents when news related to the torture of Muslims was highlighted on the front page of newspapers and headlines of top television shows while blaming Hindus for the same even when it was not certain that Hindus are the culprits behind such incidences. On the other hand, news related to Hindu sufferings is either not given the necessary coverage or it occupies a little space somewhere in the corner of the middle or last pages of the newspapers. Electronic media either discards it or shows it in their mundane shows giving minimum duration to the program.

If majority is not given importance then the treatment should at least be equal to the other communities. But neither media finds it sensational, nor Hindus. Both still keep quiet or shut their eyes to the persecution of the Hindus, which is much more than the persecution of Muslims anytime.

Media jumps the gun on the minor attacks on churches but Hindu temples are broken, contaminated, and remain neglected in dilapidated conditions. They fail to attract the cameras to show the persecution of Hindus.

Few Hindu activists also claim that the church seems

to be governing the Indian media while highlighting the Hinduphobia and suppressing the news about persecution of Hindus by the Christian missionaries. The same is the case at the commercial front. Somewhere the international influence too has a paralytic effect on media. The corporate goals of the profitable benchmarks in the international brands restrict the media from highlighting the authentic pros and cons of international strategies and brands that are harmful for Indians in future.

Evils of the Hindu religion get the buzz all over the news platforms. For instance, problems of the Hindu Dalits are highlighted to create sensation but no journalist exposes the similar conditions of the lower caste Muslims. Offering milk to Shiva Lingam becomes the talk of the town and anti-human, as milk is wasted for prayers but killing of thousands of animals on Eid is considered as sacred. The Hindu pyres are seen as violation of environmental agendas whereas occupying acres of land for the graves is acceptable. News of constant conversions is missed but if a Hindu raises his voice against the same then it is considered as anti secularism.

The movie makers continue to glorify the persecutors like Akbar, Shahjahan, and Jahangir while completely being unaware of the heroes of the Hindus. These people are shown as heroes and icons of romantic endeavors with the Hindu princesses where the reality was completely different.

As mentioned earlier, we must learn from the other countries as to how they dealt with the history related to the persecution of their ancestors. Look at Europe that neither forgets nor forgives the atrocities of the Nazi rule under Hitler. There is hardly any positive reference to either Hitler or his army in the present day text books on European History. No one there talks about the the qualities of Hitler as a great commander or an inspiring leader or a great orator, who could influence Germans with his hypnotic speeches. His name is deleted from the public discussion. No films are made showing Hitler as a romantic hero singing songs and his mistress as a heroine.

The current generation is exposed to the evil deeds perpetrated by his regime. The untiring work of politicians, journalists, historians and film producers did justice to the European consciousness. The present day Europeans do not even think of seeing any virtue in Hitler or Nazis.

Europe and America produced at least a few thousand films highlighting the human misery caused by Hitler and his army. The films expose the horrors of Nazi regime and reinforce the beliefs and attitude of the present day generation towards the evils of the Nazi dictatorship.

On the other hand, we produced films like Mugal-e-Azam, Anarkali, or Taj Mahal which romanticize the Mughal rulers, depicting them as great heroes of noble virtues oozing with kindness, romance, secularism and love for the humanity! The hero of Anarkali was as involved in persecution of Hindus as any other Muslim persecutor. He also gave a hand to the British to establish their foot in India, who continued to persecute the Hindus even when Mughals bid farewell to this world. The hero of Taj Mahal was no less than his father and cruel to the Hindus, who produced a son like Aurangzeb, who terrified the Hindu and Sikh community. The hero of Mughal-e-Azam was as responsible for the holocaust of Hindus as Khilji and Qasim. But people are made to see them as romantic heroes and remember songs from these movies with great nostalgia!

No films are produced on how Mohammad bin Qasim began the chapter of persecution of Hindus by Muslims. No film idealized Raja Dahir who fought with this monster for securing the Hindu community till he was beheaded by the wild animals from the Middle East. No movie even remembers King Marthanda Varma who saved India from the persecution of Dutch and no movie ever listed the names of the plundered temples and universities of the Hindus by Muslims.

We highlight Aurangzeb but miss the contribution of Guru Gobind Singh and his sons, Fateh Singh and Zoravar Singh, the two children who lost their lives for setting a heroic example of living and dying for their religion and not accepting a forcible conversion.

We see a thousand of Rama's and Sita's interpretations catering to the commercial interests. Rama's character and Sita's personality are defined by what the audience watch. To make the movies interesting the writers take full liberty to tamper with history. This is only possible with the Hindu scriptures. No other religion will allow an inch of tampering with their religious history. Even if you use the name of their idea of God respectfully, it becomes a national sensation. The movie titled as Mustafa was changed to Gulam-e-Mustafa where Krishna and Durga were used freely without even considering the sensitivity involved. To make the stories interesting, Peshwa Bajirao is projected in front of the new generation as a Romeo, contrary to his real image of a genius military general with great strategic and political wisdom and the cruel Muslim looters are showcased with adjectives like 'the great'. Our religious values and rituals which are purely based on scientific reasons are often showcased as superstitions in movies while attempting to humiliate our sentiments for Hindu deities. These movie makers cannot exercise the same liberty with other religions. Movies like PK and God is Great, though with a great message for the audience, humiliated many Hindu rituals which could have been extremely offensive if done to the other communities. For instance, statements like *'Jo dar gaya samjho mandir gaya'* which means the one who fears goes to a temple'. This has been the extent of religious persecution by media, but we watch the movie and make it houseful and let the movie makers earn money and boost their morale to repeat this. No one would dare to make this statement for a mosque or a church. If they do, they will have to pay for it. The problem is that the Hindu doesn't even know how badly and how often he is being slapped in public and he just offers his other cheek and giggles on top of it. If this is not curse than what is it?

The Hindu journalists are busy pleasing the leaders who openly admit to appeasement politics. The remaining favours are granted to the other bureaucratic communities and leftists. The media should be intimidated for their anti-hindu approach which is resulting from their selective vision so they further shrink the space for raising questions.

The 'pseudo secular' journalism limits their role of a catalyst or of a watch dog to only people who stand for Hindutva. The so-called liberals stay reluctant to claim their Hindu identity leading the fringe to monopolize Hinduism. The press, dominated by the Left-leaning fails to report on the grievances of the Hindu upper castes. It is also seen that Muslim journalists and activists both are contributing to their communal interests but the Hindu's obsession of being politically correct is governing the Indian media. It is a warning sign for the Hindus and the Indian media to fasten their seatbelts as we are certainly on a wrong track.

Indian movie makers also refrained from their national duties by funding the artists from a country that is killing our soldiers. Yes, we are talking about Pakistan. We invite them on the best of our platforms and we sign them for big budget movies shrugging off from our responsibility towards the nation. They defend themselves with an argument that they are artists and therefore are beyond these political games; shame on us. Does our border secure only politicians and not the artist's lives? Don't they know that the money that we pay them as fee or rewards directly goes to their government as taxes and is spent in maintaining nuclear labs, purchasing fighter planes, bombs, and RDX with the intention to kill our soldiers. There is no art, culture, civilization, and harmony greater than the life of those who are killed by terrorists, women who become widows and children who become orphans.

Can we compensate for a soldier's leg that was amputated during the war or who lost his eyesight? But we want to simply make money at the cost of this country and spend it irresponsibly.

Indian media needs to wake up and know its responsibility towards the nation because 70 per cent of their profits come from the Hindu pocket. Every Hindu should watch the watchdog of society and correct it when it is required. Till the time he doesn't do it, this curse will never go away.

Call to Action: Wake up Hindu

WHAT WERE THE reasons that laid the foundation for the foreign invaders to rule us for more than 1000 years? For sure we were not just victims but equal participants in the persecution of the believers of Sanatan Dharma. It may not be an over statement that we gave our head to them on a silver platter. However, we defend ourselves with our humble civilization that inspired us to embrace all, forgive and forget, and say that the world is one. But this is not the reality. The Hindu must accept his own fault because till the time you do not identify the disease, it's impossible to cure it. It's high time we look inwards rather than outwards and stop blaming others and find out how our ancestors allowed those 'uncivilized' invaders who managed to persecute the heirs of a 'thousand-year-old civilization'.

God would have cursed the Hindus for his Fatalism

The most important reason why God would have cursed the Hindu was his fatalist approach to everything. Prolonged paralysis of someone who doesn't bother about what is happening to his religion and eventually he has lead others to put the gun on his head. We as a community diverted towards fatalism and unconditional non-violence for more than a thousand years, which was never the essence of Hindu ideology or theology.

Our culture, rituals, civilization, temples, scriptures, and deities never preached unconditional non-violence. Hindusim as a religion taught us to be action oriented but we interpreted it as per our own convenience which was our destiny. We wait for God to set things right for us but God has clearly stated in our scriptures that he has nothing to do with our destiny. We only reap benefit of our own actions. What we do is what we get. Our life is our own karma. Period!

We go to temples so that God answers our prayers. Having faith is good but being fatalist is bad. We keep waiting for God to change things. Who knows probably God is waiting for us to change them? We go to the temple and expect that before going out our wish should be fulfilled. We think that by offering a prasad of 51 rupees God will do what we want. And if it doesn't work, we change the God.

Shri Krishna forgave Shishupala for 100 sins but then he decided that he should be punished. But aren't we crossing the limit of those 100 sins now or we have already crossed it and that is why it is happening. 'Survival of the fittest' is a reality even today. If you are not powerful the outsider will attack you and persecute you.

God would have cursed the Hindus for superstitions and evil practices

People light *diyas* near trees to get the blessings, but they keep it so close that these diyas often burn the roots of the tree. As if, closer the diya is to the root, higher the devotion is. We leave milk, curd, and sweets on the idols of deities that invite flies but we only bother about blessings. We pollute the rivers to get rid of our sins but is contaminating rivers not a sin? We misunderstand Karma as destiny when it's clearly defined in Geeta as one's Action. The Hindus somehow lost their Kshatriya spirit and everyone has become a trader.

God would have cursed the Hindus for not respecting this land of wonders and bliss of life that we are bestowed with. All sorts of climatic conditions and a number of rivers made it a heaven as everything was available to lead a happy and contented life. But we contaminated them with sins.

God would have cursed the Hindus for not valuing our scriptures and wisdom of sages. We hardly know about our intellectual wealth. Millions of documents are still left in dilapidating libraries.

India gave zero, decimals, astronomy etc. to the world, so our civilization was completely scientific and open to challenges. More than that, our Gods gave us freedom to amend them from time to time when they do not serve our purpose. But we could not respect them.

God would have cursed the Hindus for their lack of integrity: Hindus lacked integrity since forever. This has been repeated in our entire past, again and again. We never knew what oneness is? In spite of belonging to a religion that was based on a concept of 'yoga' that means being united, we were always isolated in the name of caste, region, language, culture, and for individual motives. We evolved from a united civilization as Bharat Varsha but we were never united nor did we act as one nation.

God would have cursed the Hindus for caste discrimination: If we did not restrict the knowledge of Vedas and knowledge of weapons to a limited section of society our strength would have been unbeatable and the content would have been alive in the minds of the populace passed on from their ancestors. God would have cursed Hindus for torturing a massive section of society known as Dalits for thousands of years. These humans for thousand years were treated like animals by the upper caste. He would have cursed us for denying them equal right to live, eat, drink, study, prosper, and most importantly learning the divine Vedic knowledge which was their fundamental right.

God would have cursed Hindus for Gender discrimination: God must have cursed Hindus because we nurtured gender discrimination by abusing women, killing the female fetus in the womb or as an infant, committing honor killings, torturing them for dowry, and committing innumerable crimes against them. He would have cursed us for preventing half of his creation from knowledge and being equal to men. What if we equipped our women at par with men? The history would have been different. We would have had more of Laxmibais than those who committed Jauhar and were persecuted in other brutal ways.

It seems he even cursed women for not standing for their dignity. They were burning stoves in the kitchen but they seldom burnt the ones who did injustice to them. They did not use the knife to cut them into pieces. They chose Jauhar rather than fight. They forgot the Sita of the Ramayan who chose to bury herself ignoring her husband's cries for her dignity. They forgot Draupadi who lead the Mahabharata getting millions of people killed for her dignity. They forgot the Durga Saptashati in which the Goddess killed Mahishasura and Shumbh and Nishumbh.

Ramayana, Mahabharata, Geeta, and Durga Shaptashati were kept in their homes but they never learnt anything from them and prayed to them only for a proposal of marriage, a boy child, a tender, or a job for their father, brother, son, or husband.

God would have cursed Hindus for corruption and missing patriotism: For small gains we are staking our lives

It's not only the government's duty or army's duty to solely maintain our defense apparatus. We are equally responsible for that because every Indian is a stakeholder. It's an Indian's duty and a Hindu's duty. It's our duty to safeguard ourselves and our coming generations. But we only restrict ourselves to make judgment about others and keep blaming others. We steal taxes, bribe the government officials to get our work done, do not raise our voice against corruption, spend money on foreign brands, and completely depend on government and defense forces for our well being.

So may be God is ashamed of us and has cursed us. He turned his back because he can't see this nonsense that we are doing and he left us on our own to kill each other one day and the planet be freed from our fatalism, indolence, and ignorance. May be we do not deserve the life he gave us.

It is a harsh statement but true that the biggest persecutors of Hindus have been Hindus themselves because they allowed the others to persecute them in spite of being blessed with the best of the gifts of nature and knowledge. A segment of Hindus debarred other Hindus from their culture, scriptures, and divine knowledge. The outcome of this sin is still borne by their offsprings and God knows how many more generations will have to pay the price for it.

So many battles have happened in 1000 years. Innumerable numbers of people were present around the battleground waiting to know the outcome but no one intervened and fought along with the injured soldiers thinking that it was only the warrior's duty to fight battles for the motherland.

For instance, in the battle of Plassey, it is said that there were ten times more Hindus who were waiting for the result of the battle outside the battleground. Had they even picked up a stone and hit the enemy, they would have made a difference. May be they could have prevented what happened.

There were very few people from some communities who raised weapons to support the other fighters. But whenever that happened the opponent had to run away. Warriors like Maharana Pratap gathered the forces from tribes and other castes and succeeded in giving a tough fight to Akbar through his guerrilla war strategy. But it was not a common scenario in the Indian subcontinent. Most times, the ordinary Hindu was dependent on the destiny of the warriors. When they won they were secured and when they lost they were not. Why this dependency on one community? Why didn't a common Hindu come out in the battleground influenced by the knowledge of scriptures like Shrimad Bhagavad Gita? For 1000 years we were dependent on others to decide our security and well being.

We can't even blame anyone because we did not let our own people read the scriptures so they were roaming around in darkness to such an extent that when the enemy attacked us, they were mentally and physically incapable of safeguarding the civilization; thanks to the Brahmin's dominance on the Hindu scriptures.

Our wealth was concentrated in few hands that were tied and all the others were enslaved. We ourselves converted our strengths into weaknesses and opportunities into adversities. Had we allowed the scriptures to reach the masses since the beginning, they would have existed in our ancestor's minds and passed on to generation after generation even if the invaders had set our libraries ablaze. We were okay with letting the invaders burn our knowledge but not to share it with our own people. As a result, though we have a vast intellectual inheritance, our minds were always superstitious, bewildered, and ignorant.

We kept our women behind and taught them to immolate themselves when men fail to protect them. We taught them to jump into the fire of Jauhar, but not to push the enemy into it. Had we been fair to our women, there would have been a number of women like Queen Lakshmi Bai of Jhansi, Padmavati of Mewar would have slain Alauddin Khilji and threw him into the fire rather than jumping into it with thousands of other women. However, we reverently bow down to these women who had the courage to burn themselves alive in fire to preserve their dignity and sanctity.

The story that became a story of fear and darkness was not the one that the Arabs started or the Mughals or even the British. We Hindus only started this never ending tale of persecution. If pyres of Kashmiri Hindus are still smoldering in Hindu hearts, it is only because we allowed the outsiders to oppress our own people and contaminate our rivers with blood.

But the irony is that we learnt nothing in the 1000 years that destroyed our very existence by the relentless and barbarous atrocities of these invaders. Nothing has changed till date; the scenario remains the same today. We forgot those martyrs who sacrificed their lives and highlighted those who are often questioned for their political decisions or the ones who massacred, looted, and destroyed India. Why Subhas Chandra Bose was forgotten? Why the freedom that was attained by the sacrifice and lives of martyrs like Bhagat Singh is credited to only a particular section of people that still influence the country. And above all, we often forgave and even forgot those who lead to the deaths, casualties, and even rape of our women; the height of the tolerance of Hindus.

Like before, we still depend on the forces to defend the country or the government to make decisions for us. We sit in an air conditioned living room, wearing foreign brands, eating continental food, and judging what the army should have done and what the government should have done. This also includes those who prefer to sleep or go for long drives on the day of voting.

We learnt nothing from the persecution of 1000 years. We forgot that when the Kshatriyas lost the battles it was not only the Kshatriya women who were raped, but women from all castes had to bear the torture. Not only Kshatriyas were enslaved but all castes were enslaved. Not only Kashtriyas were converted and massacred, but each and every caste was the victim of this holocaust. We should be ready to face the same consequences if we are committing the same mistakes.

The same will happen today. We don't even realize what is going on in the country. Only the means have changed but persecution is still going on. Foreign policies are continuously hijacking our minds in a way that we give our talented workforce to foreign countries and pay our hard earned money to them.

Why have we forgotten King Hemu, Marthanda Varma, Bappa Rawal, and other Indian soldiers who contributed to the Hindu dignity. Why do we have more accumulations of the Mughals than of Shivaji? Why are so many Hindu kings who fought valiantly buried under history? Why are we served sheer lies in the name of history and education and we are watching like fools.

God must be ashamed of us. People to whom he preached the Gita and gifted Vedas simply witnessed the persecution as silent statues. What the hell are we doing? How can we just watch everything as if we don't exist. It's not a fiction for heaven's sake. It's a reality; you and me are at stake.

We fight between regions and they conquer other countries. We fight over whether women will go to a particular temple or not in spite of knowing that God is not limited to a particular temple.

To repeat, no one talks about why Muslim women can't go to the mosque. No one raises a question on Christianity about why there is no female pope but Hinduism is the only religion that could be twisted, altered, questioned, criticized, and manipulated by anyone and everyone; in fact by its own people, what an irony.

Why everyone intrudes the Hindu territory geographically, intellectually, emotionally, and mentally? Everyone can come on this pitch and bat with no rules, no ethics, and no permission because there is nobody to prevent it. Can Hindus intrude into other's domain? No. You try it and you will be shown your place. We allowed British and Mughals to tamper our scriptures which are eternally valuable.

Politicians are thinking of their political careers; pleasing the minorities again and planning for another persecution of Hindus; we forget that if seen globally Hindus are becoming a minority. *Vasudhaiva Kutumbakam* invited invasions, *atithi devo bhava* allowed them to captivate our land and *ahimsa parmo dharma* made us blind to the torture happening around us. They have been the ideal philosophies of Hindus but they turned into a curse.

The Hindu is allowing invasions; he is living them and broadening the scope for them in future. The form of invasion changed from slaughter to economic, mental and philosophical slavery. But aren't we keeping a foundation of slavery for our future generations.

We couldn't even protect our land. The discrimination and cultural evils within us served our nation on a silver platter to the outsiders who were not even warriors but dacoits from some far away land that was not as resource abundant as ours.

Every secular Hindu must know that secularism can't be carried on the Hindu's shoulder alone. Other religions should equally carry the weight of it only then it may survive in the long run. India was always economically a progressive country. High standard of literacy and higher education was never a challenge for India. But still the light of this prosperity was diminished by the dawn of cruelty of the Muslim invaders. Nalanda University is the biggest example of when there was no dearth of prosperity, literacy, higher education, and refinement. A cruel invader succeeded in demolisihing the temple of knowledge and human well being for his insanity.

Then how do you expect that our MBA degrees, IIT admissions, and H1B visas will prevent history from being repeated?

We are calling Mughals 'the great', and naming our streets after them. Delhi is full of such roads and one has to see the names of the murderers and rapists painted over our streets. Aurangzeb to Akbar, all are alive in independent India. If you go a few kilometers ahead you find the best of the locations having their graves for which our taxes are spent to maintain. People say it doesn't matter but it does. Naming those roads and buildings after them affects the psyche of the modern and coming generations. What message we are conveying to our future generations? Can Germany give such treatment to Hitler? No. The so-called liberals whose minds are still imprisoned by the persecutors defend retaining those names and graves in the name of history with their so-called intellectual and secular but insane arguments while everyone knows that they are simply catering to appeasement politics.

Apart from being the oldest religion of the world, Hinduism is also pro democracy, it has flexibility, gender equality, in-built secularism and acceptance. Hinduism or Sanatan Dharma is a belief system that endorses an ideology that God manifests itself in various forms. A being that is a part of the Supreme Being is free to draw his own picture of God as per his devotion. In Hinduism, there is acceptance of God in every form, from every place, and from every concept or religion which is missing in all the other religions that restricts the evolution of the idea of God in devotees. They are bound to obey what is preached, they see their God through other's filters, and follow what others want them to follow with no scope of questioning.

In short, Hinduism says 'My belief about God is true but your belief is also true so I accept your ideology with reverence and I expect you to accept mine'. Whereas in other religions they say

'Its only my belief that is true, my idea of God is true, if you do not identify with my belief you are a Kafir, an infidel or an atheist and you deserve to die and go to hell'.

This is the fundamental factor that differentiates the Hindu religion from any other religion. A Hindu loves the Almighty and bows his head in reverence. If Hindus become a minority in India; there will not be any democracy anymore as this is the only religion that embraces all other religions and communes with respect and compassion. This is the only religion that keeps gender equality to the core unlike many other religions. It is the only religion that worships Gods in feminine form by having the female goddesses. This is the only religion that gives anyone the power to question, practice, or not practice a religion. It allows a person to marry in any religion. It teaches unconditional compassion for other beings. It teaches flexibility, and grants permission to be a human and to behave like a human and not God. He is accepted with all his variation or you can say in a layman's language, flaws.

But how will this religion that is oriented on human grounds survive, as none of the current generation of Hindus stand up for their ancestors. The Hindu converted to Islam is absolutely intolerant of his original belief system for he is so conditioned by the foreign imprints in the name of the religion. The Christian too is ignorant as he is looking for his foreign aids and acceptance by an opulent community as his own. People made his life nothing but miserable. And the Hindu who remained a Hindu for namesake, is scared to speak for his religion, fearing he would be called anti-secular, a Hindu terrorist and fundamentalist and this would lead to social mayhem. He would be trolled on social media and would be targeted by the activists.

Hence, the ancestor's spirit is suffering and waiting for our plundered temples to smell the incense again and value this civilization that they died protecting . It's a call to action, else history will repeat and we must be afraid of the fact that one day entire India would be a Kashmir and all Hindus would become Kashmiri Pandits.

It is also a time to set strict boundaries around our religion because open doors have invited troubles in the past! Its flexibility has made it vulnerable in Kalyuga. Hence, we should stop calling it a way of life! Yes it is a way of life but it is also a well defined code of conduct that should be followed, preserved, and taught. Its name is Sanatan Dharma, the eternal duty of a human being is to lead a successful life irrespective of the religion he is born in while not allowing others to challenge it at every step.

'It is a Call to Action!'

Jai Shri Ram!

Citations

Reference Number	Reference Details
1	Mahabharata - Udyoga Parva, the fifth of eighteen books of the Epic Mahabharata
2	Russia Insider, 2015-Jun –19/Mike Weatley.
3	XINHOANET 2017-07-30 Editor Zhang Dongmiao
4	DeccanHerald, 2014-July—04/Citation
5	David T. Smith, *Religious Persecution and Political Order in the United States*. Cambridge University Press. pp. 26–. ISBN 978-1-107-11731-0.
6	Nazila Ghanea-Hercock (11 November 2013). The Challenge of Religious Discrimination at the Dawn of the New Millennium. Springer. pp. 91–92. ISBN 978-94-017-5968-7.
7	Census 2011, Hindu.com
8	Census 2011, Hindu.com
9	Mahabharata
10	Wright 2010
11	McIntosh, Jane in *The Ancient Indus Valley: New Perspectives*
12	Professor Childe, *Discovery of India* by Nehru

13	Vedicsciences.net, RickBriggs Roacs, NASA Ames Research Center, Moffet Field, California
14	K. N. Jha, *Chanakya: the pioneer economist of the world.*
15	Pt. Jawaharlal Nehru, *Discovery of India.*
16	Instructions given to Muhammad bin Qasim by Hajjaj-Derryl N. MacLean, *Religion and Society in Arab Sind.*
17	Dr B.R. Ambedkar writes in *Pakistan or The Partition of India*
18	From a letter by Hajjaj to Muhammad bin Qasim. MacLean, *Religion and Society in Arab Sind.*
19	Kufi, the author of the *Chachnama*
20	Lal, K. S. (1992). *The legacy of Muslim rule in India.*
21	Al Biruni
22	Minhaj-i-Siraj in *Tabakat-I-Nasiri* (Tabaquat-i-Nasiri)
23	Politician, writer and educationist from Gujarat, Shri Kanaiyalal Maneklal Munshi, Jay Somnath
24	Politician, writer and educationist from Gujarat, Shri Kanaiyalal Maneklal Munshi, Jay Somnath
25	Asoke Kumar Majumdar in his book, *Chaulukyas of Gujarat* Nizam-ud-din, Badauni, Firishta
26	Satish Chandra (2006). *Medieval India: From Sultanat to the Mughals-Delhi Sultanat (1206-1526).* Har-Anand. Firishta, Roy, Kaushik (2004). *India's Historic Battles: From Alexander the Great to Kargil.* Orient Longman.
27	D.C. Ganguly
28	Vincent A Smith, *The Oxford History of India: From the Earliest Times to the End of 1911*
29	William Wilson Hunter, *The Indian Empire: Its Peoples, History, and Products*
30	*The Cambridge Economic History of India: c.1200-c.1750,* Edited by Tapan Raychaudhuri, Irfan Habib
31	Ziauddin Barni, *Tarikh-I Firoz Shahi.*
32	*Zafarnama,* Sharafuddin Yazdi, Elliot & Dowson,

33	*Tarikh-i Firishta*, Muhammad Kasim Hindu Shah, Firishta (b. 1570).
34	*Khwājah Nizāmu'd-Dîn Ahmad bin Muhammad Muqîm al-Harbî: Tabqāt-i-Akbarî* translated by B. De, Calcutta, 1973
35	*Srivara, Zaina Rajtarangini*
36	Lawrence, Walter Roper (1895), *The Valley of Kashmir*
37	*Tarikh-i Mubarak-Shahi*, Yahya bin Ahmad
38	*Zubdatu-t Tawarikh*, Haig 1928
39	*XXXIII - Táríkh-i Dáúdí, of Abdu-lla, The History of India, as Told by its Own Historians: The Muhammadan Period, Volume 4 -* Henry Miers Elliot, Edited by John Dowson
40	*XXVIII - Túzak-i Bábarí; or, Wáki'át-i Bábarí: The Autobiography of Bábar, The History of India, as Told by its Own Historians: The Muhammadan Period, Volume 4 -* Henry Miers Elliot, Edited by John Dowson
41	*Prepare Or Perish: A Study of National Security*, K.V. Krishna Rao
42	Elliot and Dowson, *The History of India, as Told by Its Own Historians - The Muhammadan Period*
43	Schimmel, Annemarie, *The Empire of the Great Mughals*
44	John F. Richards, *The Mughal Empire*
45	Smith, *Akbar the Great Mogul* *K.S. Lal, Studies in Medieval Indian History*
46	K.S. Lal, *Kishori Saran. Indian Muslims: Who Are They*
47	Husain, S M in *Structure of Politics Under Aurangzeb*
48	Smith, Vincent in *The Oxford History of India: From the Earliest Times to the End of 1911.*
49	*Ayalon and David* in *Studies in Islamic History and Civilization.*
50	Heathcote, T. A
51	Sultan, Tipu (1811). *Select letters of Tippoo Sultan to various public functionaries*
52	Miller, Roland E, *Mappila Muslims of Kerala: a study in Islamic trends,*

53	Kamath, M. V. *Tipu Sultan: Coming to terms with the past*. The News Today. Chennai. Archived from the original on 13 August 2009. Retrieved 1 October 2017.
54	Rao, C. Hayavadana, ed. (1930). *Mysore Gazetteer. Volume II, Part IV*. Government Press.

Foxes from the west (Special Thanks To Dr. Shashi Tharoor)

55	M. O. Koshy, *The Dutch Power in Kerala*
56	Jabez T. Sunderland, *India in Bondage: Her Right to Freedom and a Place Among the Great Nations*, New York: Lewis Copeland, 1929
57	F.J. Shore
58	William Digby, *Prosperous British India: A Revelation from Official Records, London*: T. Fisher Unwin,1901.
59	Jon Wilson, *India Conquered: Britain's Raj and the Chaos of Empire*, London: Simon &Schuster, 2016
60	*Era of Darkness*, Shashi Tharoor, Will Durant
61	Henry W. Nevinson, *The New Spirit in India*, London: Harper & Brothers, 1908
62	*Era of darkness*, Dr Shashi Tharoor
63	Jinnah various speeches
64	*Era of darkness*, Dr Shashi Tharoor
65	Ranjan Borra in 1982, in his piece on Subhas Chandra Bose, the Indian National Army and the war of India's liberation
66	Digital interview online with Sr Journalist Pushpendra Kulshrestha
67	Television Interview, Anil Sahstri, Lal Bahadur Shastriji's son Television interview, Kuldeep Nayyar, Seniour journalist & Author
68	Postcard.news
69	Jindal, T.P. (1995). *Ayodhya imbroglio*. New Delhi: Ashish Pub. House.
70	Indiatoday.in

71	*A Grain of Sand in the Hourglass of Time*, the autobiography of Arjun Singh
72	*The Times of India*. 12 August 2008. "India Assessment 2014". Retrieved 28 December 2014.
73	Tarek Fateh Inteview/Various television channels